Cabinet

For my sisters, Kathleen Townsend,
Terry Farr and Maureen Smith

Cabinet

PETER HENNESSY

Basil Blackwell

Copyright © Peter Hennessy 1986

First published 1986
Reprinted 1986, 1988, 1990

Basil Blackwell Ltd
108 Cowley Road, Oxford OX4 1JF, UK

Basil Blackwell Inc.
3 Cambridge Center,
Cambridge, Massachusetts 02142, USA

British Library Cataloguing in Publication Data
A CIP catalogue record for this book is available from the British Library.

Library of Congress Cataloging in Publication Data
Hennessy, Peter, 1947–
  Cabinet.
  Includes index.
  1. Cabinet system – Great Britain. 2 Great Britain –
Politics and government – 1945–   . I. Title.
JN405.H45   1986   354.4104   86-6844
ISBN 0-631-14968-6
ISBN 0-631-14969-4 (pbk.)

Phototypeset by Dobbie Typesetting Service, Plymouth, Devon
Printed in Great Britain

Contents

Preface

The majority of Cabinet Ministers come to Cabinet overburdened with briefs, and with life generally . . . it is important now for Ministers, when they come to the Cabinet, to realise that it is a place where great issues ought to be decided and discussed. *Lord Butler, 1965*[1]

Most books contain an element of autobiography, a sliver of concealed prejudice which should be declared to the reader as if it were a financial interest. Within weeks of Lord Butler displaying, in his radio interview with Dr Norman Hunt, the accumulated wisdom of sixteen years as a Cabinet minister under Churchill, Eden, Macmillan and Douglas-Home, I was fortunate enough to receive as a prize at Marling School in Stroud a shiny copy of Anthony Sampson's *Anatomy of Britain Today*.[2] His chapters on the Treasury and the Civil Service aroused what has so far proved to be a lifelong interest in Whitehall and the hidden processes of government. His section on the Cabinet helped put into shape particles of memory acquired from a decade of reading the newspapers. When it comes to sorting out complexity for the keen but untrained mind, Sampson has never been equalled. I cannot have been the only eighteen year old for whom he unlocked a treasure house.

It was in reading Sampson that I first came across Bagehot. Though I did not read *him* for another year. By this time I was an undergraduate at St John's College, Cambridge. The Fontana Library edition of *The English Constitution* with an introduction by R. H. S. Crossman,[3] which I went so far as actually to buy, was a treat. Both Bagehot and Crossman wielded a pen like a sword. Their language had bite. Phrases remained with one. The book was entirely free of the Teflon factor, the non-stick quality of so many works on undergraduate reading-lists.

Studying history rather than political science (Cambridge did not offer it as a subject in the late 1960s) meant that the pleasure of encountering Mackintosh[4] and Jones[5] on Cabinet government was what might be called a deferred gratification. The running dialectic between Crossman and Mackintosh, who believed collective Cabinet government had succumbed to personalized prime ministerial government, and George Jones, who did not, was a rarity in political-science terms. For it stimulated a genuine debate on a big issue among political scientists *and* practising politicians such as Lord Butler ('on the whole the Prime Minister had tended to stop being an equal among equals'[6]) and Ian Gilmour ('the writers of the Prime Ministerial School made the same mistake about the Premier as the Whig historians made about George III and the Monarchy: they overrate his power today and underrate the power he had in the past'[7]). It must be remembered that Crossman himself was a Labour MP from 1945 to 1970, as was Mackintosh from 1966 until his tragically early death in 1978. Both scholarship and political life in Britain would be healthier if the 1980s were to witness serious debates of such quality about central themes.

Cabinet government did not intrude into my thoughts until five or six years after the Jones–Mackintosh–Crossman debate had run its course.[8] In 1976 I spent a short spell at Westminster as Lobby Correspondent of the *Financial Times*. I was there but seven months, since I acquired a powerful aversion to the lobby system of non-attributable mass briefings as the institutionalized channel of communication between government and governed.[9] But the spring, summer and early autumn of 1976 contained a succession of sufficiently dramatic events to rekindle a personal interest in our system of Cabinet government. I arrived in the Press Gallery just in time to witness the beleaguered Wilson Government lose a vote on its expenditure plans in March 1976, followed inside a month by Wilson's surprise resignation and the contest for the Labour leadership which propelled James Callaghan, with his different style of Cabinet government, into No. 10. Callaghan's first months in the premiership were punctuated by successive economic setbacks, culminating in the collapse of sterling in the early autumn, when the smell of panic in Whitehall could be detected strongly in the press corridor in the Palace of Westminster, across Parliament Square from the Treasury.[10] Whatever else it was in September and October 1976, the Callaghan Cabinet was not the command post of a robust, smooth-running system of government.

Watching the Callaghan Cabinet from my Westminster observation post during the currency slide of 1976 awakened my interest in what political scientists call the 'overload' problem. The quotation from Lord

Butler which crowns this preface is a firm reminder that the problem predates the stress under which British government was placed by the economic dislocation caused by the quadrupling of the price of oil by the Organization of Petroleum Exporting Countries in 1973–4, the so-called 'oil-shock' effect. Indeed, one of the biases in my treatment arises from the fact that my reporting of British government as a journalist has almost entirely postdated the oil shock, which may, in terms of a longer perspective, mean that I have been over-influenced by what Lord Rayner has called 'the fatigues and disappointments of the British political and economic systems'.[11] Perhaps inevitably, coverage of government since 1973 has been dominated by what Peter Riddell, Political Editor of the *Financial Times*, has described as 'the case-work of decline'.[12]

In October 1976 I returned to *The Times* as its Whitehall Correspondent. Eighteen months later, after Callaghan, a prime minister I rather admired, ordered the senior Civil Service to have no more dealings with me (a pair of leaks had aroused his anger), I started the practice of 'blowing' his secret Cabinet committees, their membership and functions – a process which had all the thrills of the chase as well as being constitutionally revealing. Just over a year later, Mrs Thatcher moved into Downing Street and subjected the conventions of Cabinet government to their greatest hammering since David Lloyd George refashioned the Cabinet system at the height of the First World War.[13] She reopened all the issues to an extent which requires the standard examination questions on prime-ministerial versus Cabinet government to be rephrased and a new set of one-line quotes to be minted for exam purposes.

Much use is made in this book of a set of edited conversations on the quality of Cabinet government with five insiders possessing personal experience of the system at work. They involve two former prime ministers, two former Cabinet ministers and a retired permanent secretary. They were recorded in February and March 1985 and broadcast on BBC Radio 3 under the title *The Quality of Cabinet Government* in June and July 1985. They are reproduced here with the kind permission of Lord Home of the Hirsel, Lord Wilson of Rievaulx, the Rt Hon. Peter Shore, PC, MP, the Rt Hon. David Howell, PC, MP, and the Rt Hon. Sir Frank Cooper, PC, GCB.

The book begins with an introduction to the theme of Cabinet government, stating what I think it is (a subject of endless dispute almost worthy of the arguments on transubstantiation which accompanied the Reformation) and why its healthy functioning is so crucial to the 56 million British citizens who are affected by its output. Chapter 1 is a snapshot of the Cabinet machine in autumn 1985, the structure of the Cabinet Secretariat and the range of Mrs Thatcher's Cabinet committees. Chapter 2 is a survey of developments since 1945. Mrs Thatcher, for reasons already outlined, deserves, and receives (in chapter 3), a section to herself. New material available at the Public Record Office, coupled with information obtained from conversations with Lord Wilson and Sir Frank Cooper and from private sources, makes this an opportune moment to reconsider the now venerable issue of how far full Cabinets are allowed to influence nuclear-weapons policy; this is addressed in chapter 4. Chapter 5 discusses the quality of Cabinet government; and, finally, chapter 6, 'The Reform Agenda', is my attempt to entice the political scientists and the politicians, and perhaps a journalist and a historian or two, back on to the field of discussion, argument and debate on the issue of Cabinet government.

Special thanks are due to Anne Winder of the BBC, who produced *The Quality of Cabinet Government*; to Dr Anthony Seldon, who provided me with my first opportunity for airing the themes of this book before the Politics Society of Whitgift School, and who afforded me constant advice and support; and to the Politics Department of Nottingham University, the Extra-Mural Department of Manchester University, the Department of Law at Durham University, the Department of Government and Economics at Birmingham Polytechnic, the PPE candidates at Lady Margaret Hall, Oxford, and John Benyon and the Department of Adult Education at Leicester University for successive airings, all of which produced thoughts and comments of great benefit.

Thanks, too, for detailed criticism, to Professor George Jones of the London School of Economics who disagrees with the thrust of my views and who never fails to stimulate me to greater exertions by the candour and clarity with which he expresses them; to his colleague John Barnes for help on Conservative administrations in the 1950s; to Dr Peter Morris of Nottingham University, for his precise comments on content and presentation; to Dr Brian Hogwood and Mr Tom Mackie of Strathclyde University for shared interest and constant encouragement; and to Miss Gillian Peele of Lady Margaret Hall and Professor Colin Seymour-Ure of Kent University, participants in a session of the Machinery of Government sub-group of the International Political Science Association at its 1985 Congress in the 'Science-Po', Paris, when a semi-finished version of this work was presented. I am grateful to Sir Charles Carter, Editor of *Policy Studies*, for accepting a section of my work on Cabinet government for publication;[14] and to John Benyon for stimulating an updating of my unofficial Cabinet-committee list;[15] and to Bill Jones of the Politics Association for advice and encouragement. As usual, a private word of thanks goes to my anonymous army of informants, both elected and non-elected, who are engaged in keeping the Cabinet system on the road.

I would like to thank the Public Record Office and Cabinet Office for permission to reproduce material from Crown© *Questions of Procedure for Ministers* (1952), Public Record Office: CAB 129/52; and the author and publishers concerned for permission to quote from Barbara Castle, *The Castle Diaries 1974–76* (Weidenfeld and Nicolson Ltd and Holmes and Meier, 1980).

A huge debt of gratitude is owed to the Policy Studies Institute, my intellectual home since October 1984: to John Pinder, who took me in, and to Donald Derx, who kept me there; to Robin Guthrie and the Trustees of the Joseph Rowntree Memorial Trust, who have provided funding for my Senior Fellowship at the Institute; to Sandra Jeddy, Stephanie Maggin and Michelle Rayner, who have processed the words; to Sue Johnson and Mary Cassels for finding the books, and to Nick Cox, Duncan Chalmers and Hilary Jones for steering me towards the documents. Thanks finally to Sean Magee of Basil Blackwell for making the book happen and to the unconventional scholarship girl from Grantham who made Cabinet government interesting again.

Walthamstow   Peter Hennessy
January 1986

Introduction

The most curious point about the Cabinet is that so very little is known about it. *Walter Bagehot, 1867*[1]

It is easier to know what the Cabinet was than what it is now. *Professor Colin Seymour-Ure, 1971*[2]

The underlying principle is, of course, that the method adopted by Ministers for discussion among themselves of questions of policy is essentially a domestic matter, and is no concern of Parliament or the public. *Miscellaneous Questions of Procedure, Note by the Prime Minister, 8 August 1945*[3]

Procedure is all the Constitution the poor Briton has. *Sir Kenneth Pickthorn, MP, 1960*[4]

The origins of Cabinet government are uncertain. No seventeenth-century equivalent of a systems analyst, realizing that a kind of pattern had emerged after the restoration of the monarchy in 1660, ever sat down and produced a flow chart of the decision-making process or attempted to codify the relative powers of monarch, ministers and Parliament. The system, in so far as it justifies that description, has always been something of an affront to the tidy-minded, but is all the more interesting for that.

In essence, the Cabinet emerged as, by the standards of the age, a small, businesslike committee of that truly ancient institution the Privy Council, which, incidentally spawned the older Whitehall departments, which began life as boards of the Privy Council. The prototype Cabinet was known variously in the 1660s and 1670s as the Foreign Committee or the Intelligence Committee of the Privy Council.[5] By the 1690s the inner group of Privy Counsellors who counted, because they enjoyed the trust of the monarch *and* carried clout in Parliament, were becoming known as Lords of the Committee, and their collectivity was already being described as the full Cabinet.[6] For Patrick Gordon-Walker, successive refinements showed Cabinet to be the practical and lasting eighteenth-century solution to the perennial power struggle between sovereign and Parliament which had bedevilled the seventeenth.[7]

Bit by bit the problem of the monarch diminished as the King ceased to attend Cabinet, investing, as it were, the Cabinet with the authority of the Crown by putting his powers into commission. The last known appearance of the monarch at Cabinet was George III's in 1784, 'but for practical purposes after 1717 the Cabinet ceased to be a body meeting in the presence of the King'.[8] Intriguingly, the doctrine of collective Cabinet responsibility, used by modern prime ministers to squash dissent and to keep internal procedures and discussion secret, was, originally, a typically practical English invention, an anti-monarch device, as Richard Pares explains in his *King George III and the Politicians*:

The King did nearly all business with the Ministers in the room called his closet. He normally saw them one by one. . . . A Minister had no strict right to discuss anything in the closet but the business of his own department; but a senior Minister – especially if he were Leader of the House of Commons or had pretensions to consider himself as Prime Minister – could range more freely. . . . The business of the closet does not appear, at first sight, to have afforded the Ministers much opportunity for collective action. But they knew how to counteract the tendency to separate and confine them. On any question of general political importance, they would agree beforehand what to say, and then go into the closet, one by one; and repeat the identical story.[9]

By the beginning of the nineteenth century the bone structure of the modern Cabinet system was visible. But it took extensions of the franchise and the emergence of organized political parties to complete the transformation of the Cabinet into the commanding height of the British system of government for which rival sets of politicians compete. Once the mass parties had come into existence in the 1860s and 1870s, 'The Cabinet was', writes Gordon Walker, 'outstandingly the highest political prize in the country'[10] – though, as we shall see, some of its more amateurish practices, such as the absence of minutes, staggered on through successive premierships until a combination of the Kaiser's war and the arrival of David Lloyd George in No. 10 enforced a degree of modernization upon the system. The primary purpose of this book is to illuminate the reality of that system since 1945.

British political parties win power by mobilizing prejudice more success-fully than their rivals. Once in government, the political task facing them splits into three: (1) mobilizing Whitehall for the purpose of converting manifesto pledges and party philosophy into practical strategies, statutes or administrative schemes; (2) retaining the support of the House of Commons, without which government cannot be sustained; and (3) mobilizing consent among the electorate, whose continuing favour can never be taken for granted, and securing the acquiescence, if not consent, of interest groups great and small, from powerful nation states such as NATO allies or EEC partners, to lobbies such as the Trades Union Congress or Confederation of British Industry, or single-issue groups such as Shelter and the National Listeners' and Viewers' Association.

When in government, therefore, ministers must look constantly in three directions: inward to the Civil Service machine, across Whitehall to Parliament, and outward to the party beyond Westminster, to institutions, professions, the country as a whole and to other nations. The Cabinet spans and, with luck, reconciles the three activities. It reaches and frames its conclusions with an eye to the real world outside. Once committed to paper by the Secretary of the Cabinet, the economically worded Cabinet minutes are the trigger for action down the length and breadth of Whitehall.

On the performance of the twenty-two men and women round the Cabinet table depends directly the security and well-being of 56 million people in the United Kingdom. And, given the size of the British economy and the firepower of its arsenal, the public enterprise based on 10 Downing Street also has an effect, albeit often indirect, on the lives of countless more overseas. Yet great pains are taken in official circles to keep the procedures of the Cabinet process a secret and to maintain the validity of Bagehot's 1867 appraisal. Ministers and senior civil servants, with a few cherished exceptions such as a Michael Heseltine, are determined to keep what the current Cabinet Secretary, Sir Robert Armstrong, has called 'the marvels and mysteries of Cabinet Government'[11] hidden in the traditional secret garden of the British Constitution. Indeed, the Cabinet's secret rule-book, *Questions of Procedure for Ministers* and its equivalent for Cabinet secretariat staff, *Talking about the Office* (which coaches Cabinet Office civil servants in what to say when asked at parties what they do),[12] are imbued from beginning to end with the spirit of closed government. For Whitehall's insiders, the Cabinet system is *not* the business of Parliament or the public unless ministers choose to make it so, as every edition of *Questions* from Clement Attlee to Mrs Thatcher has stated plainly.

Yet Cabinet Government remains a putty-like concept. A prime minister can make of it very largely what he or she will, provided colleagues do not baulk at their treatment. Twentieth-century political historians could, if so minded, produce a scatter diagram of prime ministers since Lord Salisbury from the presidential and the commanding (Lloyd George and Thatcher), on the one side, to the collegiate and retiring (Baldwin and Attlee), on the other. It would not be a very satisfactory exercise. Attlee was once described as achieving a *coup de repos* in Cabinet,[13] yet he had the bite of an adder when he chose to strike. Churchill could be immensely commanding. Yet, as we shall see in his handling of the hydrogen-bomb issue, he was a romantic traditionalist when it came to the notion of collective Cabinet responsibility.

The plasticity of Cabinet government has proved, too, a considerable job-creation scheme for scholars. An endless process of definition and refinement awaits the student of the standard literature. The Cabinet-committee structure, a practical device for relieving the burden of business falling upon the full Cabinet, is easily enough traced thirty years after, when the relevant papers have been declassified (the preceding twenty-nine years present a would-be anatomist with severe problems, however). It is when the notion of the inner Cabinet, the small group of ministers on the inside track, arises that the fun starts. What do you call them? Wilson, the master of camouflage, called his the Parliamentary Committee.[14] N. A. Gibbs, referring specifically to the Attlee years, described them as 'Minor Cabinets'.[15] Patrick Gordon Walker called them 'partial Cabinets': 'A partial Cabinet is the very opposite of Prime Ministerial government: it presupposes that the Prime Minister carries influential Cabinet colleagues with him, and that these will, with the Prime Minister, convince the Cabinet if policy is questioned when the Cabinet is informed.'[16] But Mackintosh thinks the taxonomy of such groups can be overdone:

Too much must not be made of the talk of inner Cabinets. There is no group of offices which confer any special status on their occupants and no machinery which formally separates an inner from an outer ring. The point about Ministers who are said to be in an inner Cabinet is that they are markedly and regularly consulted (often one by one rather than as a group) by the Prime Minister.[17]

It might be thought that reaching an agreed definition of what the full Cabinet is and what it does would be easier than playing around with concepts of partial, inner or minor Cabinets. After all, it consists of twenty-two known politicians and meets most Thursday mornings in No. 10 with a carefully filtered version of what transpired reaching the newspaper-reading public on Friday mornings after political journalists have received a non-attributable briefing from the Prime Minister's press secretary the evening before. *Questions* defines the Cabinet in terms of functions: it is concerned with matters engaging the notion of collective responsibility because they are major issues or are politically sensitive, and questions reflecting inter-departmental conflicts which cannot be settled in a lower forum.[18] Mackintosh offers several definitions, one of which is very close to *Questions* itself: 'the Cabinet holds the central position because, though it does not often initiate policy or govern in that sense, it is the place where disputes are settled, where major policies are endorsed and where the balance of forces emerges if there is a disagreement'.[19] A second Mackintosh definition is rather more prolix and complicated:

the major task of the Cabinet is not to lead the party, to manage Parliament or to think out policy; it is to take or review the major decisions, to consider (though not necessarily at the formative stage) any proposals that might affect the future of the government and to ensure that no departmental interests are overlooked, thus giving the work of the government a measure of unity.[20]

At his tersest, Mackintosh saw Cabinet as simply 'the most senior Committee' of the Government.[21] In its simplicity, that definition is almost worthy of that uncluttered gentleman with direct experience, Lord Home, who said, 'Cabinet government is designed to concentrate the attention of a small number of people, rather like the board of directors of a company, on the essential business to be done.'[22]

At the other extreme sits Professor Colin Seymour-Ure. Writing in 1971 and heavily influenced by the experience of the Wilson administrations of 1964–70, he took a line similar to one of the Mackintosh definitions: 'the importance of the Cabinet *as an institution* appears to have diminished to the point where it ought properly to be described as no more than *primus inter pares* among other Government committees, just as the Prime Minister used to be called *primus inter pares* among his colleagues'.[23] But he went further.

Building on Max Nicholson's description of the Cabinet (in his fascinating, neglected book *The System*) as an 'abstract and partially fictitious mechanism'[24], Seymour-Ure suggested 'that the Cabinet is becoming a *principle* of government and barely an institution at all'.[25] For him, the Cabinet system, if it ever deserved such a designation, had disintegrated to the point where, when it came to taking decisions,

the role of the full Cabinet is quite arbitrary. Its members are all important. But the ministerial combinations in which decisions are effectively made rarely coincide with Cabinet membership. Some of the combinations do not recur at all (e.g. Prime Minister plus a few colleagues *ad hoc*). Others recur and have been institutionalised in varying degrees.[26]

Having asserted in 1971 that Cabinet was a principle, an approach to government rather than a system (the definition that most clearly reflects the putty-like quality of British Cabinet government), Professor Seymour-Ure, some fourteen years later, produced some helpful 'basic rules' for those who subscribe to the plastic school of thought:

(1) The political leadership takes responsibility collectively for the consequences of decisions taken in its name, regardless of who actually 'takes' them.
(2) This leadership is drawn from Parliament and is ultimately dependent on the House of Commons.
(3) The Cabinet is the highest authority in which *administrative* considerations of government (and administrative notions of efficiency) are reconciled with *political* ideologies and possibilities (and political notions of efficiency).[27]

He stressed the 'supremacy of the political'[28] in the decision-taking cocktail of Cabinet government – a necessary and salutary reminder to a member of the 'policy studies mafia'[29] such as I, who can easily fall into the trap of downgrading the political in favour of the administrative aspects and thereby distorting reality.

But, in offering one's own definition of Cabinet government there are even greater dangers, because, as Seymour-Ure pointed out in 1971, 'one Cabinet exists primarily to embody certain political and governmental values'.[30] Any individual's definition of Cabinet government, therefore, is suffused with his or her personal value system and beliefs about what best suits British society. Such definitions try to freeze the most desirable forms of procedure and to turn them into canons of the Constitution. In their way they are just as self-serving as the blinkered closed-government philosophy contained in *Questions of Procedure for Ministers*. Like *Questions*, they must be taken with a large pinch of salt. Here is my definition.

Cabinet is a blender. It must try and reach rational, practical decisions from a most unpromising mixture of ingredients: political calculation and political hunch; a sometimes wide range of choices each appraised with the best technical and financial analysis Whitehall can produce; judgement about the knock-on effect of choices on other policies and a constant sensitivity to the law of unintended consequences; a reconciliation of short-term requirements with medium-term needs and long-term strategy; and a balancing of the twin pulls on central government from administrative requirements and political imperatives. This is asking a great deal from twenty-two ordinary men and women – ordinary in every sense except, usually, their level of personal ambition. As the most glancing look at any of the Cabinet diaries will show, the reality is messy, a cocktail of calculation, self-delusion, defiance, desperation, opportunism, pathos and bathos. Yet, in a mature democracy, a collective approach to decision-taking in the highest forum in the land has its advantages. It goes with the grain. It is a kind of guarantee against an over-mighty leader and an overweening ideology. Cabinet government does not suit tyrants.

At least one of Mrs Thatcher's Cabinet ministers accepted the Pickthorn interpretation of the British Constitution quoted at the head of this chapter. Norman St John Stevas – like Sir Kenneth himself, no mean scholar of the British system of government[31] – plagiarized his famous one-liner nearly twenty years later when unveiling to the House of Commons in 1979 the Government's plan for a new set of parliamentary select committees. 'Procedure', said St John Stevas, 'is the best constitution that we have.'[32] Both Pickthorn and St John Stevas were referring to *parliamentary* procedure as publicly enshrined in Erskine May, a volume of some bulk formally known as *A Treatise on the Law, Privileges, Proceedings and Usage of Parliament*. The Cabinet equivalent, *Questions of Procedure for Ministers*, is much slimmer and is classified 'confidential'. It is the first document a new Minister is handed by his private secretary. And, if one accepts the Pickthorn–St John Stevas view of procedure, it is the nearest thing we have to a written constitution for British Cabinet government.

Questions, has expanded in line with the growth of post-war government. Attlee's new ministers received their copy in two instalments on 8 August 1945, the day after the first Cabinet meeting of the 1945–51 Labour Government.[33] It was circulated then, as it still is, as a formal Cabinet paper. The Attlee Mark I version was entitled *Cabinet Procedure*, and consisted of twenty-three paragraphs over four smallish pages.[34] Ministers received simultaneously *Miscellaneous Questions of Procedure*, fourteen paragraphs over four pages.[35] Together the two Cabinet papers amounted to thirty-seven paragraphs over eight pages. A revised and expanded version promulgated by Attlee in May 1946 had grown to forty-five paragraphs over ten rather larger pages.[36] Within a year, twenty extra paragraphs had been added.[37] In April 1966, *Questions* consisted of eighty-five paragraphs and sixteen pages.[38] Ten years later, when James Callaghan was in No. 10, it was a document of 132 paragraphs and twenty-seven pages.[39]

For the purpose of treating *Questions* as a surrogate constitution for British Cabinet government, I shall use the 1952 version circulated to ministers by Winston Churchill. More recent and still classified versions contain identical wording in key sections dealing with Cabinet business, conclusions, committees and collective responsibility. As *Questions* is the Cabinet's own book of rules, it should be absorbed, initially anyway, neat and without embellishment.

I.   Cabinet Procedure

Preparation of Business for the Cabinet
  1. The business of the Cabinet consists, in the main, of:–

  (i) Questions which engage the collective responsibility of the Government, either because they raise major issues of policy or because they are likely to occasion public comment or criticism.
 (ii) Questions on which there is an unresolved conflict of interest between Departments.

All questions involving more than one Department should be examined inter-departmentally, before submission to Cabinet, so that the decisions required may be clearly defined. When there is a conflict of interest between Departments, it should not be referred to the Cabinet until all other means of resolving it have been exhausted, including personal correspondence or discussion between the Ministers concerned.
  2. Proposals which involve expenditure or affect general financial or economic policy should be discussed with the Treasury – and, if agreement

cannot be reached between officials, with the Chancellor of the Exchequer – before they are submitted to the Cabinet or to a Ministerial Committee; and the result of those discussions should be indicated in the memorandum.

3. Matters which fall wholly within the Departmental responsibility of a single Minister and do not engage the collective responsibility of the Government need not be brought to Cabinet at all. A precise definition of such matters cannot be given, and in borderline cases a Minister is well advised to bring the matter before his colleagues.

4. These rules do not limit the right of Ministers to submit to the Cabinet memoranda setting out their views on general issues of policy.

5. When a Minister wishes to raise a matter orally at the Cabinet, the Prime Minister's consent should be sought through the Secretary of the Cabinet.

6. Memoranda for the Cabinet should be as brief and as clear as possible. Time spent in making a memorandum short and clear will be saved many times over in reading and in discussion; and it is the duty of Ministers to ensure that this is done by personal scrutiny and, where necessary, revision of memoranda submitted to them by their officials.

The model memorandum explains at the outset what the problem is, indicates briefly the relevant considerations, and concludes with a precise statement of the decisions sought. It is sometimes useful to include a summary of the main points brought out in the body of the memorandum, but such a summary should never exceed a few lines. Prefatory covering notes should be avoided. To facilitate reference in discussion, paragraphs should be numbered.

If it is necessary to refer repeatedly to a body with a long title, an abbreviated version may be used if on the first mention the full title is given and the abbreviation added in brackets, *e.g.*, 'The North Atlantic Treaty Organisation (NATO).'

7. Save with the Prime Minister's permission, which will be granted only for reasons of extreme urgency, a memorandum may not be set down on the Agenda for discussion by the Cabinet until two working days after it was circulated.

8. Cabinet memoranda (as distinct from memoranda for Cabinet Committees) are normally reproduced by the Cabinet Office, the text being sent by the originating Department to the Cabinet Office for the purpose. If for any reason a Cabinet memorandum is reproduced by the originating Department, all copies should be sent to the Cabinet Office, and application should be made to the Cabinet Office for any additional copies required by the reproducing Department. The same rule applies to memoranda reproduced by Departments for consideration by Cabinet Committees: all copies made should be sent to the Cabinet Office for circulation. If an originating Department so wishes, a standing arrangement may be made whereby the Cabinet Office will automatically supply for its use a fixed number of additional copies of memoranda.

9. In no circumstances, other than those mentioned in the preceding paragraph, are Cabinet memoranda to be reproduced or copied in Departments. If a Department requires additional copies of a memorandum, application must in every case be made to the Cabinet Office.

Attendance at Cabinet

10. Cabinet meetings take precedence over all other business. If a member of the Cabinet, or a Minister summoned for a particular item, is unable for any reason to be present at a Cabinet meeting, he should notify the Secretary, who will inform the Prime Minister and will also consider whether any rearrangement of business is required.

11. Ministers' private secretaries can help the Secretary of the Cabinet by indicating, when asking for a subject to be placed on the Cabinet's Agenda, which Ministers other than members of the Cabinet are likely to be concerned, so that arrangements may be made for their attendance.

12. The Prime Minister's Private Secretary is responsible for ensuring that the proceedings of the Cabinet are not disturbed. To assist him, Ministers should give instructions that messages are not to be sent to them while in Cabinet unless they are so urgent that they cannot wait until the end of the meeting.

13. The Secretary should be informed of Ministers' out-of-town engagements, and also of their week-end and holiday arrangements so that, if some sudden emergency arises, he may be able to inform the Prime Minister at once which Ministers are immediately available.

Cabinet Conclusions

14. The record of the Cabinet's proceedings is limited to the decisions taken and such summary of the discussion as may be necessary for the guidance of those who have to take action on them. The Secretary is under instructions to avoid, so far as practicable, recording the opinions expressed by particular Ministers. Matters of exceptional secrecy may be recorded in a Confidential Annex.

15. Any suggestions for amendment of Cabinet Conclusions must reach the Secretary not later than the next day but one following that on which the Meeting was held. Thereafter the Conclusions will be sent to be printed.

16. Ministers are responsible for giving such instructions to their Departments as may be necessary to give effect to the Conclusions of the Cabinet, and for communicating to subordinate Departments or branches decisions of which they should be made aware. Where an urgent matter arises in Cabinet unexpectedly, and a decision is reached requiring immediate action by a Department not represented at the meeting, the Secretary will ensure that the Department concerned is notified forthwith.

17. When a Department has to take action upon, or is otherwise directly affected by, a particular Conclusion, the actual decisions of the Cabinet on

that matter may be copied in the Department, together with so much of the record of the discussion as is essential to a proper understanding of them, and these extracts may be passed to responsible officers in the Department, as may be necessary. The distribution of such extracts within a Department should be limited to the occasions on which it is strictly necessary for the efficient discharge of public business, and care should be taken to see that extracts are sent only to those officers of the Department who need be acquainted with the actual terms of the decision. Where action has to be taken at once by a Department, application may be made to the Secretary for an advance copy of the relevant Conclusions.

Return of Cabinet Documents

18. Cabinet documents are the property of the Crown. Ministers relinquishing office should hand over to their successors those Cabinet documents which are required for current administration and should return all others to the Cabinet Office. A former Minister may at any time have access in the Cabinet Office to copies of Cabinet or Cabinet Committee papers issued to him while in office.

To facilitate the recovery of Cabinet and Cabinet Committee papers and to ensure their safe custody Ministers are asked during their tenure of office to arrange for the regular return to the Cabinet Office (at intervals of, say, three to six months) of such Cabinet documents as are not required for current administration.

On a change of Government, the outgoing Prime Minister issues special instructions about the disposal of the Cabinet papers of his Administration.

Cabinet Committees

19. The procedure outlined above applies *mutatis mutandis* to Ministerial Committees of the Cabinet.

While Committee meetings provide a useful forum for the discussion of policy and for enabling Ministers to ensure that their points of view are understood and to make a contribution to the formulation of policy, their prime object is the despatch of business and the making of decisions. Attendance should be restricted to the permanent members and other Ministers who have a major interest in the question under discussion.

Collective Responsibility

20. Decisions reached by the Cabinet or Cabinet Committees are normally announced and defended by the Minister concerned as his own decisions. There may be rare occasions when it is desirable to emphasise the importance of some decision by stating specifically that it is the decision of Her Majesty's Government. This, however, should be the exception rather than the rule. The growth of any general practice whereby decisions of the Cabinet or of Cabinet Committees were announced as such would lead to the embarrassing result that some decisions of Government would be regarded as less

authoritative than others. Critics of a decision reached by a particular Committee could press for its review by some other Committee or by the Cabinet, and the constitutional right of individual Ministers to speak in the name of the Government as a whole would be impaired.

21. The method adopted by Ministers for discussion among themselves of questions of policy is essentially a domestic matter, and is no concern of Parliament or the public. The doctrine of collective responsibility of Ministers depends, in practice, upon the existence of opportunities for free and frank discussion between them, and such discussion is hampered if the processes by which it is carried on are laid bare. For these reasons it is also the general practice to avoid, so far as possible, disclosing the composition and terms of reference of Cabinet Committees and, in particular, the identity of their Chairmen.

II. Precautions against Unauthorised Disclosures of Information

22. Disclosures in the Press of matters under discussion by the Cabinet or its Committees damage the reputation of the Government and impair the efficiency of its administration.

23. Ministers who share the collective responsibility for the Government's programme must be kept generally aware of the development of important aspects of Government policy. But outside this narrow circle knowledge of these matters should be confined to those, whether Ministers or officials, who are assisting in the formulation or execution of the particular policy concerned, or need to know what is afoot because of its effect on other aspects of public business for which they are responsible.

24. Government policy should not be discussed with persons outside Government service unless this is necessary for the transaction of public business. Care should be taken to see that no discussions of Government policy are held in places where they may be overheard.

25. Ministers are personally responsible for ensuring that all members of their staffs understand the need for exercising the strictest discretion, and for seeing that the appropriate precautions are strictly observed in their Department. The following considerations should be borne in mind:–

(i) While it is within the discretion of Ministers to decide which of their advisers or subordinates should be shown Cabinet papers, the normal rule is that such papers should not be seen by any save their immediate advisers concerned in the formulation of policy. In particular, Cabinet papers should not be circulated as a matter of course to Information Officers or their staffs.

(ii) A Minister who is a member of the Cabinet has responsibilities wider than those of his own Department, and will in that capacity receive some documents which are of no concern to any of his subordinates.

(iii) A Parliamentary Private Secretary is not a member of the Government; and the information given to him should be correspondingly limited. Only exceptionally, and with the express authority of his Minister, should he be shown Cabinet or Cabinet Committee papers or other secret official papers. The information given to him should be limited to what is strictly necessary for the discharge of his Parliamentary and political duties.

(iv) Documents reflecting the personal views of Ministers are in a special category, and their handling requires special care. It is contrary to the doctrine of collective responsibility to make known the attitude of individual Ministers on matters of policy.

(v) If occasions arise on which it is necessary that any considerable number of officers should be consulted on particular issues arising out of Cabinet memoranda, this should be done by means of minutes addressed to the officers concerned, confined to the particular points on which they are required to advise, thus avoiding a wide circulation of the memoranda themselves.

(vi) Experience has shown that leakages of information have often occurred as a result of the skilful piecing together, by representatives of the Press, of isolated scraps of information gathered from several sources, each in itself apparently of little importance. The only safe rule is, therefore, never to mention such matters even in the form of guarded allusions, except to those who must be informed of them for reasons of State, until the time has come when disclosure, in whole or in part, is authorised. Reasons of State may require, in appropriate cases, the confidential communication of some information to a responsible editor, lobby correspondent, &c., for purposes of guidance; but such communication is only justified where it can be assured that the confidence and the terms on which it is made are respected.

26. Secrecy cannot, however, be secured solely by rules restricting the circulation of papers. Public business cannot be transacted without a fairly wide dissemination of confidential information within Government circles, and the essential need is for the observance of a high standard of discretion by all who acquire knowledge of such information in the course of their duties – an attitude of mind which puts first the interests of the Government as a whole and subordinates everything to that end. It is the duty of Ministers to set this standard of discretion in regard to all confidential matters which come within their knowledge, to give an example to others, and to see that their example is followed.

The remaining sections of *Questions* deal with the constitutional position of junior ministers and parliamentary private secretaries, the procedure for making statements in Parliament, publishing White Papers, setting up committees of inquiry, making speeches, broadcasting, writing articles for the press, holding press conferences, granting interviews to individual journalists, making visits at home and abroad, accepting gifts and the handling of private financial business while in office.[40] Nothing is left to chance. Ministers are subject to a discipline comparable to a member of the Armed Forces. Taking the Queen's Shilling, in the political sense, involves a substantial loss of liberty. It is surprising that so few ministers have complained at the time or subsequently. Tony Benn is a rarity. For him, a prime minister's 'power to secure compliance with them [the rules contained in *Questions*] rests upon his power to dismiss those who breach them', and such patronage for him is a key exhibit in his case for a more 'constitutional premiership'.[41]

What I regard as the essence of Cabinet government was captured by Lord Hunt of Tanworth (Secretary of the Cabinet, 1973-9, under Heath, Wilson, Callaghan and Thatcher) in a public lecture on election day in June 1983 (the timing was genuinely coincidental). 'I accept', he said, 'that Cabinet Government must always be a somewhat cumbrous and complicated affair and that this is a price well worth paying for the advantage of shared discussion and shared decision – provided the system can keep up with the demands put upon it.'[42] In chapter 1 I dissect the system before going on to weigh the demands placed upon it since the Second World War.

1

The Cabinet Machine

Now that the Cabinet's gone to its dinner,
The Secretary stays and gets thinner and thinner,
Racking his brains to record and report
What he thinks what they think they ought to have thought.
Anonymous verse, undated[1]

Historians reading this fifty or a hundred years hence will get a totally
false picture. They will be filled with admiration and surprise to find
that the Cabinet were so intellectually disciplined that they argued each
issue methodically and logically through to a neat set of precise
conclusions. It isn't like that at all you know. *Harold Macmillan to
George Mallaby on the style of Cabinet minutes, early 1950s*[2]

Heavens no. I couldn't have stood the intrigue! *Lord Wilson, 1976, on
being asked if he regretted not becoming a permanent civil servant in
the Cabinet Office after the Second World War*[3]

Preparing, in 1976, a 'Times Profile' of the Cabinet Office in the closing
months of Harold Wilson's last premiership, I was struck, after talking
to one veteran minder of the Cabinet machine, by the solace that its
routine could bring at times in the face of vicissitudes and disturbance.
I did not have his permission to attribute his reflections. But they led
me to write the following, concluding comment: 'So long as Cabinet
government survives, the minutes will be taken, typed and distributed,
prodding the rest of Whitehall into action after every Cabinet and
Cabinet Committee meeting. At eight, one and five precisely, the brown
vans will go out carrying the green boxes. Whatever the circumstances,
like Wells Fargo, they will always get through.'[4]

Routine is dull but no Whitehall watcher can afford to ignore it.
It can be very revealing. Indeed, a common criticism of the British
Civil Service is that it places more importance on procedure than getting

the right answer, 'an over-concern with form at the expense of content', as Dr Tessa Blackstone, a former 'think-tank' member has put it.[5]

The origins of 'modern' Cabinet procedure lie in the great political crisis of the First World War, which projected David Lloyd George into the premiership. In the space of a week in December 1916, Lloyd George and Sir Maurice Hankey streamlined the Cabinet system along lines pioneered by the Committee of Imperial Defence. Though it is scarcely credible now, there were no such things as formal Cabinet minutes before the Lloyd George–Hankey reforms. As John Grigg, Lloyd George's biographer, notes,

No less significant than the creation of the War Cabinet – indeed more significant in the longer run – was the attachment to it of the Old War Committee's professional staff under Hankey, which became the War Cabinet Secretariat. The War Committee had worked to an agenda, and a record was kept of its meetings. But at the same time the Cabinet continued to be run without a formal agenda and without minutes. Under Lloyd George's new model government the businesslike procedure of the War Committee was applied to the War Cabinet, and in due course the Cabinet Secretariat became, in peacetime, a permanent institution. No single change was more necessary to enable the executive to function efficiently, and it is one of Lloyd George's outstanding contributions to the modernisation of the British State.[6]

The story of how the Cabinet Secretariat survived the fall of Lloyd George in 1922 – just – is well known. Indeed, the history of the Cabinet Office, its difficult relationship with the Treasury, its shape and performance under successive inter-war prime ministers has been authoritatively told in the Captain Roskill's superb biography of Hankey, the first Cabinet Secretary.[7]

Hankey was a remarkable Royal Marine, a great despatcher of business who applied the craft he had learned as Secretary of the Committee of Imperial Defence to the construction of the Cabinet Office. Sir Robert Vansittart, Permanent Secretary at the Foreign Office in the 1930s, captured in typically colourful language the combined effect of Lloyd George and Hankey on the Whitehall bureaucracy:

Here was one [Lloyd George] never likely to grow grey in the service of assistants, a nature fizzling with those constant transformations of energy which make up conduct. He had only faced the cacophony of war at the last minute, but thenceforth his oratory could be as inspiring, though not quite of the same quality, as Winston's in our second extremity. It could hardly be said that 'he mobilized language and made it fight', but his speeches stand like superannuated spells. A new spirit was upon us.

He had his way by forming a small inner Cabinet in constant session: it was provided with agenda so that Ministers might know what they were going to talk about, and with minutes so that they might remember what they had decided – tremendous innovations.

A secretary was admitted to the arcana and it was Maurice Hankey, who progressively became secretary of everything that mattered. A marine of slight stature and tireless industry, he grew into a repository of secrets, a Chief Inspector of Mines of Information. He had an incredible memory . . . an official brand which could reproduce on call the date, file, substance of every paper that ever flew into a pigeon-hole. If St Peter is as well served there will be no errors on Judgement Day.[8]

That tribute would strike some who knew Hankey as excessive. Vansittart wielded a turbo-charged pen. He and Hankey were allies in fighting Appeasement in the late 1930s. Yet there is justice in the appraisal. Hankey suffered a deal of bureaucratic snobbery from the more traditional Whitehall high-flyers, being only a temporary himself (though he served as Cabinet Secretary from 1916 to 1938). And he did build up what was, by the standards of the time, a Rolls Royce of a machine. It brought, in Sir George Mallaby's words, an element of 'indispensable articulation'[9] to the machinery of government.

Hankey was a machine-minder *par excellence*. There have only been six Cabinet secretaries. One of them has developed a rough-and-ready rule-of-thumb: the job oscillates between efficient machine-minders (Hankey, Brook, Hunt) and rather more artistic policy-makers (Bridges, Trend, Armstrong).[10] Hankey took care of five prime ministers – Lloyd George, Bonar Law, Baldwin, Ramsay MacDonald and Chamberlain – in five sorts of administration: wartime Coalition, post-war Coalition, Conservative, Labour and National. He passed the torch to Edward Bridges in 1938 at the height of Appeasement.

Bridges, whose tenure (1938–47) spanned three prime ministers (Chamberlain, Churchill and Attlee) and four kinds of administration (National, Coalition, Caretaker and Labour), was a Treasury man to his fingertips. In many ways, Edward Bridges was the finest flowering of the Victorian public servant – high minded, politically neutral, a gifted all-rounder who believed that government was best served by crowding the higher Civil Service with latter-day Rennaissance men. He preached this philosophy in a beautifully articulated lectured at Cambridge in 1950 called 'Portrait of a Profession.'[11]

Bridges was a crucial figure from 1940 to 1945, running the 'Home Front' while Churchill got on with the war. Only he and Sir Hastings Ismay, universally known as 'Pug' because of his bulldog features, remained in the same job for the duration. On Victory in Europe Day, when the War Cabinet went to Buckingham Palace to celebrate and to be photographed with the royal family, King George VI, Ismay recalled, 'remarked that he and Bridges and I ought to be taken together as the only three who had kept their jobs throughout the war. But, alas, the proposal was not pressed.'[12]

For about eighteen months after the war, Bridges was a Pooh-Bah figure serving simultaneously as Secretary of the Cabinet, Permanent Secretary to the Treasury and Head of the Civil Service. During the Attlee years he was somewhat eclipsed by Norman Brook, who formally succeeded him at the Cabinet Office in 1947, though he had been Cabinet Secretary in all but name for a year.

Brook, who held the Hankey succession from 1947 to 1963, was an enormously influential figure under four prime ministers – Attlee, Churchill, Eden and Macmillan. He was quietly forbidding, an austere pipe-smoker, a great despatcher of business, a stickler for correct dress. Bridges would playfully aim punches at the stomachs of colleagues and say of some piece of work, 'Isn't this fun?' Such behaviour from Brook would have been inconceivable. Harold Macmillan once told Lord Moran, Churchill's physician, that Brook's position in the constellation was all the more remarkable given his humble origins (direct grant school in Wolverhampton, scholarship boy at Oxford): 'Norman has most wonderful judgement. He was always right. Pure in-born judgement because, as I expect you know, he had no background.'[13] Macmillan had been at Eton, an institution for which he had unstinting praise.[14] Brook was Hankey-like in his attention to procedure. In 1947 he invented a system of 'steering-briefs' for the Prime Minister. Using these he would advise Attlee on the order in which business should be taken at meetings of the Cabinet and Cabinet committees, the points that needed to be brought out in discussion and the outcome he thought most desirable. Set the briefs alongside the minutes, taken and circulated by Brook, and one detects a similarity of thrust. This could, of course, simply reflect Brook's gift for reading accurately the mind of his prime minister and the Cabinet collectively. John Hunt, the next but one Cabinet Secretary, served as Brook's private secretary for two years in the late fifties. His style directly reflected his mentor's.

Burke Trend, who worked as Brook's deputy from 1956 to 1959, was a very different breed, though he shared Brook's passion for total discretion. He succeeded Brook early in 1963 after a fond farewell in Cabinet, as Macmillan's diary for 3 January records: 'I made a short-speech about him and he replied; I have sent him a nice piece of plate as a mark of esteem.' Macmillan wrote in his memoirs of 'the loyal support of this remarkable civil servant [i.e. Brook], who commanded the confidence and affection of all my colleagues'.[15] Lord Trend, a tall, immensely courteous man with a precise, almost clipped, speaking-manner, had a warm, companiable air about him. Yet people reach for glacial metaphors when describing him in operation. 'Absolutely cool under pressure', says Lord Home.[16] 'The epitome of ice-cold judgement and utter dedication with the occasional lapse into impish humour', says Sir Derek Mitchell, who was Principal Private Secretary in No. 10 during the Home–Trend partnership of 1963–4.[17]

Lord Trend was famous in Whitehall for his ability to draft White Papers in his head.[18] He once described his thought process when white-papering. In 1970 Edward Heath had firm views on what to call the jewel in the crown of his new style of Government: 'I wanted to call it the "Think Tank". The secretary of the Cabinet won and we called it the "Central Policy Review Staff"!'[19] Why did Lord Trend object and how did he persuade his prime minister to agree?

It became known as the 'Think Tank'. But they weren't quite the words you could see on the front of a White Paper. I remember scratching my head and sucking my pencil and thinking 'What on earth are we going to call this thing?' And then it seemed to me that if you took the words which we finally did adopt, they came as near as I could come to being accurate about it. It *was* central; it *was* concerned with policy; and it *was* concerned with reviewing policy centrally and it consisted of a staff, not a political unit.[20]

Seldom could Burke Trend be drawn into a discussion of the Cabinet Secretary's art. Ironically, it was an interview in the *Listener* to mark the start of the *Yes, Prime Minister* television series in January 1986 which brought him out on the subject. He offered some advice to

Sir Humphrey Appleby, who was about to move with his minister, Jim Hacker, from the fictional Department of Administrative Affairs to the very centre of power. Humphrey, said Lord Trend, had to remember two things:

He's not the Prime Minister's exclusive servant. He's the servant of the full Cabinet. He's got to have no truck with the idea of a Prime Minister's Department, a 'Kitchen Cabinet' or a 'Garden Suburb' [a reference to Lloyd George's Prime Minister's Secretariat housed in huts on the No. 10 lawn]. I can't believe in them as a source of advice to the Prime Minister in the sense of being a rival to the Cabinet Office. There has got to be one centre round which the rest of the official machine can come together.

He's got to develop a rather different style. He's got to be a bit more detached, not taking sides in departmental squabbles, ensuring that they all get a fair hearing. And he has to deal with that endless upward surge of business, driving it downward as much as he can.[21]

Lord Home remembers the Trend passion for accuracy. 'He had thought about everything to the last detail before putting his conclusions to the Prime Minister. He knew the case backwards.'[22] But not every occupant of No. 10 warmed wholly to the Trend style. Heath wished his officials had more about them of the French Civil Service method of strong policy advocacy. Trend would sometimes infuriate him by sticking to the traditional British style of displaying the options, the pros and cons of each, and insisting it was the Prime Minister's job to do the choosing.[23] Douglas Hurd, inside No. 10 as Heath's Political Secretary from 1970 to 1973, alluded to this in his *An End to Promises*. Shortly after Lord Trend's retirement in the autumn of 1973 (he left in September, a few days before the Yom Kippur War), there was a meeting in No. 10 about the handling of the impending fuel crisis and worsening industrial relations in the coalfields. Hurd recalls,

On 27 November a meeting was called at No. Ten to brief the Prime Minister for his meeting with the Miners' Executive the next day. It should have provided a chance for that clear-headed analysis of the options before the Government, which was then badly needed. Instead there was silence on the big issues and a confused, bitty discussion of trivial tactical points. I felt critical of the senior civil servants present, whose duty it should have been to force the discussion into some coherent channel.

This was the third and final occasion when I felt that at a crucial moment they fell below what was required. The others had occurred after Bloody

Sunday in Londonderry in 1972, and during the discussion of inflation in the summer of 1973. No one who was present at any of these three meetings could believe that the Civil Service runs this country.[24]

Burke Trend was succeeded by his deputy, John Hunt, who was well placed to advise the Heath Cabinet on its deepening winter crisis. Hunt had been asked by Heath and Trend to review, with Lord Jellicoe, the Lord Privy Seal, the Whitehall Emergencies Organization after its inadequate performance during the 1972 miners' strike. Out of this emerged a new arm of the Cabinet Office, the Civil Contingencies Unit (CCU), which Hunt ran until he replaced Trend in the Cabinet secretaryship.[25]

John Hunt was an immensely energetic figure, a dynamo rather than an intellectual, a great gripper of policy areas which had fallen into mess and confusion, and in the Heath, Wilson, Callaghan and Thatcher years from 1973 to 1979, which were his span, he was not short of material on which to apply his talent. 'Burke was feline', said one very senior minister: 'John is a Borzoi'.[26] A senior official reached for even more vivid imagery: 'Trend was Byzantine . . . Hunt is a sixteenth-century cardinal [Lord Hunt is a Catholic and brother-in-law of a real cardinal, Archbishop Hume] with a touch of the Borgias.'[27] For Joe Haines, Wilson's Press Secretary from 1974 to 1976, Hunt was simply 'the most powerful man in Whitehall'.[28]

Power flowed into the Cabinet Office during the Hunt stewardship. There were new units for contingencies, devolution to Scotland and Wales (contained in a so-called Constitution Unit) and Europe (which became a fully fledged secretariat). Hunt worked very closely with Sir Kenneth Berrill, the second Director of the Central Policy Review Staff (CPRS), and used him as something approaching a personal economic adviser.[29] Power also accrued to the more orthodox branches of the Cabinet Office, as one secretariat member explained, albeit cautiously, in early 1976:

If there are signs that the department which is leading on a particular subject has got into a bit of a muddle or has got too close to things, you need a sharp eye and a good nose for discovering just the right moment to ring up and say 'Why not have a meeting?' Very often this generates an almost spontaneous desire to pull the thing together even though the department concerned may have sweated blood in getting it this far'.

The managerial approach developed by John Hunt, particularly in economic affairs, means that the Cabinet Office tends to be in all the front-line fights. But we always have to carry the rest of Whitehall with us. If the departments ganged up on us, we would always be defeated.[30]

The last sentence is a bureaucratic mirror-image of the Prime Minister's power *vis-à-vis* his or her colleagues. Hunt exuded an air of confidence and power that went with his administrative style. When he walked from Whitehall through to Horseguards Parade, soldiers on sentry duty in Horseguards Arch would snap to attention, thinking him a General in transit from the Ministry of Defence to the Headquarters of the London District.[31] Hunt was a machine man *par excellence*, though he did possess a streak of non-conformity. The story is told in Whitehall of an act of defiance when he was Norman Brook's private secretary. When Brook was out of the office for a day, Hunt would sometimes turn up to the office in a tweed jacket with his dog in tow.[32]

Robert Armstrong, who succeeded John Hunt in late 1979, is a very different operator – smoother, less pushy, less overtly power-conscious. 'Mrs Thatcher', said one senior official who knows them both well, 'had an enormous respect for John. But she thought he tended to push her along when she was not quite ready. She trusts Robert's judgement, trusts him to get a solution, to smooth out problems. She listens to him a good deal about what is going on in Whitehall and about summitry. John was always sorting things out; Robert behaves in a less autocratic manner.'[33] But, as we shall see in chapter 3, Mrs Thatcher places less demand on her Cabinet machine and its minders than did any of her recent predecessors. These days it is, as often as not, her Downing Street Private Office rather than the Cabinet Office to which senior men elsewhere in Whitehall turn when they want to find out what is going on. 'There is warmth', said one well-placed official. 'They [Sir Robert and Mrs Thatcher] get along fine. But she is not the sort of person who uses the official machine to do things for her.'[34] The Prime Minister has referred to him as 'my oracle'.[35] There are signs that Armstrong does not mind too much that the Cabinet Office has lost some of the horsepower of the Hunt era. He would tell his friends in the late seventies that he thought too much power was being sucked into the Cabinet Office from the departments where it properly belonged.[36] He did not relish Hunt speaking out on the deficiencies of the Cabinet machine in his lecture on 'Cabinet Strategy and Management' delivered on election day 1983.[37] Intriguingly, though, there were highly discreet indications that Burke Trend approved of Hunt's initiative and diagnosis.[38]

Armstrong himself is not a secrecy fanatic, though he can get irritated when Cabinet committees are 'blown'.[39] He favours a code of practice on open government as a halfway house to full freedom of information, which he dislikes fiercely.[40] Occasionally, he has talked about the subject in public: 'Government ought to explain the decisions which they take as fully as possible to Parliament and to the public, and, if possible, more fully than they do now. I would like to see more open government, and I have made no secret of that, in a variety of respects.'[41] In the same interview with Marcel Berlins on the Channel Four *Questions* programme on 1 July 1984, he spelled out the requirements of a good civil servant in what were clearly auto-biographical terms: 'You need to be dispassionate, you need to be fair-minded, you need to be thorough, you need to be able to subordinate your personal and political views to the work of your department and to the service of the government of the day. And you need to be discreet.'[42]

Discreet he certainly has been. As for those 'personal and political views', they are small-'c' conservative but not Thatcherite. Those who know him well see him standing where the Earl of Stockton stands in the mid-eighties.[43] And on individual policies he has differed from his prime minister. He tried hard to fashion a voluntary 'no strike' agreement for the Government Communications Headquarters (GCHQ) in early 1984.[44] He thought Mrs Thatcher should have accepted the Civil Service unions' offer of one, and then have deunionized the intelligence centre at the first instance of industrial action at Cheltenham or one of its many out-stations.[45]

Robert Armstrong has a nice touch in self-irony and describes himself as 'impatient, self indulgent and rather lazy'.[46] He is not lazy. But he is not an earth-mover like Hunt, nor is he a reformer or a policy entrepreneur. 'I don't want to be out there in front', he told Marcel Berlins. 'I feel much happier, much more sure that I'm in a role that suits me where I am in a kind of back room.'[47] But he loves being Cabinet Secretary, close to the centre of power where the great decisions are taken:

It's very hard work and the hours are very long, and you can use almost any epithet you like to describe the activity except 'boring'. It's fascinating and sometimes it's infuriating; sometimes it's frantic; a lot of it is tremendous fun in the sense that Edward Bridges, my predecessor, used to say that things were 'fun' because they were very stimulating and exciting to do.[48]

Sir Robert will almost certainly be a unique figure in the history of the Cabinet secretaryship. He is due to retire at Easter 1987. Barring the unforeseen, Mrs Thatcher will still be in No. 10. As Secretary of the Cabinet he will have served only *one* prime minister, compared to Hankey's five, Bridges's three, Brook's four, Trend's four and Hunt's four. Old Cabinet secretaries do not, however, fade away. Very often they are called back to do 'special' tasks, as Trend was in 1974: in this instance, to investigate the case of the late Sir Roger Hollis, the former Director General of MI5, who was under suspicion of having spied for Russia.[49] And from what kind of places are they recalled? Hankey became a director of the Suez Canal Company (he returned as a minister during the Second World War); Bridges chaired the British Council, Brook the BBC, Hunt the Banque Nationale de Paris in London; and Trend became Rector of Lincoln College, Oxford. Where will Armstrong go? Perhaps a college, maybe the provostship of Eton, and there is always the opera, a constant solace: 'Covent Garden is a good contrast to the Civil Service. At 7.30 each evening the curtain has to go up on a performance to be judged by 2000 people. There is no tomorrow. In the Civil Service there is always tomorrow and a tomorrow.'[50]

Over what kind of empire does Sir Robert preside in between trips to *Figaro* and *Il Trovatore*? His inheritance from Hunt was pretty hefty. Two years later the bounds of his domain grew wider still and wider. In November 1981 I mapped his kingdom for *The Times*:

At the beginning of this month Sir Robert Armstrong . . . was already the most powerful public servant in the Kingdom, calibrating the flow of business through the Cabinet and its committees and supervising the work of the security and intelligence services on behalf of the Prime Minister.

In the second week of November, thanks to Mrs Thatcher's desire to disband the Civil Service Department and the departure of Sir Ian Bancroft into early retirement, Sir Robert, as Joint Head of the Home Civil Service with Sir Douglas Wass of the Treasury, acquired responsibility for senior appointments in the public service, the honours system, the efficiency, management and security of the Civil Service, and another substantial tranche of influence.

Whitehall has not seen such a concentration of administrative power into a single pair of hands since the period 1956–62 when the late Lord Normanbrook combined the offices of the Secretary of the Cabinet and Head of Home Civil Service.[51]

That description still stands, subject to two changes which have further concentrated power onto his person. At Easter 1983 Sir Douglas Wass retired, leaving Sir Robert the sole head of his profession. And, having fought off an attempt early in 1982 to merge the Downing Street Policy Unit and the CPRS under the direction of Sir John Hoskyns, Head of the No. 10 Unit, Sir Robert in the week after the 1983 election had to assist at the disbandment of the CPRS, a development which he strongly regretted.[52] Though he wished the 'think-tank' to continue, its demise did remove an alternative supply of rival advice to Prime Minister and Cabinet. The CPRS's scientists and technologists are now housed in a Science and Technology Secretariat reporting to Sir Robert. In fact, Sir Robert's domain is a federation of six secretariats each with its own head. They are as follows.[53]

The Economic Secretariat This is led by Brian Unwin, a deputy secretary seconded from the Treasury. It deals with economic, industrial and energy policy.

The Oversea and Defence Secretariat Christopher Mallaby, a senior diplomat on loan from the Foreign Office runs this secretariat. It blends foreign and defence policy-making with the output of the intelligence agencies.

The European Secretariat EEC business has become so bulky across a wide span of Whitehall departments that it merits a secretariat of its own, separate from the rest of foreign and economic policy. The Ministry of Agriculture, an EEC-dominated department, provides its chief, in the person of David Williamson, a deputy secretary.

Home Affairs Secretariat This covers social policy, law and order, environment, education, housing and local government. The planning of the Government's legislative programme also falls to Home Affairs, which is run by Anthony Langdon, an under secretary from the Home Office.

Science and Technology Secretariat Mrs Thatcher, the first British Prime Minister to have a science degree, takes a close interest in the work of the secretariat, which is led by Sir Robin Nicholson, a deputy secretary who came into Whitehall from industry.

Security and Intelligence Secretariat This is the most sensitive secretariat of all. It is headed by Sir Colin Figures. Sir Colin chairs the Joint Intelligence Committee, which meets weekly to sift the product from all secret sources and to present a report, the 'Red Book', to ministers, chiefly those who sit with the Prime Minister on the Oversea and Defence committee who 'need to know'. The JIC has its own Assessments Staff with a battery of current intelligence groups, which between them cover the globe. In constitutional terms the JIC is a freak. It is the only Cabinet committee on which foreigners sit. Intelligence allies from the United States, Canada, Australia and New

Zealand attend the first part of its regular Wednesday-morning meeting, when material is pooled and discussion shared. They leave before the second half, when UK-only issues are tackled.

At the end of each week Sir Robert meets with his heads of secretariat and Nigel Wicks, Mrs Thatcher's Principal Private Secretary, to prepare a three-week forward look of business coming to Cabinet and Cabinet committee. Agendas and dates are arranged accordingly.

Civil servants brought into the Cabinet Office to join a secretariat are handed a document called *Talking about the Office*. This coaches them in cover stories to be used at parties when asked what they do for a living. It also contains the justification used by successive prime ministers and cabinet secretaries for preserving the secrecy of the system:

The work of the secretariat [is] . . . essentially confidential. This stems directly from the secrecy which properly surrounds Cabinet business and the advice given to Ministers, and, by extension, the business of Cabinet Committees.

It has always been maintained by successive administrations that disclosure of the processes by which Government decisions are reached weakens the collective responsibility of Ministers, which is what welds the separate functions of Government into a single Administration. The first rule, therefore, is that *even the existence of particular Cabinet Committees* should not be disclosed – still less their composition, terms of reference etc. [Emphasis added.][54]

The Thatcher Machine

The Cabinet-committee network had in the winter of 1985–6 at least 160 groups within its span. Mrs Thatcher has acknowledged the existence of four. In a written parliamentary answer shortly after her re-election in 1983, she disclosed the four main standing-committees of Cabinet: Home and Social Affairs, chaired by Lord Whitelaw, Lord President of the Council; a Legislation Committee chaired by John Biffen, Leader of the House of Commons; and two committees chaired by herself, on oversea and defence policy and on economic strategy.[55] In announcing this quartet, which she first did in 1979, she was going much further than any other prime minister in recent times. But it left the citizen and the backbench MP some 156 committees short. Junior

Table 1   Mrs Thatcher's engine room

Committee initials	Chairman	Functions
Economic, Industrial and Scientific		
EA	Margaret Thatcher (Prime Minister)	Economic affairs and strategy, energy policy, changes in labour law, the most important EEC matters
E(EX)	Margaret Thatcher	Export policy
E(NI)	Margaret Thatcher	Public-sector strategy and oversight of the nationalized industries
E(NF)	Nigel Lawson (Chancellor of the Exchequer)	Nationalized-industry finance
E(LA)	Margaret Thatcher	Local-government affairs
NIP	Nick Monck	Official committee on nationalized-industry policy
E(PSP)	Nigel Lawson	Public-sector and public-service pay policy
E(DL)	Nigel Lawson	Disposal and privatization of state assets
E(PU)	Leon Brittan (Trade and Industry Secretary)	'Buy British' policy for public purchasing
E(CS)	John MacGregor (Chief Secretary, Treasury)	Civil Service pay and contingency plans for Civil Service strikes
E(OCS)	Anne Mueller (Cabinet Office official)	Official committee for preparing contingency plans
PESC	John Anson (Treasury official)	Committee of finance officers handling the annual public expenditure survey
OCS	Sir Robin Nicholson (Chief Scientist, Cabinet Office)	Official Committee of Chief Scientists
OCS(I)	Sir Robin Nicholson	Offical Committee of Chief Scientists on International Policy
IT(O)	Sir Robin Nicholson	Official Committee on Information Technology
Oversea and Defence		
OD	Margaret Thatcher	Foreign affairs, defence and Northern Ireland
OD(O)	Sir Robert Armstrong (Cabinet Secretary)	Permanent secretaries' group shadowing OD
OD(E)	Sir Geoffrey Howe (Foreign Secretary)	EEC policy
EQ(S)	David Williamson (Cabinet Office official)	Committee of deputy secretaries servicing OD(E)
EQ(O)	M. R. H. Jenkins (Foreign Office official)	Official committee on routine EEC business

Table 1   Mrs Thatcher's engine room (continued)

Committee initials	Chairman	Functions
Oversea and Defence (continued)		
OD(SA)	Margaret Thatcher	Committee on the South Atlantic, the so-called 'War Cabinet' of 1982
OD(FAF)	Margaret Thatcher	Committee on future arrangements for the Falklands
OD(HK)	Margaret Thatcher	Future of Hong Kong
Home, Legislation and Information		
L	John Biffen (Leader of the Commons)	Legislation
QL	John Biffen	Preparation of the Queen's Speech
H	Lord Whitelaw (Lord President)	Home affairs and social policy, including education and housing
CCU	Douglas Hurd (Home Secretary)	The Civil Contingencies Unit of the Cabinet Office, which prepares plans for the maintenance of essential supplies and services during industrial disputes
H(HL)	Lord Whitelaw	Reform of the House of Lords (abandoned after a few meetings in 1982–3)
HD	Douglas Hurd	Home (i.e. civil) defence
HD(O)	Christopher Mallaby (Cabinet Office official)	Official committee shadowing HD
HD(O)L	Not known	Updating wartime emergency legislation
HD(P)	David Heaton (Home Office official)	Updating of central- and local-government civil-defence plans
TWC	Sir Robert Armstrong	Transition to War Committee, which updates the 'War Book' for the mobilization of Whitehall and the Armed Forces in a period of international tension
EOM	Anne Mueller	Monthly meeting of Whitehall establishment officers on personnel policy
MIO	Bernard Ingham (Press Secretary, No. 10)	Weekly meeting of chief information officers
MIO	Bernard Ingham	Special group for handling economic information. Meets infrequently owing to persistent leaking
Intelligence and Security		
MIS	Margaret Thatcher	Ministerial steering-committee on intelligence which supervises MI5, MI6, the Defence Intelligence Staff and GCHQ and fixes budget priorities
PSIS	Sir Robert Armstrong	Permanent secretaries' steering-group on intelligence; prepares briefs for ministerial group

Table 1   Mrs Thatcher's engine room (continued)

Committee initials	Chairman	Functions
Intelligence and Security (continued)		
JIC	Sir Colin Figures	Joint Intelligence Committee, which prepares assessments for ministers, collating intelligence from all sources and circulating them weekly in the 'Red Book'
JIC(EA)	Sir Colin Figures	Economic-intelligence assessment
SPM	Sir Robert Armstrong	Security and policy methods in the Civil Service
Official Committee on security	Sir Robert Armstrong	Permanent secretaries' group on internal Whitehall security
Personnel Security Committee	Sir Robert Armstrong	Official group supervising the working of positive vetting, polygraphs, etc.
Ad hoc		
MISC 3	John Dempster (Lord Chancellor's Department official)	Public-records policy
MISC 7	Margaret Thatcher	Replacement of the Polaris force with Trident
MISC 14	Nigel Lawson	Policy innovation
MISC 15	Formerly head of CPRS; post now defunct	Official group for briefing MISC 14
MISC 21	Lord Whitelaw	Ministerial committee which meets each autumn to fix the level of rate- and transport-support grant for local authorities
MISC 32	Robert Wade-Gery[*a] (Cabinet Office official)	Deployment of the Armed Forces outside the NATO area
MISC 42	Robert Wade-Gery[*a]	Military assistance (for example, training of personnel) for the armed services of friendly powers
MISC 51	Robert Wade-Gery[*a]	Commodities needed for strategic purposes (for example, oil)
MISC 54	Lord Soames[c]	Future of Civil Service Pay Research
MISC 57	Robert Wade-Gery[*a]	Contingency planning for a miners' strike
MISC 58	John Dempster	Liberalizing the declassification of official documents
MISC 62	Lord Whitelaw	The 'Star Chamber' for forcing spending-cuts on departmental ministers
MISC 79	Lord Whitelaw	Alternatives to domestic rates; rate-capping
MISC 83	David Goodall[b]	Internal constitutional arrangements for the Falkland Islands

Table 1 Mrs Thatcher's engine room (continued)

Committee initials	Chairman	Functions
Ad hoc (continued)		
MISC 87	Nigel Lawson	De-indexing of benefits
MISC 91	Margaret Thatcher	Choice of ALARM anti-radar missile
MISC 94	Peter Gregson (Cabinet Office official)	Detailed preparation for a miners' strike
MISC 95	Mrs Thatcher	Abolition of the GLC and the metropolitan counties
MISC 97	Nicholas Barrington (Foreign Office official)	Preparation for 1984 London Economic Summit
MISC 101	Mrs Thatcher	Day-to-day handling of the 1984–5 miners' strike
MISC 103	Unknown	Public-sector housing policy
MISC 107	Lord Young (Employment Secretary)	Training of 14–18 year olds
MISC 108	Lord Young	Freeing small businesses from red tape
MISC 111	Mrs Thatcher	Future of the Welfare State
MISC 115	Lord Young	Tourism and Leisure
MISC 117	Lord Whitelaw	Acid rain
MISC 119	Lord Young	Deregulation
MISC 121	Mrs Thatcher	Inner cities
MISC 122	Mrs Thatcher	Handling of the teachers' dispute, 1985–6

[a]Sir Robert has since left the Cabinet Office.
[b]David Goodall has since left the Cabinet Office.
[c]Lord Soames resigned from the Government in September 1981.
Source: The bulk of this table and the explanation provided for it have to be cited as private information.

ministers have a very incomplete picture of the Cabinet's committees. Only a handful of Cabinet ministers know most of them. To help fill the gap, table 1 presents the best intelligence on the Cabinet machine in December 1985. The table and the machine need some breaking down into their constituent parts.

Harold Macmillan once called committees 'the oriflamme of democracy'. He dipped into his knowledge of heraldry in a Cabinet paper written in 1953 in the hope of persuading his colleagues to set up a Cabinet committee on air pollution.[56] These days, Cabinet committees come in five types. *Standing committees* are permanent for the duration of a prime minister's term of office. *Ad hoc committees* meet to handle a single issue such as Trident, or are convened spasmodically (an example is MISC 62, the so-called 'Star Chamber', which gathers each year in early autumn in an attempt to force economies on reluctant spending departments). There are *ministerial committees*, at which the civil servants present take the minutes but do not participate. These can be either standing or ad hoc as can the purely Civil Service groups known as *official committees*. Some of these, such as OD(O), shadow ministerial groups (in this case OD), and some, such as EQ(S) – European Questions (Steering) – do the regular spadework for standing ministerial committees. Some, such as E(OCS) – Economy (Official Civil Service) – are called into being to handle a specific problem: in this case the Civil Service strike of 1981, in which it acted first as a planning group and then, once industrial action had begun, as an executive body. After the strike ended E(OCS) lay dormant until the next burst of confrontation between the Government and its direct-labour organization. Finally, there are *mixed committees*, in which both ministers and civil servants participate. Heath favoured these as part of his attempt to improve the efficiency of the Cabinet system in the early 1970s. They did not work particularly well, as officials were generally reluctant to contradict their ministers. Wilson, himself a former Cabinet Office civil servant and a traditionalist in such matters, got rid of nearly all of them when he returned to power in 1974. The only important mixed committee to survive from the Heath era is the CCU, or Civil Contingencies Unit, which sits as an executive body taking hour-by-hour decisions when strikes are in process that threaten the essentials of life.

Some committees, usually though not exclusively those in the MISC (miscellaneous) series, have a short but very significant life. For example, MISC 111, the Prime Minister's high-level group which oversaw the progress of Norman Fowler's reviews of social security in 1984–5, went to abeyance as soon as the Green Paper was published, in June 1985. Indeed, when Cabinet Office files are declassified under the thirty-year rule, the best way of determining the ebb and flow of an administration's business is to trace the life-cycle of its MISCs. (Just to confuse matters, they change to GENs, or 'general' committees, on the arrival of a new prime minister.)

Even when Sir Robert Armstrong's Cabinet Committee Book is available at the Public Record Office, it will still be a complicated matter tracing the progress of certain issues. Take, for example, a spectre which has haunted the Conservatives ever since the National Union of Mineworkers (NUM) brought down the Heath Government in the winter crisis of 1973–4.[57] After entering Downing Street, Mrs Thatcher took some time to be persuaded of the need to plan in the finest detail possible for coping with and eventually breaking a miners' strike. Events did the persuading.

In February 1981, Mrs Thatcher and David Howell were forced into a climbdown on the question of pit closures, the very same issue which precipitated the 1984–5 dispute. Smarting under the defeat, she commissioned an ad hoc group, MISC 57, under the chairmanship of Robert Wade-Gery, to prepare the ground so that a similar result could be averted next time. At that time Wade-Gery took the chair at the Civil Contingencies Unit when it met as a purely Civil Service body for planning-purposes. Traditionally, the task of servicing the CCU and its offshoots has gone to a special section of the Oversea and Defence Secretariat, led first by Brigadier Dick Bishop and currently by another retired military man, Brigadier Tony Budd.

MISC 57 met in conditions of extreme secrecy for most of 1981. It looked at ways of preventing a miners' strike and of minimizing damage to the nation if the prevention strategy failed. The files on Heath's three-day week in 1973–4 were examined and lessons learnt about the most efficient use of rota cuts to eke out supplies of electricity. The idea would be to maintain power for essential services and supplies once the Government had taken the emergency powers it needed to issue instructions to industry and consumers. MISC 57 forwarded its findings to ministers in December 1981. As a result of the Wade-Gery report, ministers adopted early in 1982 a three-point strategy.

(1) Bigger coal stocks at the power stations might discourage the NUM from taking industrial action. Cash limits on the Central Electricity Generating Board were eased to facilitate this, and rail deliveries from pits to power stations were stepped up.
(2) If the deterrent failed, the stockpiles would ensure the miners suffered hardship during a protracted dispute. This would encourage a drift back to work and put pressure on miners' leaders to settle.

(3) During the strike there would be a switch from coal-fired to oil-burning power stations where possible. If the railwaymen backed the miners, coal stocks would be replenished by convoys of private hauliers.[58]

This piece of contingency planning led one senior civil servant to remark, as the miners' strike collapsed in March 1985, that Wade-Gery (by this time Sir Robert Wade-Gery, British High Commissioner in Delhi) 'deserved a peerage'.[59]

Yet when the strike began it was not the CCU which swung into action. That was held in reserve in case the Government needed to declare a State of Emergency and ration power supplies. In that event, the CCU would have become the focal point of an elaborate operation using regional emergency committees in provincial centres, as it had in 1973–4 and again in 1979 during the Callaghan Administration's winter crisis, when a lorry-drivers' strike hit food supplies. The key Cabinet committee during the year-long miners' dispute was not the CCU but MISC 101, a ministerial group chaired by the Prime Minister which met several times a week to review developments and plan counter-measures. MISC 101 was serviced not by the Oversea and Defence Secretariat (though Brigadier Budd and other members of it had important advisory roles) but by the Economic Secretariat (then under Peter Gregson), which, as we have seen, has responsibility for energy matters. The Government got by without a State of Emergency and the CCU's executive network did not need to be activated.[60]

Just how Mrs Thatcher uses her Cabinet Office and its engine room, and how it meshes with her very personal style of government will be discussed at length in chapter 3. Before that, it is necessary to describe the personalities and postwar events which shaped the machine she inherited in May 1979.

2

Overloading the Engine,
1945–79

Today our image of government is more that of the sorcerer's apprentice. The waters rise. The apprentice rushes about with his bucket. And none of us knows when, or whether, the magician will come home. *Professor Anthony King, 1975*[1]

I have . . . often been worried that we are imposing more and more on a system of collective ministerial decision-taking that was designed for quite a different era. *Lord Hunt of Tanworth, ex-Cabinet Secretary, 1983*[2]

The Cabinet is not a place where decisions can be formulated. *David Howell, ex-Cabinet Minister, Thatcher Administration, 1985*[3]

It's amazingly difficult to discuss anything serious in a group of twenty-two, twenty-three men and women. *Sir Frank Cooper, ex-Permanent Secretary, 1985*[4]

The general calibre of ministers is normally low. Their irrelevant experience, coupled with the impossible burdens of office, have contributed to thirty years of policy failure. *Sir John Hoskyns, ex-Head of Mrs Thatcher's Policy Unit, 1983*[5]

There are dangers involved in the writing of contemporary history quite apart from the standard objection that distance and hard evidence are required if a true perspective is to be gained. Hindsight throws a retrospective shadow over people and events which distort light and shade as they were actually perceived at the time. The period of the Attlee governments of 1945–51 was particularly prone to retrospective retouching by the ideologically driven in the mid-1980s, as Paul Addison noted in the Preface to the second of his two outstanding studies of the 1940s:

When the Marxist Left and the radical Right emerged in the 1970s there was one point on which they were agreed: that many of the seeds of decline were planted in the immediate post-war years. According to the Marxist Left, this was because socialism and the class struggle were betrayed. According to the radical Right, it was because free market forces had been stultified by the welfare state and the managed economy. . . .

I do not believe that either of these theories is plausible as a reading of post-war history or workable as a means of governing Britain. . . . Yet each theory illuminated a disturbing corner of reality neglected by conventional opinion. The Marxist Left drew attention to the fact that the sources of industrial conflict were just as explosive as ever. The radical Right drew attention to the fact that the public sector sheltered powerful vested interests whose claims for greater resources were theoretically boundless.

These were truths and remain so in spite of the fallacious ideological baggage with which they are mixed up. Neither problem reached critical proportions between 1945 and 1951, but with hindsight they cast a shadow over the period.[6]

Identical pitfalls await the student of what political scientists call the 'overload' problem in government[7] when he or she attempts to read into the past harbingers of difficulties which subsequently became acute. In fact, this is a double-headed danger. For example, the period 1945–51 has come to acquire a retrospective glow which it may not altogether deserve. Anthony King, in his seminal article on overload, published in 1975, commented on 'the increasing difficulty that both major political parties seem to have in carrying out their election manifestos' and cast his mind back thirty years to find the standard from which subsequent administrations had fallen: 'The fit between what the Labour Party said it would do in 1945 and what the Labour Government actually achieved between 1945 and 1951 is astonishingly close. Most of *Let Us Face the Future* reads like a prospective history of the immediate post-war period. Since about 1959, however, the fit has become less close.'[8]

The best antidote to myth-making is, as R. B. McCallum, pioneer of the Nuffield Election Studies, once said, to photograph events in flight.[9] This becomes technically possible for Cabinet government, a private practice carried on between appointed adults, only when the Cabinet Office archive has become available under the thirty-year rule. But, even with the files at one's disposal in the Public Record Office, it is still perfectly possible to go astray.

Attlee did not expect to win the general election held on 5 July 1945 (though the result was not declared until 26 July, to allow the votes of the Armed Forces to be garnered from around the globe). He told John Colville, one of the junior private secretaries he inherited from Churchill, 'that in his most optimistic dreams he had reckoned that there might, with luck, be a Conservative majority of only some forty seats'.[10] In fact, Labour accumulated a majority of 146. Attlee, the least affected of post-war politicians, with the possible exception of Sir Alec Douglas-Home, made one concession to his new and unexpected status, as Colville recalls:

On August 2nd the new Prime Minister returned from Potsdam with all too little settled by the Big Three and completed the formation of his Government. He thought he should acquire a sober 'Anthony Eden' black Homburg hat and asked me where to buy one. With deliberate irony I took him to Lock's in St James's Street, the most aristocratic hat-maker in London. He bought a hat that suited him well.[11]

Thus armed, Attlee assumed his political inheritance. On any measurement of overload, the pressures and problems were overwhelming. Britain was probably the most efficiently and successfully mobilized combatant in the Second World War. But the very thoroughness with which British industry had been converted to war work, the degree to which overseas investment had been sold to pay for the war effort, and the war-weariness accumulated over six years of privation created a twin dilemma: public expectations of a better post-war world had increased in reverse proportion to the capacity of the British economy to finance it. Keynes spoke of a 'financial Dunkirk'.[12] Five million men and women in uniform had to be demobilized and found work, minus those needed to maintain Britain's commitments overseas as an imperial power and one of the 'Big Four' at the United Nations.[13] The problems were daunting. Expectations soared. The outlook was grim.

Yet the Attlee Cabinet enjoyed some very real advantages. Of all new administrations this century, it was probably the best prepared for office. Virtually all the faces around Attlee's Cabinet table had served in the wartime Coalition (Aneurin Bevan was the most important exception). Attlee and Ernest Bevin, the Foreign Secretary, had sat on the key Coalition Cabinet committees on post-war reconstruction at home and overseas.[14] They started their jobs running. The country was spared the follies that all too often accompany the first six months of a new government while tyro-ministers clamber up what the Civil Service likes to call their learning-curve.

Attlee could and did capitalize on another legacy bequeathed by the war years. The political nation his administration inherited in July 1945 was, by historical and subsequent standards, a highly self-disciplined one. Almost six years of total war had left no citizen untouched by its rigours, whether in the form of the siege economy on the 'Home Front' or by military service abroad. The population was used to receiving orders and to strict regulation in face of shared danger and privation. From the Government's point of view, the condition of the people was a policy-maker's boon, all the more so as such self-restraint and national unity initially took the habitual pessimists in Whitehall by surprise. 'However ingeniously and wisely the civil and industrial controls and rationing schemes may have been devised', wrote Sir Richard Hopkins, Head of the Civil Service and Permanent Secretary to the Treasury from 1942 to 1945, 'they would not have achieved that full success but for the goodwill with which amid the strain and stress of war they were accepted by industry and by the community as a whole.' This goodwill, Hopkins added, 'went beyond – in my judgement much beyond – any forecast which could reasonably have been made before hostilities began'.[15]

Furthermore, Attlee inherited a highly efficient Whitehall war machine,[16] with a variety and quality of machine-minder unparalleled in the history of the British Civil Service (though most of the gifted outsiders who had served as wartime temporaries would soon depart[17]). Addison has encapsulated the result by observing accurately that 'for a few critical years after 1945, the home front ran on without a war to sustain it, and Britain was reconstructed in the image of the war effort'.[18] Attlee and his ministers, despite being a radically intentioned government, did not embark on a reform of the Civil Service because they knew the wartime machine personally and liked what they saw. They had seen the recent administrative past and it had worked.

Yet there is a danger here in over-gilding the memory of Attlee's Whitehall – a danger that even familiarity with the formerly secret record of his government cannot entirely eradicate. It is the danger of imposing reason and order where it was not always present. I have to plead guilty to this. In the 1970s, as a Whitehall journalist with a historical background and an interest in political science, I found myself reading the Cabinet papers of the Attlee Administration as each new batch was declassified and comparing the performance of the Labour governments of 1945–51 with those of Wilson (1974–6) and Callaghan (1976–9) which I was engaged in reporting. Wilson in particular did not shine in comparison. I was sufficiently impressed by the performance of 'the diminutive, monosyllabic former solicitor from Stanmore',[19] to co-author a study of his Cabinet-committee structure.[20]

Nothing has happened in the interim to alter substantially the conclusion of *Mr Attlee's Engine Room* that

Perhaps the virtue most appreciated, with over 30 years of hindsight, is his sheer effectiveness. Late 1940s Britain like early 1980s Britain felt itself strapped for cash. Yet Attlee's Whitehall achieved things, substantial things, on very little money. . . . One way and another, Attlee looks better with every passing year – a kind of benevolent public school master, whose sense of duty and justice raised him above the sectional partisanship of class or party.[21]

The study's thesis was that Attlee built on the Whitehall machine constructed in the Second World War and used it to implement the Labour Party's reform programme. Lord Hunt, at the time a young official in the Dominions Office, offered a similar interpretation in his 1983 survey of what had happened to Cabinet government since Lloyd George and Hankey invented it in its modern form. Speaking of the machinery-of-government implications of Beveridge, Keynesian economics and Labour's programme of public ownership, he said,

The field of government activity and interest extended rapidly, and the size of the Cabinet with it; and at the same time Ministers found – particularly with an economy weakened by the war – that these new problems were both more complex and inter-related than they had perhaps expected. How then could one get the necessary co-ordination at ministerial level and make a reality of collective discussion and responsibility?

The answer was to develop the system of Cabinet Committees to reduce the load on the Cabinet by settling minor matters and, in other cases, sharpening up the issues for decision. Indeed it has been argued that 1945 to 1951 was government by committee – hundreds of them – rather than Government by Cabinet. The system worked remarkably smoothly.[22]

New material, both archival and interpretative, requires these judgements to be modified to some degree. First, internal Cabinet

Office files suggest that Mr Attlee's engine room was not quite as clean a machine as I had portrayed it. In fact, within a year of the formation of the Labour Government, senior officials in the Cabinet Office, Treasury and Board of Trade had become seriously alarmed by the cumbersome nature of the organization supporting the Attlee Cabinet, the proliferation of committees and the prolix and indecisive performance of some ministers. Attlee took their concern seriously, and a review of Cabinet machinery was commissioned which took place in the summer and autumn of 1946.

The initial impetus for the rethink came not from the officials but from Sir Stafford Cripps in the summer of 1946. Cripps, at that time President of the Board of Trade, had long had a penchant for machinery-of-government matters and had been active as a minister in the wartime Coalition on reconstruction committees established to consider the issue.[23] The beginning of the story is recorded in a minute exchanged between the two dominant figures in post-war Whitehall, Sir Edward Bridges, Head of the Civil Service and Permanent Secretary to the Treasury, and Sir Norman Brook, Secretary of the Cabinet. On 5 July 1946 Bridges wrote to Brook,

I happened to see Sir John Woods [Permanent Secretary to the Board of Trade] tonight and he told me that Sir Stafford Cripps had been reading the minutes of Cabinet committees during his absence [in India, where he had been for nearly four months trying to reach a settlement which would lead to independence] and had been depressed by the amount of time and energy taken up in the Ministerial Committees with the discussion of quite minor matters which individual Ministers ought to settle in their discretion. He asked whether anything could be done about this.[24]

Bridges reckoned that, in every new administration, ministers had a tendency in their first year 'to bring matters to the committees which with greater experience they would settle themselves'. Shortage of supplies was also forcing more decisions to be taken centrally. But he thought Attlee ought to consider the problem 'and send a little note to his colleagues or address some remarks to them in Cabinet about the working of the committee system'.[25]

Lower down the hierarchy and, apparently, quite independently of his seniors, the young William Armstrong (who was to head the Treasury in the 1960s and the Civil Service in the 1970s) was, as Brook's private secretary, trying to make sense of the proliferation of committees, some of which had been inherited from the Coalition while others had been created at a considerable rate by the new government. There is a note of despair in his minute of 19 July 1946 to Alexander Johnston, under secretary in Herbert Morrison's Lord President's Office, about the contents of the Cabinet Committee Book, the Cabinet Office's instrument for tracking the growth of its machine:

Another point which has given me some concern is that the present book is supposed to be a directory of Cabinet Committees. So far as I know there is no definition of what constitutes a Cabinet Committee and, as the practice has grown, I believe there may be among the 70-odd Committees in the book some with less title to be treated as Cabinet Committees than some of the 700-odd interdepartmental committees of which we have no detailed information at all.

The point is of some importance since a number of rules of procedure are growing to be applicable to Cabinet Committees and we ought to know where there is a real, useful distinction or whether it is merely the pragmatical difference that some are serviced by the Cabinet Office and some are not. If there is anything in the distinction I believe that the term Cabinet Committee ought to be kept for Ministerial committees and perhaps for committees of officials directly subordinate to a Ministerial committee; but I am far from certain that the distinction is worth making.[26]

Back at the stratospheric level of government, Bridges pursued the problem of the performance of the Cabinet system with Attlee and recorded a note of the conversation which took place in No. 10 on 26 July 1946:

In a talk with the Prime Minister this morning he asked whether I thought too much time of Ministers was taken up by Committees and whether there were too many Committees. I said I thought a great deal of time was taken up with Committees. The [Parliamentary] recess would be a suitable moment for having an overhaul of the committee system and seeing whether any could be reduced. It might also be appropriate for him [the Prime Minister] to issue instructions to the Chairmen of Committees to see that time is not wasted in the discussion of irrelevant matters.

The Prime Minister also asked whether I thought that Ministers brought matters unnecessarily to the Cabinet. I said I thought there was a tendency to do this.[27]

Armstrong, meanwhile, was doggedly struggling to create some sort of classification system, a Domesday Book in miniature, for the Cabinet committees. On 23 July 1946, in a minute to W. S. Murrie, Brook's deputy, he wrote that

I am attracted to the idea of a printed Directory of Committees in a number of parts:

   I Standing Ministerial
  II Ad Hoc Ministerial
 III Standing Official
 IV Ad Hoc Official

I should also be prepared to include in the appropriate sections, committees which, though not Cabinet Committees, in fact perform closely similar functions.[28]

At this stage the Bridges–Brook review of Cabinet procedure and the Armstrong exercise on committees came together. On 30 July, while Brook was away on holiday, Bridges sent Murrie the note of his conversation of 26 July with Attlee, adding, 'It all sounds to me frightfully reminiscent of proposals which have been made before and, I think, discussed.'[29]

Murrie prepared for Brook's return an assessment of the factors contributing to the overloading of Mr Attlee's engine room. Starting from scratch in July 1945, the Government had embarked on a huge legislative programme and laid the foundations for another big instalment in 1946–7. This had necessitated a large number of meetings, particularly for the Socialisation of Industries Committee and the Social Services Committee: ministers had tended to bring too many items to committee; senior ministers had wanted to keep an eye on their more junior colleagues, and as a result a heavy burden fell on a handful. Murrie suggested Attlee should be encouraged to scrutinize carefully the number of committees being created and to circulate a memorandum discouraging ministers from raising questions unnecessarily.[30]

The review went largely according to Murrie's specifications, with Armstrong and, from November, his successor, David Hubback, pruning the committees and Bridges and Brook handling the procedural aspects. In the course of his committee cull, Armstrong came up with a phrase which deserves a permanent place in any anthology of Civil Servicese. Writing to Brook about the Palestine Committee, a survivor from the Coalition, he said that its nominal chairman was Herbert Morrison but that it had ceased to function, its work having shifted to the Middle East Ministerial Committee under Ernest Bevin. Bevin and Morrison detested each other. The MEMC, Armstrong noted, 'is not an active body either. It has never had any papers circulated to it and never met. But it may be well to keep it in existence.' Armstrong continued, 'Actually on account of the personalities involved, I think it might be better to take no action about the Palestine Committee but allow it gradually to sink into *the limbo of forgotten things*' (emphasis added).[31]

The need for a more efficient Cabinet machine was discussed in No. 10 on 4 September at a meeting between Attlee and Hugh Dalton, Chancellor of the Exchequer.[32] Attlee saw Bridges the following day. The Prime Minister told the Head of the Civil Service (who was still nominally in charge of the Cabinet Office, too, to avoid a conflict of status between Brook and General Sir Hastings Ismay, who had been Military Secretary to the Cabinet throughout the war and did not leave Whitehall till 1947) what he wanted as the ingredients of reform:

1 When the Government was newly formed it was perhaps natural for many matters to be discussed in Ministerial Committees which, with growing experience, should now be settled by the individual ministers concerned. Alternatively, if there are differences between Ministers, these can often be resolved by a meeting of two or three Ministers, if need be under the chairmanship of a Minister-without-Portfolio.
2 Papers for Committees must be short and must contain a concise summary of the proposals put forward for consideration. It is the responsibility of all Ministers to see that papers are drawn up on these lines.
3 Ministers when they come to Committees should assume that other Ministers have read their papers and time should not be spent on an oral regurgitation of what already appears in writing in the paper.
4 Fewer papers should be taken at very short notice before there has been time for the Departments to comment on them.[33]

Brook proceeded to turn Attlee's proposals into the more statuesque prose of the standard Cabinet paper. Armstrong urged Brook to persuade Attlee to announce simultaneously the abolition of a number of Cabinet committees. Brook ruled this out: 'I do not, however, favour this suggestion – we could not adopt it without undertaking a review of the Cabinet Committee organisation and that always takes a substantial time, as so many Ministers and others have to be consulted.

Nor do I think that there are at the moment Committees which cause unnecessary work.'[34]

Brook clearly thought this anti-committee mania was getting out of hand and sent Bridges a minute to this effect:

I should rather like to have an opportunity of putting to the Prime Minister some of the arguments *in favour* of handling business through Cabinet Committees. I suspect that at the moment he sees all the disadvantages and none of the advantages of committee work. I should like, in particular, to explain that if, as he himself desires, the size of the Cabinet is to be restricted [it had twenty members, more than twice the number in Churchill's War Cabinet, which oscillated between five and nine[35]], the Committee structure affords a useful means of preserving the collective responsibility of Ministers as a whole.

Another point which should not be overlooked is that Committee papers are read by a good many Ministers who do not attend the meetings, and these papers are often the only means they have of keeping themselves abreast of developments in policy.[36].

Bridges agreed. It is not clear which of the pair put these points to Attlee. But somebody did. The ploy worked. The Cabinet paper circulated on 26 September 1946 was in the Prime Minister's name but was imbued with the Cabinet Secretary's philosophy. In addition to classic injunctions such as 'I look for a marked reduction in the number of problems put forward for discussion in Ministerial Committees', in the terse Major Attlee style, the paper contains a passage which is pure Brook: 'The Cabinet Committee system has a valuable part to play in the central machinery of government, both in relieving the pressure on the Cabinet itself and in helping to give practical effect to the principle of collective responsibility at times when the Cabinet does not include all Ministers in charge of Departments.'[37]

Attlee's 1946 directive did not solve some of the more important machinery-of-government problems of his administration. It needed a sterling crisis and two ministerial reshuffles, the first caused by Morrison's demotion as economic overlord after the convertibility crisis of August 1947, and the second triggered by Dalton's resignation the following November, before the Cabinet machine adequately adapted itself, with the creation of the Economic Policy Committee, to tackle the fundamental problem confronting the Government. Under Attlee's chairmanship the new Cabinet committee became the most important in the system, the one where all the big economic issues – domestic and overseas – were handled.[38] Armstrong, by this time back in the Treasury, had the belated satisfaction of witnessing a modest committee cull.[39]

The relevant internal Cabinet Office organization files in the CAB 21 series at the Public Record Office do not seem to have been used by previous commentators on British Cabinet government. They are an important source for two reasons: they indicate that the overload problem has been a constant since the Second World War and is not peculiar to the sixties, seventies and eighties, and that even what has come to be regarded as the most efficiently run administration since 1945 had serious difficulties in the handling of business.

Recent material also illuminates another intractable problem: the quality of the pool of talent from which ministers are chosen – something no amount of reboring the Cabinet machine can remedy. Sir Alec Cairncross, a former Chief Economic Adviser to the Treasury, heaps praise on the Attlee governments at the end of his highly regarded study *Years of Recovery*: 'Whether one tries to look forward from 1945 or backwards from forty years later, those years appear in retrospect, and rightly so, as years when the government knew where it wanted to go and led the country with an understanding of what was at stake.[40] Yet even he concedes,

the economic problems encountered by the government were not, as a rule, those which it had expected. Equally, the solutions to the problems were rarely of the government's devising. There were exceptions, as when Bevin grasped at what became the Marshall Plan. But more commonly ministers were the reluctant pupils of their officials. On one economic issue after another – the American Loan, the coal crisis, the dollar problem, devaluation, the European Payments Union – they were slow to grasp the true options of policy and had great difficulty in reaching sensible conclusions.[41]

Hugh Gaitskell, an economics don and wartime civil servant who was elected to Parliament in 1945 and in six years rose from backbencher to Chancellor of the Exchequer, illustrates with his diary entry for 14 October 1947 (when he was Minister of Fuel and Power) just how little impact Attlee's directive of a year before had had on the performance of individuals:

Sometimes Cabinet meetings horrify me because of the amount of rubbish talked by some Ministers who come there after reading briefs which they do not understand. I do not know how this can be avoided except perhaps by getting more things settled at the official level, and when they cannot be settled there having the issues presented plainly to ministers.

Also, I believe the Cabinet is too large. A smaller Cabinet, mostly of non-Departmental ministers, would really be able to listen and understand more easily and hear the others arguing the matter out.[42]

But it was Sir Norman Brook who identified what to 1980s eyes is the most startling of the missing links in the Cabinet process of the late forties: the lack of any systematic attempt to review long-term public-expenditure trends and the future spending-implications of current policies. In a file graphically labelled 'Cabinet Procedure. Memorandum on classes of business not regarded as appropriate for Cabinet discussion' is a minute from Brook to Bridges dated 21 April 1950, two months after Labour had been returned to power with a slim majority of six and two months before the Korean War stimulated a huge increase in defence spending. Brook wrote,

It is curious that in modern times the Cabinet, though it has always insisted on considering particular proposals for developments of policy and their cost, has never thought it necessary to review the development of expenditure under the Civil Estimates as a whole.

It is remarkable that the present Government have never reflected upon the great increase in public expenditure, and the substantial change in its pattern, which has come about during the past five years in consequence of their policies in the field of the social services.[43]

Brook added that his analysis confirmed the importance of the proposal to submit twice-yearly forecasts to the Cabinet on the trend of future spending. He urged that a review procedure should be devised to assist ministers to ponder 'its distribution between the various services'. Very little seems to have come of the initiative until five years later, when the Treasury created something along these lines for the Conservative Chancellor, R. A. Butler, as part of an examination of spending on the social services.

By the time Labour left office in October 1951, its Cabinet machine – what might be called the Attlee–Brook model – was enormous. It consisted of 148 standing committes and 313 ad hoc committees. So much for Armstrong's attempt at rationalization five years earlier.[44] One of Brook's first tasks when Churchill re-entered Downing Street was to explain what had happened to the Cabinet system since 1945. In fact, Brook had prepared the brief before the election result was declared. It opened with his favourite theme: 'During the past ten years the system of standing Cabinet Committees has proved its value as a means of relieving the Cabinet of a great weight of less important business.'[45] He suggested the new prime minister should establish immediately 'a Defence, Legislation, Lord President's and Economic Policy Committee before reviewing existing sub-committees at his leisure'.[46]

Brook was not averse to extending his advice into the heartland of prime-ministerial patronage – the shape and composition of the Cabinet. Later, when his relationship with Churchill was particularly close, Brook, took it upon himself, on at least two occasions, to advise on which minister should hold what portfolio – his advice extending even to Sir Anthony Eden, the number-two man in the government.[47] Constitutionally, this was, to say the least, a controversial activity for a career civil servant.

In October 1951 Brook, in addition to his paper on Cabinet committees, supplied Churchill with a brief on the composition of the Cabinet. The document has a dual interest: its own intrinsic historical value; and the insight it provides into the thinking of perhaps the greatest technician of the Cabinet machine in Cabinet Office history. 'The composition of your Cabinet', Brook told Churchill, 'must be influenced by personal and political considerations.'[48] But some points were important 'to the smooth running of Cabinet machinery':

The advantages of a relatively small Cabinet are obvious. And the system of Standing Cabinet Committees, which was developed in the War Cabinet days, now makes it possible to work with a smaller Cabinet, on the lines of your War Cabinet and 'Caretaker' Cabinet,[49] without impairing the principle of collective responsibility. The ideal size, in peace, is probably somewhere between 12 and 16.[50]

Brook then sketched the outline of a suggested Cabinet:

It is convenient that, in addition to the Prime Minister and the Minister of Defence, the Cabinet should include at least one, and preferably two, Ministers without Departmental duties who can act as Chairman of Standing Committees. The old offices of Lord President and Lord Privy Seal may conveniently be used for this purpose. . . . The Lord Chancellor is, traditionally, included in the Cabinet. And it is convenient in practice that he should be a member, since this obviates the frequent summoning of the Law Officers for advice on points of Law.

The Foreign Secretary and the Chancellor of the Exchequer are key members of a peace-time Cabinet; and public opinion will expect that the Commonwealth and Scotland should be represented in it. Personalities apart, it is convenient that at the present time the following Departments should also be represented in the Cabinet – Home Office, Ministry of Labour and Board of Trade.[51]

Surprising omissions from Brook's list are Housing and Local Government, Health, and Education – all three ministries even then conduits for large amounts of public spending. The Cabinet Secretary went on to elaborate the case for keeping 'under a single Minister the supervision of both economic and fiscal policy, and both internal and external economic questions'.[52] For, like Attlee before him, Churchill originally had it in mind to curb the Treasury by parcelling out the functions of economic policy-making to a team of ministers, of which the Chancellor of the Exchequer would be a member, but not an over-mighty one.

In fact, Churchill attempted in October 1951 to refashion Cabinet government in a fairly dramatic fashion by peacetime standards. In essence, it was to be the War Cabinet of 1940 to 1945 by another means. The old warrior was harking back to what John Grigg has called 'the heroic, and in a way surreal, interlude of 1940 and 1941, when Britain, as it were played its finest match before relegation to the second division'.[53] It was a case, as Colville put it, of 'Auld Lang Syne . . . ringing out along the Whitehall corridors'.[54]

Like Attlee and his senior ministers in 1945, Churchill had seen the wartime machine and it had worked. His attempt to re-create it embraced both method and people. His main interest was foreign and defence policy (for a time he was both Prime Minister and Minister of Defence, as he had been from 1940 to 1945). Domestic policy he tended, with a few exceptions such as social security (where he would reprise his old refrain about the law of averages coming to the rescue of the millions), to regard largely as a matter of 'drains'.[55] He appreciated the difficulties of the economic position but was content to devolve the chairmanship of the Cabinet's Economic Policy Committee to his Chancellor, Butler. The distinction between overseas and defence policy in 1951–5 was for Churchill almost as clear as that between the Defence Committee, which, with the Chiefs of Staff, he used to prosecute the Second World War, and the Lord President's Committee under Anderson and Attlee, which he allowed to get on with handling the Home Front.[56]

Churchill, too, wanted a smaller Cabinet, one dominated by 'overlords' who would co-ordinate the work of clusters of departments. He sought out members of his old winning team for the purpose. His original idea was to appoint four peers, which is how they acquired the nickname 'overlords'.[57] One, John Anderson, Viscount Waverley, a wartime Chancellor and Lord President, was to be Lord Privy Seal and 'overlord' for supply and raw materials and of the Treasury and Board of Trade. He declined the offer.[58] Three of the peers accepted: Lord Woolton, the hugely successful wartime Minister of Food and begetter of 'Woolton Pies', became Lord President, with responsibility for co-ordinating the Ministry of Agriculture and Fisheries and the Ministry of Food; Lord Leathers, former Minister of War Transport, became overlord for the Ministry of Transport and Civil Aviation and the Ministry of Fuel and Power; Lord Cherwell, 'the Prof', Churchill's personal boffin in wartime, returned to his old post of Paymaster General with responsibility for co-ordinating work on the Bomb,[59] scientific research and development generally, and Churchill's revived personal think-tank, the Statistical Branch.[60]

It is worth lingering over Churchill's 'overlord' experiment, as it was put back on the agenda of reform by Sir Douglas Wass, former Permanent Secretary to the Treasury, in his 1983 Reith Lectures.[61] Memories flickered in late August 1984 when Mrs Thatcher appointed Lord Young of Graffham, the former Chairman of the Manpower Services Commission, Minister-without-Portfolio with responsibility for 'enterprise', with his own Enterprise Unit in the Cabinet Office. Shrewdly, he insisted on calling himself an 'underlord'.[62] There were tensions, however: most notably with Tom King, Secretary of State for Employment. Just over one year later, King was in the Northern Ireland Office and Lord Young was in the Department of Employment.

Churchill's 'overlords' certainly enabled him to slim down the Cabinet to sixteen members.[63] But, the memory of their efforts is blighted. 'An unsuccessful experiment', Colville called it.[64] Whitehall's Big Two, Brook and Bridges, had disapproved of the idea from the start.[65] Constitutionally it had not been thought through. Parliamentary answers intended to explain the phenomenon left a messy impression. Woolton told the House of Lords on 30 April 1952 that 'the work of the co-ordinators is not a responsibility to Parliament;

it is a responsibility to the Cabinet'.[66] That answer, at least, is consistent with the passage in *Questions of Procedure* which makes it clear that the internal arrangement of Cabinet business is no concern of Parliament or public. But it ignores entirely the question of Parliamentary accountability and its division between co-ordinator and co-ordinated. A month later, Churchill told the Commons that the role of the 'overlords' had developed naturally from the functions of Cabinet-committee chairmen in the Second World War and that 'the co-ordinating Ministers have no statutory powers. They have, in particular, no powers to give orders or directions to a departmental Minister.'[67] By this stage, Field Marshal Lord Alexander of Tunis had been dragooned by Churchill to become Minister of Defence and, in effect, 'overlord' of the Admiralty, War Office and Air Ministry.

In practice, it was left to each overlord to co-ordinate according to taste. Woolton was an exponent of *laisser faire*, Leathers a rather unsuccessful interventionist, Alexander ineffectual all round, and Cherwell what he had always been, a highly intelligent courtier to his chief, though he did succeed in driving through his pet project of hiving off atomic energy from the Ministry of Supply into what became the United Kingdom Atomic Energy Authority.[68] He was also very active on the economic front and played a prominent part in killing off a proposal to float sterling in 1952.[69]

The experiment faltered bit by bit. By the spring of 1953 Leathers and Cherwell wanted to leave the Government. Woolton told Churchill his supervisory role had largely ceased to function.[70] Anthony Seldon has written the overlords' epitaph: 'Thus the Conservatives reverted to the former system of co-ordination of policy in Cabinet Committees and in the Cabinet. . . . Churchill's idea of overlords had proved an ineffective (and largely untested) luxury.'[71] The system died formally with the Cabinet reshuffle of 4 September 1953, after barely two years.

The 'overlord' experiment should not be allowed to create a distorted impression of Churchillian style. He was a great Cabinet-government man. Meetings were conducted with a sense of occasion. 'He regarded the Cabinet', wrote Anthony Seldon, 'as extremely important, even sacrosanct, and would only rarely ride roughshod over it to get his way.'[72] He was keen for more business to be taken at full Cabinet level and set about dismantling parts of the Attlee machine.

The Churchill Government inherited a highly efficient system of Cabinet and offical committees, but within a few months officials were complaining that the neat system consolidated by Clement Attlee was in disarray. Churchill simply disliked working through committees, the Defence Committee excepted. In particular he disliked the two-tier system of committees, Ministerial and Official, with identical terms of reference, and attempted to cut away as many official committees as possible – twenty in a day according to a contemporary rumour – and also instigated a review of all committees in Whitehall and the Cabinet Office.[73]

Churchill's assault on committees yielded results. Attlee's tally it should be recalled, was 148 standing Cabinet committees and 313 ad hoc, accumulated over six and a quarter years. Churchill's complement was 137 standing and 109 ad hoc over three and a half years, representing a substantial economy among the GEN groups. Dr Seldon is right to exempt the Defence Committee from Churchill's strictures. The old warrior treated it as a kind of personal adventure playground where he could drive through cherished projects such as the revival of the wartime Home Guard or toy with trifles such as the age of entry to the Royal Naval College at Dartmouth.

The classic illustration of Churchill's reverence for Cabinet government is his insistence on taking to the full Cabinet in 1954 the decision to build a hydrogen bomb (see chapter 4). The last Churchill Cabinet was brimming with independent spirits. The old man, though accurately described by Lord Kilmuir as having 'enjoyed a wonderful Indian Summer in the House of Commons. Partisan hostility seemed to disappear miraculously',[74] had to navigate some fairly rough passages in the privacy of the Cabinet Room. The worst occasion from Churchill's point of view occurred in July 1954, after he had indulged in a piece of private diplomatic enterprise in an attempt to thaw the Cold War. Travelling home on the *Queen Mary* after a visit to Washington and discussions with President Eisenhower, he despatched a telegram to the post-Stalin leadership in Moscow proposing a meeting. On his return Churchill had to endure several difficult Cabinet meetings, and threats of resignation from Salisbury and Crookshank.[75] Colville's diary shows just how shaken the Prime Minister was and how grim the mood that occasionally intruded at Chequers over the weekend of 24–25 July 1954, during the 'stag party' to celebrate Oliver Lyttelton's retirement from the Cabinet:

There was a crucial Cabinet on Friday July 23rd, at which Lord Salisbury threatened to resign and was supported by Harry Crookshank. We did not therefore send off the telegram he had drafted to Molotov, more especially as he had received from Eden a cold and almost minatory minute just before the Cabinet began. The matter was adjourned till Monday, with the threat of Lord S's resignation hanging over everybody and the still more alarming possibility that Winston, if thwarted, would resign, split the country and the party and produce a situation of real gravity.[76]

The crisis blew over. Churchill heeded his Cabinet dissenters. Foreign policy tended to be the area where Churchill kept full Cabinet somewhat at arm's length, as Anthony Seldon notes:

When foreign affairs were discussed, few would offer their comments. Indeed, the Cabinet was scarcely used as a forum of discussion in foreign policy, although Eden kept Ministers informed at all times. Salisbury, and occasionally Lyttelton and Macmillan, would offer comments on foreign affairs, but on major policy matters Eden preferred to deal with Churchill direct.[77]

A fascinating example of this, with hindsight at any rate, is the secret despatch, on Churchill's instructions, of a small task force to the South Atlantic in February–March 1952 after the Argentine dictator, General Perón, had made threatening noises about the Falklands. The initiative was confined to a small circle – Churchill, Eden and the Chiefs of Staff – and I described the episode in *The Times*, after the 1952 papers had reached the Public Record Office in January 1983, as 'one of the best kept secrets in the 1950s'.[78]

No account of Churchill's stewardship of Cabinet government is complete without mentioning the swiftest and most comprehensive Cabinet leak in the long history of unauthorized disclosure. The problem arose because of Churchill's increasing deafness. He could not hear the mumblers around the Cabinet table. So microphones and loudspeakers were installed. Lord Home takes up the story:

Winston put these machines in front of everybody and there was a button that you pressed when you spoke and you released when you listened. . . . Anyhow, it had been going for a very short time, not very satisfactory, because none of us really were very successful with our machine, and then a . . . messenger came in to say that a [radio] taxi driver had come into No. 10 to say he's heard everything going on in his taxi in Whitehall. So that was the end of that experiment![79]

The memory of Churchill's last premiership is suffused with a golden haze – the England of the Ealing comedies, of amelioration in social and economic life. To be sure there was stress in government. Churchill's stroke in June 1953 put a dent in the working of the Government. Fortunately for those who wanted him to continue in Downing Street, his period of incapacity and recovery coincided with the Parliamentary recess. Colville is candid enough to recognize the highly unorthodox expedients – unorthodox in constitutional terms – to which he and Christopher Soames, Churchill's son-in-law and Parliamentary Private Secretary, resorted while the old man was out of action.

Colville, Soames and Brook played an intimate part in keeping the show on the road while Churchill recovered. 'My colleagues and I', wrote Colville, 'had to handle requests from Ministers and Government departments entirely ignorant of the Prime Minister's incapacity. Discussion of how best to handle such enquiries, whether by postponement, by consultation with the Minister or Under Secretary responsible or, in some cases, by direct reply on the Prime Minister's behalf were the subject of daily discussion with the Secretary of the Cabinet.'[80] Thus arose the delicate question of whether Soames should be allowed access to secret documents and Cabinet papers. The rules were waived.[81] 'Before the end of July the Prime Minister was sufficiently restored to take an intelligent interest in affairs of state and express his own decisive view. Christopher and I then returned to the fringes of power, having for a time been drawn perilously close to the centre.'[82]

The health of individuals apart, overload was not a severe problem in the early fifties, as Lord Thorneycroft, at that time Mr Peter Thorneycroft, an energetic and successful President of the Board of Trade, recalled in an interview with Terry Coleman more than thirty years after Churchill's retirement. While a Cabinet minister, Thorneycroft was in the habit of attending the life class at Chelsea School of Art on Tuesdays and Thursdays between six and nine. 'Could that happen today? "I don't know. In an earlier dispensation, they liked to foxhunt or something. Now they work incredibly hard." There was less government in those days. "Now there's too much. We try and do too many things."'[83]

Churchill was succeeded by Eden, like Thorneycroft a bit of an artist, and like Churchill vulnerable to illness. The torch was passed from the grand old man to the heir-apparent at a touching little ceremony at the end of the Cabinet meeting on 5 April. Brook recorded it in his usual dry fashion:

The Prime Minister said that it remained for him to wish his colleagues all good fortune in the difficult but hopeful situation which they had to face. He trusted that they would be enabled to further the progress already made in rebuilding the domestic stability and economic strength of the United Kingdom and in weaving still more closely the threads which bound together the countries of the Commonwealth or, as he still preferred to call it, the Empire.

Eden, saying he had been asked to speak by the Cabinet, said 'they would remember him always – for his magnanimity, for his courage at all times and for his unfailing humour, founded in his unrivalled mastery of the English language'.[84]

Eden began his premiership in a businesslike fashion even though he had decided on an instant election. He wrote to all his senior departmental ministers asking, 'have you any problems to which we shall have to give our early attention?' The replies yielded little political intelligence, though Iain Macleod, Minister of Health, told the Prime Minister he was dissatisfied with the organization of the social departments.[85]

Eden was instantly plunged into industrial disputes in the docks and on the railways. While utilizing the existing Emergencies Committee, he commissioned an ad hoc group, GEN 496, on economic aspects of the emergency, under Bridges.[86] When the strikes were over he established a Standing Committee on Industrial Relations to produce suggestions for improving the collective-bargaining system and for curbing wildcat strikes.[87] Eden was the supreme foreign-affairs specialist, but he constructed a battery of new committees on the home front, of which the most important were the Ministerial Committee on Industrial Relations, IR, the Committee on Colonial Immigrants under Kilmuir, CI,[88] and a ministerial group on long-term spending on the social services.[89] When the 1955 files were released at the Public Record Office, Eden's committee-making in these areas was interpreted as evidence of vacillation and lack of grip on the part of a premier of whom Kilmuir later wrote, 'no one in public life lived more on his nerves than he did'.[90] A first leader in *The Times* on 3 January 1986, surveying, from thirty years on, the lessons of Eden's stewardship in his early months in No. 10, criticized the new Prime

Minister's tendency to kick for touch on handling coloured immigration and curbing wildcat strikes.[91] And the historian M. R. D. Foot, writing anonymously, (as is house style) in *the Economist*, declared,

Though the Cabinet is supposed to be a decisive body, much of its time [in 1955] was taken up with postponing decisions: whether to legislate against immigrants from the Caribbean or of Indian ancestry; whether to help the Egyptians build the Aswan High Dam; what to do about Cyprus or Malta, about admitting Japan to GATT [the General Agreement on Tariffs and Trade], about the textile market, about the death penalty.[92]

To upbraid Eden for failing to give the green light to the Home Office's draft four-clause Commonwealth Immigrants Bill,[93] is a bit harsh. The Cabinet was deeply divided on the issue, between those, such as Alan Lennox-Boyd, the Colonial Secretary, who argued that immigration curbs could damage 'the Commonwealth concept',[94] and those, such as Duncan Sandys, Minister of Housing and Local Government, who warned the Cabinet that 'in certain districts, such as Birmingham and Lambeth, colonial immigration had already led to serious over-crowding and consequently to social disturbance'.[95] An unnamed minister (probably the Lord President, Lord Salisbury), in the absence of control on coloured immigration, spoke of 'a real danger that over the years there would be a significant change in the racial character of the English people'.[96] There was at that time little public pressure to curb immigration. Party-managers were not sure they could carry Conservative backbenchers on a control bill, let alone the Commons as a whole. That Eden should have allowed the Cabinet a full and lengthy debate on 3 November 1955 could be construed as skilled management, and his referral of the issue for further thought to a Cabinet committee might be seen as prudent policy.

His pattern of personal leadership, as revealed by the Cabinet committees he chose to chair himself, reinforces the standard interpretation of him as a man more at ease with overseas than with domestic policy. He followed Churchill's practice and allowed Butler, the Chancellor of the Exchequer, to chair the Economic Policy Committee. Eden, naturally, took Churchill's place at the head of the Defence Committee, and the list of ad hoc committees he chaired reflects both his appetites and the intrinsic importance of their subject matter: GEN 502 on the supply of military aircraft; GEN 503 on security in Cyprus; GEN 506 on preparations for the meeting of foreign ministers of France, the UK, USSR and USA in Geneva in October 1955; and GEN 511 on a third Indian steel plant.[97]

In procedural terms, Eden was neither a reformist nor a tinkerer. His sole initiative was essentially a matter of housekeeping. On 16 December 1955 he circulated a note on 'Submission of Business to the Cabinet'.[98] Eden told his colleagues that 'on certain occasions recently a decision taken without reference to the Cabinet or a Cabinet Committee has had to be re-considered soon after it has been made public because of the weight of criticism it has provoked. This is damaging to the Government's credit and we must do all we can to avoid it.' Eden was probably referring to the unfortunate statement from Henry Hopkinson, junior minister at the Colonial Office, that Cyprus would 'never' be granted full independence,[99] and a domestic slip-up: an announcement that the manufacture of heroin would cease entirely in the UK (the medical profession subtly pointed out its legitimate uses as a drug). Eden's remedy was to encourage departmental ministers to bring to Cabinet or Cabinet committee 'any questions which are likely to occasion public controversy or criticism or may need to be carefully explained to the Government's supporters in Parliament'.[100]

But, rightly or wrongly, Eden's tenure in Downing Street is remembered as a single-issue premiership. As his wife, Clarissa, put it, the Suez Canal ran through her drawing-room.[101] Eden was tested to destruction by the Suez crisis. The ground on which he broke was his speciality – foreign affairs. But the nature of the Middle East crisis of 1956, and the interplay of diplomacy, war and personality exposed Eden's temperament in all its frailty. It also put the Cabinet system itself under severe stress. Colin Seymour-Ure, taking Korea, Suez and the Falklands as his case studies, has made a ground-breaking study of Cabinet government in small wars:

The subject is illuminating because it shows the Cabinet system under stress. In war, a Cabinet designed to manage political conflict finds itself instead directing armed force. On the one hand military action must be pursued with maximum efficiency, defined by military criteria. On the other, the uncertainties of war are likely to need the most sensitive political response in terms of the Cabinet's relations with party, Parliament and public. Cabinet business always involves a mixture of political and specialist (or administrative) considerations. Some matters are no doubt decided only by reference to their intrinsic merits, others on purely political grounds. But many must involve both; and reconciling them is a purpose to which the Cabinet is specifically suited.

In a war, however, the two considerations arguably tug in opposite directions. To intrude political criteria into military decisions risks reducing efficiency at the cost, conceivably, of disaster. Yet the resort to arms is by definition a crisis of politics, and to neglect the political response for the sake of military considerations may be just as perilous. There is a further element too – the personal stress of war. The Cabinet is only as good as its members. Eden cracked under the strains of Suez, and his Foreign Secretary, Selwyn Lloyd, came close to cracking at times.[102]

The roots and branches of the Suez war require an arboretum of their own. This is not the place to disentangle the foliage. For our purposes the story starts in the dining-room at No. 10 on 26 July 1956. Eden was entertaining his friend and ally Nuri es-Said of Iraq when news that Nasser had nationalized the Suez Canal was conveyed to the Prime Minister. As soon as his guests had left, Eden summoned his senior ministers and the Chiefs of Staff (plus Jean Chauvel, the French Ambassador, and Andrew Foster, Chargé d'Affaires at the US Embassy in London) to the Cabinet Room. The meeting lasted till two in the morning. There was to be no let-up for more than three months. Later on the 27th Eden established his version of a war Cabinet. He did not use the existing Defence Committee, which he chaired, as Attlee had done for Korea. A special Egypt Committee was commissioned which included Macmillan, Chancellor of the Exchequer; Selwyn Lloyd, Foreign Secretary; Salisbury, Lord President; Lord Home, Commonwealth Secretary; and Sir Walter Monckton, Minister of Defence.[103] The Egypt Committee's membership, despite the delicacy and secrecy of its work, was highly fluid. At least sixteen ministers attended at various stages.[104] It was liquid in other senses, too. It lacked terms of reference.[105] Initially, it handled the diplomacy of the crisis: 'an instrument for flexible political management of a particular diplomatic crisis which culminated in war'.[106] Contingency planning for the use of force was undertaken by the Chiefs of Staff. Later, once a variety of diplomatic initiatives had been tried and discarded, it became more literally a 'War Cabinet'. Seymour-Ure uses the inning and outing of Butler, a sceptic about the use of force, to illustrate the peculiar, shifting nature of the Egypt Committee:

The general impression is of a body strongly affected by political considerations. The inclusion of Butler (Lord Privy Seal and Leader of the

House of Commons) was typical: omitted from the original membership he simply turned up to the first meeting, according to Hugh Thomas, 'and of course was allowed to stay. . . .' Yet by the time the invasion neared he was one of the inner-most group of five Ministers – with Eden, Lloyd, Macmillan and Head [who had replaced Monckton as Minister of Defence] (plus Mountbatten, the Chief of Staff) – who effectively took the decision to issue an ultimatum to Egypt and Israel.[107]

Despite the gravity of the crisis, Eden in 1956 followed the practice which he had adopted in 1955, of putting the full Cabinet on ice during the summer recess.[108] 'The Egypt Committee', Selwyn Lloyd remembered, 'would, however, continue to function, but if emergency decisions had to be taken the Cabinet would be recalled.'[109]

When the Suez crisis boiled over in the autumn, the strain on ministers was immense. As Lord Chancellor, Kilmuir was part of the floating composition of the Egypt Committee. His memory of this classic outbreak of overload remained green when he was compiling his memoirs six years later:

After Eden had returned from the House, there might be another meeting of Suez Ministers at about 4.30 or 5.00 pm, and another between 10.00 and 11.00 pm, to give Sir Pierson Dixon in New York his final briefing for the United Nations, which would come to the boil about 12.30 or 1.00 am in our time, i.e. 7.30 to 8.00 in New York. If any decision required taking in regard to Egypt, one had to remember that 1 o'clock was 3.00 am on the Canal. I usually left the night meeting about 2.00 pm, but quite often after that Anthony [Eden] had long telephone conversations with Guy Mollet, the Prime Minister of France, which went on until 4.00 or 5.00 am. Even to someone like myself, who has been envied in politics much more often for my physical stamina than for my brains, it was a severe pace, and I had only a fraction of the work and strain of Anthony. His courage never faltered, but his health collapsed.[110]

After determined application of the economic weapon by the Eisenhower Administration had forced a cease-fire as British troops advanced down the Suez Canal on 6 November 1956, an exhausted Eden flew to Jamaica to recuperate on 21 November. 'We were all, Ministers and backbenchers', wrote Kilmuir, 'emotionally and physically exhausted.'[111] Eden returned to London on 14 December. On 9 January 1957 he told the Cabinet that he was about to resign on health grounds. Salisbury, Butler and Macmillan spoke kind words.[112] Kilmuir and Salisbury sounded out the Cabinet one by one in the Privy Council Office. The Chairman of the 1922 Committee sounded out the backbenchers. Macmillan was summoned to the Palace.

Before turning to Macmillan's premiership, another casualty of Suez must be mentioned. As the crisis deepened, Bridges was in his last weeks as Permanent Secretary to the Treasury. He, who had been so close to the innermost of inner circles since succeeding Hankey in 1938, was receiving only fragmentary details of the inner Cabinet's war-planning, despite having to advise the Chancellor on the financial implications. He was not even receiving the minutes of the Egypt Committee. He sent his private secretary down the corridor to see Sir Norman Brook to ask if they could be provided. The Cabinet Secretary was most apologetic. But the Prime Minister himself had compiled the circulation list and Sir Edward's name was not on it.[113]

Harold Macmillan was not a reluctant prime minister. He savoured the office, its history and its place in the scheme of things. 'He seemed', wrote his early biographer Anthony Sampson, 'to see himself as part of a fashionable play.'[114] His attention to the style of his premiership shone through even at the age of ninety, twenty years after his departure from No. 10, in a television interview with Ludovic Kennedy:

MACMILLAN   I enjoyed Prime Minister because I found it much the most relaxed of the offices I held. I didn't work so hard.
KENNEDY   Many people would find that surprising.
MACMILLAN   Yes, but you didn't have to do the work of the departments. Oh, you had the Cabinet to run and all that. I found I read a lot of books and so on, I rested a lot. It's a great mistake to get yourself into a state of nervous excitement all the time . . . nobody should ever overdo it you know . . . you should read Jane Austen and then you'll feel better.[115]

In fact he was a nervous man, particularly before making one of his unforgettable, mannered speeches whose flow continued into the mid-1980s. The unflappable image needed to be worked on – and he began as soon as he entered No. 10 in January 1957. He hung up a notice in his own writing bearing a quote from *The Gondoliers*:

Motto for Private Office and Cabinet Room.
Quiet, calm deliberation
Disentangles *every* knot.

HM[116]

His irreverent friend and Downing Street assistant (unpaid and unofficial), John Wyndham, added,

> And remember, if it doesn't
> You will certainly be shot.[117]

The new relaxed Downing Street style was instantly picked up by the Cabinet and greatly appreciated. None had relished Eden's tendency to transmit his own nervousness to colleagues. The transformation was vividly recalled by the man Macmillan pipped for the premiership, R. A. Butler:

> Eden would ring up, sometimes as often as a dozen times a day, to ask why there had been a certain speech made in the provinces by a member of the opposition, why an answer hadn't been given, and that sort of thing. When I came to Macmillan, it was with the greatest difficulty that I telephoned him at all. Because when you raised the telephone . . . he showed great irritation and pretended not to hear you, so that it immediately made you think that you'd been unwise to telephone at all.[118]

Macmillan may have appeared to treat the premiership as if he were a Whig grandee running a great estate in the gaps between his private reading. In reality 'he had a firm business-like approach to running the Cabinet', according to John Barnes and Anthony Seldon.[119] He made use of the Cabinet-committee structure as a filter for business, though he chaired very few committees himself (the main exceptions were the Economic Policy and Defence committees). He kept abreast of committee minutes and in close touch with the chairmen. Sometimes, if taking an initiative in an area he deemed crucial, he would take the chair, as he did at the Reflation Committee in 1958.[120]

In the early years of his premiership he was very sharp, though, as Iain Macleod recalled, 'he could be maddeningly discursive – it was nothing to reach a decision on an enquiry into rating via the Greek Wars and Parnell'.[121] He made Cabinet fun, as his successor, Lord Home, remembers: 'He was marvellously entertaining always. You did your business but it was great fun at the same time.'[122] All the same, Home thought he was over-indulgent: 'Harold was very clever. He was one of those prime ministers in Cabinet who let everyone talk – too much sometimes.'[123]

Inevitably, Macmillan's grip slipped as his premiership wore on and the economic problems (pay pause and EEC membership) crowded in. One Cabinet minister told Anthony Sampson that

Harold is a very good prime minister as far as taking the Cabinet goes. He takes it slowly, lets everyone have his say, and if they don't agree he doesn't mind calling an extra meeting to come back to it. As he grows older he thinks about fewer things – he is now mainly occupied with the Common Market, the cold war and the Atlantic Alliance. But he can turn his mind to detailed needs, like pensions, if he has to.[124]

Macmillan took great pains to husband his energies. He had seen Eden's health break under the strain. Reading Jane Austen was more than an affectation: it was a life-preserver. His habits of work, write Barnes and Seldon, were 'business-like. In contrast to his predecessors who worked at all hours of the day Macmillan tended to keep office hours. He made it a rule that the work which flowed in during the course of the day had to be dealt with during that day, unless there was a very good reason.'[125]

In terms of overload, though, the Macmillan years probably did add to the problem. One of the reasons was procedural. In the early 1960s the practice of fixed fifteen-minute sessions of Prime Minister's Questions twice a week was established. This development, as Professor George Jones has pointed out, contributed to the modern phenomenon where the Prime Minister is expected to be answerable for every aspect of government business virtually all the time.[126] Secondly, Macmillan adored summits and playing the world statesman. Foreign affairs and nuclear policy were among his greatest preoccupations. Not everybody believes a profusion of summits are a good investment of prime ministerial time: the results do not always justify the hours and the nervous energy spent. Lord Home for one disapproved, recalling 'the only difference I ever had with Mr Macmillan. He used to love summits. I used to say "they are the most useless thing". . . . He used to like the . . . social . . . side . . . of the . . . meeting. Well, they are rather fun. But as far as efficiency is concerned the work could be done without nearly so many.'[127]

For what will Macmillan's Cabinet stewardship be remembered? Certainly for his sacking of a third of his colleagues in the 'Night of the Long Knives' in July 1962. His unflappability deserted him in the face of by-election reverses. Lord Kilmuir's harsh recollection of his summary despatch may usefully be compared to Macmillan's sepia portrayal more than twenty years after the event. First, Kilmuir:

On the following evening [11 July 1962], as a meeting of the Committee of the Cabinet was ending, Macmillan took me aside and said 'The

Government is breaking up', and murmured something about 'You don't mind going?' I was startled but merely replied, 'You know my views.' . . . On the following morning, when I was attending another committee of the Cabinet, I was handed another message that the Prime Minister wished to see me. . . . I got the impression that he was extremely alarmed about his own position and was determined to eliminate any risk for himself by a massive change of Government. It astonished me that a man who had kept his head under the most severe stresses and strains should lose both nerve and judgement in this way.[128]

For Macmillan nineteen years later it was still, to be fair, a matter of regret. But 'It's a cruel life, politics. Somebody's got to be in charge. . . . We had nearly 14 years of continuous office and a lot of my older friends were worn out.'[129]

Macmillan's management of Cabinet will be remembered, too, for what Whitehall regards as 'the biggest bounce of all': Concorde – an enterprise which David Henderson, the former Chief Economist at the Ministry of Civil Aviation, has called one of 'the three worst civil investment decisions in the history of mankind'.[130] The genesis of the Concorde project was a meeting of boffins at the Royal Aircraft Establishment, Farnborough, in February 1954, when Macmillan was still engaged in building his 300,000 houses a year.[131] For him the issue did not become live until well after the 1959 general election. By 1962 – the critical year of decision – it had become bound up with high politics (rupturing a prestige Anglo-French collaborative project was not the best way of smoothing Britain's path to EEC membership) and the phenomenon of imperial surrogate whereby hi-tech enterprises became a substitute and a consolation for loss of empire.

True to his style, Macmillan held himself aloof while the programme crawled its way through the working-party and interdepartmental undergrowth, the estimated cost rising all the time and the Treasury losing no opportunity to attack the project on grounds of both need and expense. In the spring of 1962, Lord Mills, Macmillan's favourite industrialist from Ministry of Housing days, was invited to chair a committee to examine the pros and cons, and came out in favour. In the autumn it went before a Cabinet committee chaired by Butler. Jock Bruce-Gardyne and Nigel Lawson quote 'a senior member' of the committee summing up its conclusion thus: 'even then we thought it was going to ruin us; but also that you can't control the march of science'.[132] The Treasury and the Ministry of Aviation, now run by

Julian Amery, Macmillan's son-in-law, remained at loggerheads as the issue moved to full Cabinet on Guy Fawkes Day 1962.

The 'Europeans' lined up with the 'technologists' (and those who spoke for party opinion in the Commons) against the Treasury. At last Macmillan showed his hand: it was essential to get the aircraft companies to contribute to the cost of Concorde's research and development. But, if Britain pulled out, the French were likely to go ahead anyway.[133] Macmillan then deployed a favourite tactic: he deferred the final decision till a later meeting of the Cabinet. Between the meetings he began to operate in earnest, seeing individually spending ministers worried that Concorde would drain funds from their budgets.

The final Cabinet meeting on Concorde abounds in folklore. First, there is the lunch-break story (though it is not entirely clear that this relates to the very last meeting: it might relate to 5 November). Barnes and Seldon deploy it as a classic example of Macmillanesque subtlety in handling colleagues. He took his senior men aside at lunchtime for a *tour d'horizon* on 'the wider implications of the project for European unity, and when the Cabinet resumed matters of cost and technical detail which had caused objections that morning were swallowed up in the wider prime ministerial perspective'.[134] Bruce-Gardyne and Lawson recount the most famous anecdote of all. Reminiscences of the trenches in the First World War or Stockton-upon-Tees in the twenties and thirties (his favourite standbys) did not fit the occasion. So he turned to an aged relative for assistance:

He told his colleagues about his great aunt's Daimler, which had travelled at the 'sensible speed of thirty miles an hour', and was sufficiently spacious to enable one to descend from it without removing one's top hat. Nowadays, alas! people had a mania for dashing around. But that being so Britain ought to 'cater for this profitable modern eccentricity'! He thought they all really agreed. No one seriously dissented. It was all over in a few minutes.[135]

Ironically, Concorde travelled the crucial stage of its budget-busting passage just as Macmillan's new system for bringing both reason and control to the public-spending process was bedding down. On the recommendation of a 1958 report from the Commons Select Committee on Estimates, a technocratic team had been commissioned to build on the forward looks for social-service and defence spending pioneered by the Treasury in the mid-fifties. The committee took its name from Lord Plowden, the former head of the Central Economic Planning Staff, who chaired it. He led a team of Whitehall heavy-weights including the formidable Dame Evelyn Sharp from the Ministry of Housing and the Treasury's ebullient innovator Sir Richard 'Otto' Clarke. Plowden's recommendation in 1960[136] of greater long-term planning of public spending went very much with the Macmillan grain. Planning had been his *cri de coeur* as a Tory rebel in the thirties and was the cornerstone of his political testament, *The Middle Way,* first published in 1938.[137] As a result, the Plowden Report found favour at No. 10 and achieved a speedy and lasting impact on the machinery of Cabinet government. In terms of personality, the Chancellor was strengthened by a second Treasury minister in the Cabinet with a special spending-brief, the Chief Secretary. The first incumbent of the post, Henry Brooke, was appointed in October 1961. A Public Expenditure Survey Committee (PESC) of finance officers from twenty-four departments, with a Treasury deputy secretary in the chair, provided ministers with five-year forward looks at expenditure patterns, and the notion of a rolling programme was established.[138]

The big decisions thrown up by PESC have always been taken by full Cabinet, though Macmillan set a precedent followed by future prime ministers when he established in autumn 1960 a small Ministerial Action Group on Public Expenditure, known as 'Magpie'.[139] Its membership consisted of Brooke (still Minister of Housing at that stage); Iain Macleod, the Colonial Secretary; and John Hare, Minister of Labour.[140] In their own way they were the spiritual precursors of Mrs Thatcher's 'Star Chamber'. Unlike in the early eighties, though, Tory philosophy in the early sixties embraced the concept of public expenditure as a positive tool of progress. The establishment of the PESC system, like the way Macmillan eased the Concorde project through the Cabinet Room, is an illustration of his tactic of modernizing madly behind a smokescreen of Edwardian charm and timeless tradition. It was fun to be a Cabinet minister under Macmillan unless you were Enoch Powell. The Prime Minister rearranged the seating round the Cabinet table so that he could avoid the unnerving, penetrating eyes of his Minister of Health, as Lord Home revealed in his memoirs:

One morning I came into the Cabinet Room rather early and found the Cabinet secretary, Sir Norman Brook . . . changing all our places. I asked what had happened – 'Had their been a shuffle? – or had one of us died in the night?' 'Oh no, said Sir Norman, 'it's nothing like that. The Prime Minister cannot stand Enoch Powell's steely and accusing eye looking at him across the table any more, and I've had to move him down the side.'[141]

Lord Home, Macmillan's surprise replacement after the undignified scramble (Home himself apart) for the Tory leadership in the autumn of 1963, avoided those steely eyes, as Powell refused to serve under him.

In a sense, Lord Home was a landed version of Attlee. They are the only two post-war premiers to have had no time for the black arts of political news management and personal public relations.[142] Both were frugal in their use of energy and time. Both practised political economy around the Cabinet table. Both were tough on the prolix. As we have seen, Home thought Macmillan, whom he liked and admired, lax in this respect.[143] For Lord Home, in Cabinet 'the great thing is to be short. People can't bear – they've got enough to listen to already – and anybody who waffles is written off pretty quickly and, therefore, you lose your point. . . . To be short and concise is the secret of making an impact in Cabinet.'[144]

Another Home technique for reducing the burden on the premiership was to devolve, even in an area central to his and the Government's fortunes:

HENNESSY   You were always very honest about the one area in which you lacked expertise, which was economics. Did you try and compensate for that by the way you set up your Cabinet-committee structure? Did you chair the Economic Policy Committee, can you remember?

HOME   Oh no. No, no, I wouldn't. The Chancellor of the Exchequer did that. But I used to talk to him [Reginald Maudling] regularly, of course. I used to talk to him regularly about what he was up to. I was not familiar with economics. They had never come my way. Nor have I been encouraged ever since to think there's an exact science. But it was a weakness. If I had thought I was going to be Prime Minister, I would have taken more trouble to understand the various theories'.[145]

In No. 10 Lord Home relied on his Principal Private Secretary, Derek Mitchell, a Treasury man, for assistance in this area. 'He was very efficient. I never understood a word about economics and his strength was economics.'[146] Lord Home, who possesses a degree of candour unusual in political life, is still ambivalent about his handling of economic policy. 'If I'd taken more trouble with economics I might have been more effective as Prime Minister. But then, on the other hand, I believe in devolving your economics to the Chancellor of the Exchequer. If he can't make a go of them, nobody can.'[147]

In one area he did, reluctantly, take steps to improve upon his lack of natural gifts.

HENNESSY   It seems to be a conventional wisdom that relations with the media are absolutely crucial for a prime minister. But you, with Mr Attlee, were thought to be the most unworldly of post-war prime ministers on that. You just behaved as you, in fact, naturally were and had no time for the black arts of propaganda. Is that right?

HOME   Well, I was bored by the whole of presentation as far as television was concerned because I think television is bound to be superficial. I was wrong. Harold Wilson convinced me I was wrong because he trained himself very, very well to be a pretty good television performer, and I think it is necessary for the Prime Minister. I still regret it, but I'm afraid the Prime Minister has to appear a great deal on the media.[148]

Lord Home's remains the unknown premiership of the post-war period. One reason is that nothing very much happened between October 1963 and October 1964 in terms of high policy. Activity was concentrated on the low politics of the forthcoming election. 'There wasn't much scope for doing very much that year. . . . We had one controversial term – the Resale Price Maintenance Bill', Lord Home recalled.[149]

Resale-price maintenance (RPM) was the arrangement whereby the price of an article – an item of grocery or a washing-machine – was kept the same whether it was sold in the most efficient supermarket or the most run-down corner shop. The Board of Trade, a free-trading department down to its last paper-clip, had long opposed this restrictive practice as a conspiracy against the consumer and as a malign, artificial inflator of prices. But in the Tory Party there are a lot of votes piled up in corner shops. Board of Trade officials had tried for nearly twenty years to change the policy of RPM. But the political price was always judged too high by ministers, despite the logic of the abolitionist cause. When Home succeeded Macmillan, he moved Edward Heath from the Foreign Office (where he had been Home's number two) to the Board of Trade.

The man, the hour and the issue were met. Heath was determined to abolish RPM. Heath sold it to Home as a symbol to the country that, after twelve years in office, the Conservatives were still capable of radical action. The party's political managers thought it a ruinous ploy in election year. The Cabinet had to move swiftly, however. The Labour MP John Stonehouse had a private member's bill on the subject about to begin its passage through the Commons.

RPM reached the full Cabinet on 14 January 1964. The Cabinet was seriously divided. Quintin Hogg was highly critical of the failure to prepare party opinion: 'You must always let people see the cat before you let it out of the bag.'[150] Selwyn Lloyd, Redmayne and Blakenham warned of the effect on the party. Butler was critical. There was stalemate. Stonehouse's bill was due for a second reading in three days' time. The Government would have to be ready with a view either way. Cabinet met again on 15 January with the words of one critic, who claimed it would be 'throwing the small shopkeeper to the supermarket wolves',[151] still ringing in their ears. As Nigel Lawson and Jock Bruce-Gardyne discovered subsequently through their excellent insider links,

This time the argument was entirely over the onus of proof. Heath, in the words of one witness, 'made it eyeball to eyeball'. He refused to budge, and was given full support by Douglas-Home, whose diplomatic skills softened the rough edges of Heath's 'extraordinary resolution'. Eventually after, in all, three hours of Cabinet discussion of this one issue, the opponents conceded: Heath had won. There was to be full-blooded abolition of RPM and legislation to achieve it that session'.[152]

The furore on the Conservative side raged all year; it has been continually claimed ever since that RPM cost Home the October 1964 election, in which Labour won the slimmest majority of four seats. Twenty years later, Lord Home was as philosophical as he was phlegmatic:

Ted Heath was very keen and nobody else was very much. I thought it was right and therefore we went ahead. It probably cost us seats at the general election. That was a clear case where the Bill was right and the timing was wrong. But I didn't feel I could overrule Ted Heath on this particular occasion because he was essentially right on what the Bill proposed. . . . It certainly lost us quite a lot of Conservative votes. But then if a thing is so patently right . . . you have to take the decision and risk it.[153]

Throughout his year in Downing Street, Lord Home brooded on ways of coping more successfully with the pressures on government. He toyed with the possibility of a think-tank. 'The idea had occurred to me. But I didn't have the time to do anything except prepare for the election during that year.'[154] He developed in his mind a set of procedural reforms for implementation after the election.

HOME   It would have been a much more efficient use of the Cabinet system, the committee system. Because in my last five years before [becoming Prime Minister] I had been Foreign Secretary [and], therefore, away a lot. But nevertheless I had seen the Cabinet agenda getting more and more overflowing and, therefore, Cabinet decisions had to be taken quickly. You'd start off with parliamentary business then have a review of foreign affairs, and very important departmental things may often have to be shoved out of the way to another Cabinet. Wasn't really as efficient as it could have been.

HENNESSY   So your ideal system would have been to have a few strategic Cabinet committees beneath the Cabinet that would have done all the most controversial business?

HOME   That's right. And, what is more, I would have instructed the ministers, as far as the Prime Minister can instruct another minister, to take the decisions in their committees and only bring the really most controversial aspects of particular bills to Cabinet. In other words, a lot more decisions ought to be taken at the committee level.[155]

In the event, the problem of how to streamline Whitehall was handed by the electorate to that old Cabinet Office hand Harold Wilson.

At first glance, Wilson should have been a superlative practitioner of Cabinet government. As the young secretary of the War Cabinet's Manpower Requirements Committee,[156] he had learned his craft from Bridges and Beveridge; he was President of the Board of Trade and in the Cabinet at the age of thirty-one; he had a sense of history, he was numerate *and* he knew all the tricks of political manipulation and presentation. When he took over in October 1964, he enjoyed two other advantages: his majority of four ensured that the fractious Parliamentary Labour Party would have to behave; and, apart from Patrick Gordon Walker, whom he appointed Foreign Secretary, and James Griffiths, who was sent to the newly created Welsh Office, only he possessed Cabinet experience. This added to his ascendancy over the tyros round his Cabinet table in the autumn of 1964, as he now acknowledges. 'It was very hard work in many ways', he told me in February 1985, 'and the fact that we'd been thirteen years [in Opposition] meant that most of them, almost all of them, had no experience at all in government. To that extent it strengthened the hand of the Prime Minister in my earlier period.'[157] Peter Shore, Wilson's Parliamentary Private Secretary in 1965–6, puts it even more strongly: 'Harold's supremacy within that Cabinet in the first two, perhaps even three, years was enormous.'[158] Wilson self-consciously capitalized on that supremacy in his 'First Hundred Days' of dynamic action, a deliberate imitation of the Kennedy style in early 1960. He played, as he would later say, the centre-forward role. Included in that hundred-day programme was what at first sight seemed substantial changes in his own bailiwick – a clutch of new ministries, of which the Department of Economic Affairs (DEA) was the most important. Peter Shore, who served as its last secretary of state, believes that the creation of the DEA was an attempt to remedy 'the principal defect of Cabinet government, as well as the principal defect of economic policy, which was the overweening power of the Treasury, which was too great for . . . the full collective work of a Cabinet'.[159]

The concept of the DEA, conceived, according to legend, by Wilson and his deputy, George Brown, in the back of a taxi on the short journey between the St Ermin's Hotel and the House of Commons (a legend Wilson has demolished, though on that journey he did offer Brown the job of running the DEA[160]) had scarcely received the attention it deserved during Labour's preparation for power. Wilson did put some flesh on the bones in a television interview with Norman Hunt,[161] only to have it torn off in strips by the venerable Bridges, long since retired but still a determined advocate of a unitary Treasury dominating economic policy from the centre.[162] Yet the chaos that occurred after the election, when Brown was put into the DEA with the grand title of First Secretary of State, showed to what paltry use Wilson had put his unique background (unique, that is, since the death of his predecessor, Hugh Gaitskell) as skilled Whitehall technocrat *and* top-flight politician and parliamentarian. The chaos was physical: early meetings in the Storey's Gate offices earmarked for the new department saw George Brown on a chair while everyone else 'sat on the floor like Buddhas'.[163] It was hierarchical, with silly rows about the status and pay of its permanent secretary, Sir Eric Roll.[164] Most serious of all, chaos blighted both policy and politics as what was supposed to be the creative tension with the Treasury deteriorated into petty demarcations and empire-building.

This is not the place to attempt a history of the DEA. For our purpose it is important to note that it merely threatened to dent the Treasury ascendancy over economic policy-making. Until the introduction of deflationary measures in July 1966 (Brown wanted devaluation as an alternative, and lost to Wilson and to Callaghan at the Treasury), the DEA and its mercurial First Secretary *did* present the Cabinet with an alternative voice and, in the shape of the 1965 National Plan, a growth strategy, an emphasis on production to counter the Treasury's obsession with finance. Once Brown had departed to the Foreign Office in 1966, the life drained from the DEA. Roy Jenkins, who succeeded Callaghan at the Exchequer after the enforced devaluation of November 1967, persuaded Wilson formally to bury the DEA cadaver in 1969.

Lord Wilson's account in 1985 of the decay of what was intended to mark a sea-change in the process and outcome of economic policy-making at the highest level is best read slowly and without comment – except, perhaps, to note that, in reforming terms, an almost ideal apprenticeship for a Prime Minister is no guarantee that he will deliver the goods:

HENNESSY In 1964 when you came in you tried to recast both the structure and the thrust of Cabinet government. . . . There was a spate of new departments. There was a Welsh Office, a Ministry of Land and Natural Resources, a Ministry of Overseas Development. But, above all, there were two new bodies to tackle the fundamental problem of Britain's long-term economic decline, a Ministry of Technology to harness research and development to industry, and a Department of Economic Affairs to break the Treasury monopoly of advice. They were going to produce a National Plan, which they did. You were, in fact, a very production-minded Prime Minister. What went wrong with all that?

WILSON Sterling . . . in those days you couldn't float the pound. You had to go through all the misery and raise it with the danger of leaks all the time in some of the central international establishments in America.

HENNESSY So you think this vitiated all the economic planning that you'd so carefully prepared for?

WILSON No, it didn't vitiate it. The way the press attacked it and so on obviously made life a lot harder for us.

HENNESSY But, before the devaluation, the Department of Economic Affairs had failed pretty consistently over three years to actually break the monopoly of Treasury advice and the National Plan had all but gone under. What had gone wrong there?

WILSON All of the Treasury. They're still at it. Recently, we were having a debate in the Lords and we got on to nationalization and I said that one thing that we need to nationalize in this country is the Treasury, but nobody has ever succeeded.

HENNESSY   One thing baffles me about that, Lord Wilson: you were Prime Minister, you were the boss, you were presiding over Cabinet government. Whitehall is the direct-labour organization of a prime minister. It's the one area where his writ runs. Why couldn't you break the power of the Treasury and get your beloved Department of Economic Affairs to take off?

WILSON   Moles. Moles. 'Moles' was a phrase we very often used about the Treasury and it's been used many times since. The Treasury were very, very skilled chaps in more or less stopping you doing anything.

HENNESSY   You're suggesting they leaked against you and the departmental structure you wanted and undermined it?

WILSON   They lost it. I mean I said 'I want something by next Thursday' and, of course, they weren't there or the papers weren't done. And also they wanted harsh decisions to be taken in respect of their effects on industry.

HENNESSY   It's a very depressing conclusion that elected people, Cabinet, Prime Minister, cannot prevail against an ancient British institution at the centre of events in Whitehall . . .

WILSON   Some of us have had more success than others. I had the advantage of having been in the Civil Service in the war and [was] even offered establishment in the Treasury as a permanent thing. Anyone who had had that knew a bit about the Treasury and knew a little bit about fighting back and working round them and all the rest of it and of giving orders direct to the Chancellor and saying, 'Look, this is what we must have', and then getting the Cabinet to back it, so that it was harder for the Treasury to say 'No.' They still wheedled and played their little tricks. But, with the Cabinet decision and the Chancellor party to it, it was harder for them, and I think we had more success than most other governments in doing this just because I knew the background.

HENNESSY   Why, then, did you wind up the Department of Economic Affairs in '69?

WILSON   It was a disappointment. The Treasury, as I say, undermined it to some extent, but all the time there was duplication going on. And, well, I just felt it had been worth trying but it wasn't going to work.[165]

The fate of the DEA was symbolic of Wilson the supreme Whitehall technician – failure at every level, from the Cabinet command post to the interdepartmental bush, where drive, energy and strategy can disappear without trace. His was a hugely disappointing premiership in terms of modernizing the instruments of government. His explanation, in our 1985 conversation, of what happened to the DEA is typical too. He is an arch-practitioner of the politics of scapegoating. It was all the Treasury's fault.

As the disappointments crowded in – the economy, Rhodesia, strife within the trade-union movement – Wilson tried the expedient of a semi-formal inner Cabinet, or Parliamentary Committee, as he misleadingly liked to call it. 'Civil servants', wrote Susan Crosland, 'thought the inner Cabinet a joke.'[166] Certainly, as Wilson used it, it seems to have been as much an instrument of personnel management as one of Cabinet government. If a member crossed him on a policy issue, as Callaghan did on trade-union reform in the spring of 1969, he would be expelled, even if, like Callaghan as Home Secretary, he was a pillar of the administration. A similar fate had befallen Tony Crosland, President of the Board of Trade, a year earlier.

Every twitch in the fortune of Cabinet government under Wilson Mark I was lovingly recorded by Dick Crossman, the would-be Bagehot of the twentieth century. There he sat at home on his Oxfordshire farm every few months, behaving like a one-man Greek chorus, informing us (he had every intention even then of publishing well short of the thirty-year limit) of the vicissitudes of the British Constitution.

Initially he is overwhelmed: 'I continue to have this curious sense of fiction, the feeling that I am living in a Maurice Edelman novel. All this business of being a Cabinet Minister is still unreal to me. . . . It's as if we are taking part not in real life but in a piece of reportage on the British constitutional system' (22 October 1964).[167]

He gets shirty with Sir Burke Trend because of the impersonal way in which the Cabinet Minutes are prepared: 'I pointed this out to Burke Trend and I said, "Harold can't have said this." To which he replied, "Ah, of course, he never said it, we never do give verbatim what people say. We précis the sense and give the substance of what they say." To which I replied, "This is not the substance of what he said, and if it had been the substance he would have divided the Cabinet"' (15 December 1964).[168]

Occasionally, on the train from Banbury to Paddington, Crossman would do his Bagehot impression, as in this entry for 19 July 1965:

I came up to London last night by the last train because I had to face a Monday morning of solid Cabinet Committees. As I sat there first at EDC [Economic Development Committee] and then at Home Affairs, I reflected on the way that Cabinet Committees as well as the Cabinet itself are becoming part of the dignified element of the English constitution. This is very largely because under this Government, maybe under all governments, Ministers are more and more departmentally conditioned before they come to these meetings. . . . And no Department will prepare a brief for its Minister on anything outside the departmental purview.[169]

Crossman consulted Thomas Balogh (the Oxford economist and close friend of Wilson then residing rather unhappily in the Cabinet Office). They agreed on the need for ministers to bring in their own staff from outside to remedy this conditioning:

If I started again I would like to have . . . (1) a ghost writer, not for my speeches but for my letters and statements: he would be the kind of person who could take the Ministry's policy and translate it into the kind of words I would use; (2) perhaps an economist; and (3) a general investigator whose job it would be to brief me so that I could participate intelligently at Cabinet Committees and in Cabinet on subjects outside my own Department. All these men would not only write; they would also have to read, because the Minister is not able to read all the Cabinet agenda before he gets there, or even all the agenda of the Cabinet Committees; and if he does read the papers he reads them with an eye which often fails to understand and to spot the relevant.[170]

Crossman at heart was a traditionalist. He believed in collective Cabinet government and abhorred anything that smacked of an over-mighty premiership. For example, he took comfort from the deflationary economic measures of July 1966, which he opposed, as it gave him the chance 'to reassert collective Cabinet authority because I see how disastrous it is to allow Cabinet government to decline into mere Prime Ministerial government . . . if I achieved anything it was by asserting the right of Cabinet to take part in the making of economic strategy so that Harold conceded we must be given that right'.[171]

It did not last. The entry in Barbara Castle's diary for 3 January 1968 records a dinner at Crossman's Westminster home where she, her host, Peter Shore, Tony Benn (then Minister of Technology) and Balogh engaged in a collective whinge about Wilson's management of Cabinet:

Dick told me I had got it all wrong. None of these special Cabinet committees really *did* anything: it didn't matter a damn that people like Wedgie [Mr Benn] and me were not on SEP [Steering Committee on Economic Policy] or OPD [Oversea Policy and Defence]. The trouble with Cabinet was not that Harold ran it through little cabals, but that there was no focal point of decision-making at all. Harold operated purely bilaterally, ringing up some Ministers on some things and others on others ('And only ringing *us* up when he wants something', interjected Wedgie). Wedgie suggested that we urgently need an inner Cabinet of four: Chancellor, Foreign Secretary, Lord President and Secretary of State for Economic Affairs with, of course, the PM. 'And backed by a proper Cabinet secretariat', added Tommy. 'Burke Trend would never stand for that, it would undermine his power', said Dick.[172]

Crossman and Castle were longstanding allies. From time to time they would engage in what read like mannered conversations on whether they were acting as Cabinet ministers or as purely departmental ministers.[173]

Even the most casual reader of the Crossman and Castle diaries cannot fail to pick up the sense of exhaustion that permeates their pages. The late sixties, in soccer terms, were the era of Alf Ramsey, who placed supreme emphasis on work rate. Wilson, himself a soccer fan, was the same, as Crossman discovered when he went to see him in April 1970 about a set of lectures on Cabinet government he was preparing for Harvard:

The next point that upset him was that I said that unlike the American President, the Prime Minister was relieved of a great deal of official ceremonial by the Queen and Prince Philip. Harold said that this would be a most unhappy way of putting it. 'I hope you won't say that. After all, let's be clear about it. Macmillan was an idle man, who just didn't work as Prime Minister, and Douglas-Home was idle. I am not an idle man, I have never worked harder than I do here.'[174]

Crossman on that occasion found Wilson 'rather white and puffy'.[175] But not all Wilson's senior ministers fell into the overload trap. Roy Jenkins, both as Chancellor of the Exchequer and as Home Secretary, was expert at itemizing the workload of his high office and at time-budgeting accordingly.[176] Reviewing Mrs Castle's diaries for 1964–70, he observed loftily if accurately, 'She was always "dragging" herself to an early meeting, "crawling" with exhaustion out of Cabinet, and finally "creeping home" to a tired bed. She made exhaustion into a political virility symbol, and was foolishly critical of those who did not believe that decisions were best taken in a state of prostration.'[177]

Across the road in Parliament in the late sixties, as Wilson, Castle and Crossman wore themselves out in the cause, as they saw it, of a more modern and socially just Britain, there sat in the Leader of the Opposition's office a man who not only shared the Jenkins view of workload but was planning exactly what he would do about it if the electorate gave him his chance. Edward Heath was the most managerially minded prime minister since Attlee. As part of what he would later call his 'quiet revolution',[178] Heath made detailed preparations for a new style of government, business-like, rational and free of Wilsonian gimmickry. 'Heath', wrote Phillip Whitehead, 'was a problem solver first, and ideologue only a distant second.'[179]

Heath, in fact, was a permanent secretary *manqué*. He would tell friends that, if, after he had taken the Civil Service Competition in 1946, he had been offered the Treasury instead of the Ministry of Civil Aviation, he would have stayed in Whitehall and eschewed a political career.[180] This trait was noted by fellow politicians such as Enoch Powell: '[Ted] believes there is an answer to all problems which can be worked out by proper bureaucratic means – I'm not using that word abusively for once – by the proper approach. If all the relevant facts are assembled and put together by competent people, and logical analysis is made, then that will provide the answer.'[181] The same was noticed by the senior civil servants themselves, who, almost without exception, had a high regard for the former assistant principal in the Ministry of Civil Aviation. 'Ted', said one, 'was a technocrat. He would have been a jolly good permanent secretary. He was rather slow, rather ponderous. And, unlike Mrs Thatcher, he did not rush to conclusions. He liked to sit seeing others, including the permanent secretaries, arguing in front of him. He would make up his mind and then he was unshiftable.'[182] One insider has a view of Heath in Downing Street etched in his memory. The Prime Minister was coming down the stairs from the first floor flanked by Burke Trend, the Cabinet Secretary, William Armstrong, Head of the Home Civil Service, and Robert Armstrong, then his Principal Private Secretary – all three Treasury men. 'There's Ted', mused the insider, 'surrounded by the Treasury.'[183] Many noticed he was happier in the company of the permanent secretaries than he was with his ministerial colleagues.

In Opposition days, Heath the permanent secretary *manqué* set about preparing for government with a will. In chapter 5 below, David Howell, his leading backroom boy, describes the work of the Public Sector Research Unit, how it scoured North America for business methods adaptable to Whitehall's needs and searched for think-tanks to visit. Heath sought the advice of seasoned Whitehall figures such as Lord Plowden and Lord Roberthall, who were summoned to his flat in the Albany.[184] He had an appetite for organization very rare in a politician. As he later told Charles Wintour and Robert Carvel of the *Evening Standard* 'I find this [the machinery of government] of extraordinary interest.'[185]

The result of that extraordinary interest was a White Paper four months after Heath's surprising victory in the general election of June 1970. *The Reorganisation of Central Government*[186] marks the most systematic attempt to reform the mechanics of Cabinet government since Lloyd George. In its second paragraph it accepted the overload thesis:

This administration believes that government has been attempting to do too much. This has placed an excessive burden on industry, and on the people of the country as a whole, and has also overloaded the government machine itself. Public administration and management in central government has stood up to these strains, but the weakness has shown itself in the apparatus of policy formulation and in the quality of many government decisions over the last 25 years.[187]

There are clear signs that senior officials, such as Burke Trend, William Armstrong and Ian Bancroft, involved in drafting the 1970 White Paper went along with the Heath analysis. The remedies adopted reflected very strongly the work of Heath's backroom team of the late sixties and were intended to 'remove the need for continual changes for a considerable period in the future'.[188] There were three main strands to the Heath reform:

(1) an efficiency system, Programme Analysis and Review, designed to examine critically longstanding policy commitments and to improve policy-making at the micro-level;[189]
(2) a change in the departmental structure creating giant super-ministries such as Department of the Environment and the Department of Trade and Industry to suck back decision-taking from the centre; and the establishment of business-like organizations, such as the Property Services Agency and the Procurement Executive, to secure the better management of large blocks of Whitehall work;[190]
(3) the foundation of 'a small multi-disciplinary central policy review staff in the Cabinet Office' to help formulate and sustain a clearer overall strategy for the administration as a whole, for 'governments are always at the same risk of losing sight of the need to consider the totality of their current policies in relation to their longer-term objectives'.[191]

When his new style of government was still running in, Heath explained to Wintour and Carvel that his aim was 'a more intensive Cabinet government' rather than prime-ministerial government, 'because it's the Cabinet all the time which is dealing with the strategy'.[192] He outlined his purpose to the pair of journalists in much the same words as he had used to the members of the nascent Rothschild CPRS on the lawn at No. 10 in 1971:[193]

What was most important was for the Cabinet to be in a position to take strategic decisions. I had seen Cabinets which all the time seemed to be dealing with the day-to-day problems and there was never a real opportunity to deal with strategy, either from the point of view of the Government or the country. What I wanted to do was so to change things that the Cabinet could do that.[194]

Implementation of the thinking developed in Opposition was not totally smooth, however, as David Howell remembers:

HOWELL   Of course, once we got into government a great many of our ambitions and aims and the ideas we'd seized hold of from talking to the Americans, people like Robert McNamara for instance, of the American Department of Defense, came up against the realities of Whitehall. Nevertheless, we did find a general mood in Whitehall and amongst the senior civil servants that their system was not perfect and that the time had come for some fairly radical changes. And I think even while we'd been in Opposition, remember no one knew whether we were going to win or not, it surprised many people when we did, there had been some sort of discreet across-the-fence interest at the professional Civil Service level in some of the concepts that we were developing and I'd made it a point of writing the occasional pamphlet as our thinking went along to send out smoke signals to everyone including the civil servants as to what we were about.[195]

HENNESSY   The outcome of the exercise in the White Paper, I think, had three main parts: one was a new think-tank, the Central Policy Review Staff, which presumably reflected some of the stuff you'd seen in the United States at Rand and so on; the other was a new system of, I suppose you would call it, zero-based budgeting, where you would look at longstanding government commitments and see if they should stagger on – that was Programme Analysis and Review; and, to reduce the weight on Cabinet, there were to be big conglomerate departments, which led to the Department of Trade and Industry and the Department of the

Environment. Now, what in fact had been watered down from your original keenness in the late sixties in terms of what actually emerged in that White Paper? What had the civil servants bargained away?

HOWELL   Well, I think the form was rather similar to what we wanted. The substance, though, was not. First of all the Central Policy Review Staff. Frankly some of us actually wanted that to be a staff for No. 10, for the Prime Minister, rather more like today's Policy Unit which the present Prime Minister has in No. 10, and less a general body to serve all the Cabinet. We thought that No. 10 was under-equipped to deal with the great departments of state. So we wanted the CPRS to be less of a Cabinet-wide body more serving the Prime Minister than was actually the case. As far as the conglomerate departments were concerned, I think those came about broadly as we intended. But, of course, our idea depended on something else as well, namely the substantial delegation of functions to non-departmental bodies and indeed the privatization of functions as well. We said everything should be examined and questioned to see whether it needed to be done at all. If it needed to be done, could it be done in the private or public sector? And if it had to be done in the public sector then could it be done by a separate hived-off body or by a department? And, even if it had to be done by a department, could it be done with fewer people in a different and more managerially efficient way? So we wanted this systematic question to go right through Whitehall and to greatly reduce the functional load on departments. As it was, the functional off-loading didn't really get going, so these departments ended up huge in policy terms but huge in functional terms as well. And that I think led to some weaknesses.[196]

Heath's new style of government was tested to near destruction within three years as a concatenation of crises generated at home and abroad struck his administration in 1973. But, before we examine his 1970 model under stress, it is necessary to eavesdrop on the Heath style in the Cabinet Room. There was no lightness of touch. It was always a very serious business. As one insider put it, 'In the Cabinet he would sit there glowering and saying practically nothing. The colleagues would watch him to see what impression their words were making. Then he would come down one way or another and that was it. He wasn't terribly interested in the politics of it. He would just do it if it was right and that, in the end, was what got him into trouble.'[197] David Howell was not a member of Mr Heath's Cabinet but he was close to him. I asked him about Heath's style as Prime Minister:

HENNESSY   He's said to have been very presidential in the Cabinet Room.
I know you were only a junior minister, but one hears about things when
one's down the line, that he was very presidential, that he wouldn't let
them talk much and was very stiff and frozen. And yet he did encourage
those six-monthly sessions at Chequers when the think-tank would come
and brief the full Cabinet, and smaller ones in No. 10 for the junior
ministers. And it's never quite fitted for me that he could be so stiff and
laconic in Cabinet and yet try and be much more expansive on these set-
piece occasions.

HOWELL   Yes, as you say, I wasn't in the Cabinet so I can't really speak
with any authority at all about how he conducted affairs there. But, of
course, he was and is a fairly silent man. He's very amusing and can be
a very able speaker in public. But he's not a great conversationalist and
not a great chatterer and talker and worker out of problems, like, for
instance, Viscount Whitelaw, whose genius is that he's always absolutely
ready with many views on every single problem that's going, political,
policy and so on. That wasn't Ted Heath's style at all. He's a very silent
man and yet I think he actually, at the same time, the opposite side of
the silence and inwardness, . . . did want a great many people working
on issues and analysing them around him. I remember before he became
Prime Minister he was in charge of the Conservative re-think where I helped
him do a lot of that work and I think he enjoyed that very much. He was
very good at it. He was always waiting, very receptive to new ideas and
so he did like people and organizations to present their views and he did
like to hear discussion. But he didn't say much himself.

HENNESSY   The other thing that was said about him, particularly towards
the end, after the U-turn on economic policy, was that he'd been captured
by his officials, and that he also, in the end, rather relished the company
of the permanent secretaries more than he did his Cabinet colleagues. Is
that fair?

HOWELL   I think there is obviously a danger with all people in high office
that very able officials round them with very clear minds who are aside
from all the political pressures must be a very attractive haven. I should
think that all politicians, and I speak for myself, we all face this temptation.
You forget the political pressures and relax in the company of brilliant
minds. And I'm sure that Ted Heath was as prone to that as the rest of
us and he had some very able people round him.[198]

One aspect of bureaucratic life which did not appeal to the permanent
secretary *manqué* in No. 10 was the dense committee undergrowth.
He took the opportunity of Sir Burke Trend's retirement in 1973 to
hack it down. Cabinet committees were reduced by half from around
140 to seventy. Heath also used the opportunity of Trend's retirement

to change the nature of the steering-briefs for the Prime Minister – Brook's innovation, it will be recalled. 'Burke Trend', said one insider, 'used to say a brief should be Socratic and ask a series of questions. John Hunt developed a more stylized form of briefing. All new entrants to the Cabinet Office got a model brief. Section one would give the background and the options. Section two was on handling the problems that were likely to come up. Section three was the conclusions, the decisions needed with a bit of advice.'[199]

In addition, Heath adopted the expedient of mixed commitees of ministers and civil servants, a task-force approach to Cabinet government. He thought it wasted time to have official committees pre-processing options before they came before ministerial groups. The mixed committee experiment was generally unsuccessful. Civil servants found it very difficult to contradict their ministers or to pursue a different line.[200] There was one major exception which worked well – the Civil Contingencies Unit created after the 1972 miners' strike.[201] It gave ministers an improved intelligence system on the physical consequences of industrial disputes in vulnerable industries and services. It also fashioned an improved operational instrument for ministerial use to buy time and to distribute scarce resources once a dispute started. By and large it performed well during the miners' industrial action of 1973–4 and the concurrent 'go-slows' in the electricity-supply industry, as David Howell recalls:

HOWELL   The system of government was rather good. In fact I'm told we ran the three-day week so well that it didn't make enough impact on the country; they didn't realize the crisis and thought they wouldn't support Ted Heath.

HENNESSY   So the Civil Contingencies Unit, the Cabinet committee set up after the miners' strike of '72, which I've no doubt you were intimately involved in, in '74[202] actually delivered the goods. It ran Britain exceedingly well under duress.

HOWELL   I think it did. I think everyone says the three-day week produced some remarkable results and I think that side of things continues to be run very well indeed. I am enormously impressed. It's fashionable, and always has been, to sneer at civil servants. I think the way in which they organize that side of things is quite brilliant.[203]

The Civil Contingencies Unit does seem to have stood up well to the battering inflicted by the 1973–4 winter of discontent. Serious collapse was avoided (though, as one official involved recalled, 'it was pretty close at the end'[204]), but the new style of government as a whole did not stand up so well. As ministers grappled with a quadrupling of oil prices after OPEC's deployment of the oil weapon in October 1974 *and* mounting industrial trouble at home, exhaustion and slipshod policy-making accumulated relentlessly, one problem compounding another. Heath, a glutton for work,[205] had also to devote large chunks of energy and concentration to the EEC and to Ireland as the Sunningdale Conference on power-sharing approached. Douglas Hurd's memoir captures the reality the particular cocktail of overload mixed by the pressures of late autumn and early winter 1973:

On Sunday 8 December, for example, the Prime Minister entertained the Italian Prime Minister, Signor Rumor, to dinner at Chequers. The meal was hardly over when Mr Heath flew to Sunningdale by helicopter to preside over the last stage of the conference on the future of Northern Ireland. Three days later it was time for the state visit of President Mobutu of Zaire. Two days after that the European summit began in Copenhagen. These were four major events, two of them (Sunningdale and Copenhagen) of outstanding importance. They were all the kind of diplomatic event which in normal times Mr Heath would much enjoy and at which he would perform very well. They all involved talks, travel, long meals, extensive briefing beforehand; yet none of them had anything to do with the crisis which was swallowing us up.[206]

The officials on whom Heath relied so heavily felt the strain too. One broke under it. William Armstrong, Heath's right-hand man particularly after the U-turn in 1972 on incomes policy, public expenditure and industrial intervention, may have been, as Head of the Home Civil Service, one step removed by virtue of his office (Sir Douglas Allen was Permanent Secretary to the Treasury). But Heath raised him to a kind of economic overlordship which led Bill Kendall of the Civil and Public Services Association to dub him 'deputy prime minister', a tag which stuck. In bureaucratic terms, Armstrong was the keystone in the arch of Heath's economic strategy from the autumn of 1972. By the end of January 1974, Armstrong, a highly sensitive man, was at a conference at Ditchley Park in Oxfordshire 'talking wildly of coups and coalitions to his alarmed fellow guests'.[207] Campbell Adamson of the Confederation of British Industry went with his fellow industrialists to a meeting with Armstrong in February 1974: 'We listened to a lecture about how Communists were infiltrating everything. They might even be infiltrating, he said, the room he was in. It was quite clear that the immense strain and overwork was taking its toll, and two days later of course he had to give up and have a rest.'[208]

The proud anti-overload device, the 1970 White Paper, had not noticeably eased the burden of government when overload went into overdrive after October 1973. The system changed gear into short-term crisis management – the CPRS, whose energy study in the summer of 1973 had predicted the oil-price explosion, included.[209] No longer was it to be a question of careful, rational long-term planning of public expenditure. It was a desperate search for cuts and economies. Programme Analysis and Review was too slow and too cumbersome to inject reason into necessity. In January 1974, Heath's giant Department of Trade and Industry was broken up and a separate Department of Energy created. Heath had heeded official opinion, which argued that now too much policy-making was bottled up in the super ministry and too little was reaching Cabinet.[210] As Heath went down to electoral defeat in February 1974, the yellowing of the 1970 *Reorganisation of Central Government* White Paper was the last thing on people's mind. Heath wanted to be, in machinery-of-government and Cabinet terms, the Lloyd George of the 1970s. The National Union of Mineworkers and the oil sheikhs denied him the title. Yet, ten years later, some surprising people remembered and cared. 'Ted Heath', said Dr David Owen in November 1983, 'had some of the best ideas of any postwar Prime Minister. He . . . was a rather radical person.'[211]

One senior official with a ringside seat at the traumas of winter 1973–4 contemplated resignation during the first week of March so that he could tell the country that Heath was a serious man and had been a worthy prime minister. It was the reappearance of Harold Wilson in the driving-seat of government which prompted this. The official stayed and, in later years, coined the best metaphor for the Wilson style: Harold as the great player of Space Invaders taking the first blip to cross the screen whether it was important or not.[212] Wilson's own choice of metaphor was no longer that of the centre forward, but the seasoned centre half feeding passes to his experienced forwards and allowing them to score the goals. For those officials who remembered Harold Mark I in 1964, he was not the same man ten years later. 'I always had the impression', said one, 'that we were not seeing the best of Harold Wilson in that period. He was tired and almost bored.'[213]

He did tinker a bit with the machine. The Department of Trade and Industry was broken up still further into three separate departments: Trade, Prices and Consumer Protection, and Industry, to accommodate the ministerial dispositions he wished to make in the Cabinet. Each Cabinet minister was allowed up to two 'special advisers' drawn from outside Whitehall who would serve as temporary civil servants for the duration of the administration. Wilson therefore regularized a practice he had begun in 1964 when outsiders such as Professors Nicholas Kaldor and Robert Neild had been recruited into the Treasury, a practice which Heath had followed on a smallish scale.[214] He showed little interest in the CPRS, but was happy enough to keep it and sent Lord Rothschild a chirpy Prime Minister's personal minute on 1 April 1974 which Rothschild reproduced in his *Random Variables*:

In view of the current economic crisis, I would be grateful if you would give consideration to the following figures:

Population of the United Kingdom	54,000,000
People aged 65 and over	14,000,000
People aged 18 and under	18,000,000
People working for the Government	9,000,000
The Armed Forces	2,300,000
Local Government employees	9,800,000
People who won't work	888,000
People detained at Her Majesty's pleasure	11,998
Total	53,999,998

Balance left to do the work   2

You and I, therefore, must work harder, especially you, as I have felt no evidence of your considerable weight since I took office.

1 April 1974   HW[215]

Wilson's most important and, to date, durable innovation in March 1974 was the creation, separate from the CPRS, of a Downing Street Policy Unit under Dr Bernard Donoughue, a political scientist from the London School of Economics. It was a prime-ministerial *cabinet* in all but name[216] and plunged instantly into the economic blizzard which engulfed the new Labour administration and with which, initially, it coped so inadequately. Labour's first fifteen months back in office – the era of the Social Contract between government and unions, the partnership meant to curb soaring inflation in return for an improved 'social wage' – was a very one-sided affair. As Joel Barnett,

Wilson's Chief Secretary to the Treasury, later described 'the quaintly titled social contract', 'the only give and take in the contract was that the government gave and the unions took'.[217]

For all its experience, the Wilson Cabinet grappled scarcely at all with the realities of the post-OPEC economy. Bernard Donoughue noted 'the almost complete absence of discussion of economic policy. I think it's true that the Cabinet never really discussed economic policy before the October [1974] election; indeed didn't, as I recall, discuss it until early 1975.'[218] Its weekend strategy session in the autumn of 1974, tapping the intellectual horsepower of the CPRS, is graphically recorded in Mrs Castle's diary entry for Sunday 17 November. It is worth quoting at length for a number of reasons: it is the only detailed eyewitness account available of a CPRS Chequers presentation to ministers during the Review Staff's thirteen-year life; and, perhaps most important of all, it captures the banality and desperation of top-level discussions on intractable problems at a time of crisis. Mrs Castle opens her account[219] with a few reflections on the 'feminine' touch Edward Heath had brought to the redecoration of Chequers and some bitter-sweet memories of 1969, when she and Wilson had clashed there with trade-union leaders over the *In Place of Strife* proposals for union reform. Her note of the occasion, which took place in the library at Chequers, speaks volumes about the quality of British government in the mid 1970s:

Though the CPRS had drawn up an agenda in four parts, starting with our relationship with the external world, we soon found ourselves in the middle of a second reading debate over the whole field. Ken Berrill [Head of the CPRS] introduced the discussion succinctly, setting out the problems (the threatening world slump, the petrodollar crisis, etc.) rather than attempting to answer them. Harold Lever then spoke to his own paper. 'We have only a 50 per cent chance of avoiding world catastrophe', he told us. Getting some international machinery to recycle the petrodollar was the only hope. Everything else, like petrol rationing, was only 'frolics at the margin'. We should broadly back the Americans. Denis [Healey] admitted that it was very unlikely we could close the whole of the balance of payments gap by 1978–79, even if things went well. But unless we improved our competitiveness our balance of payments position would become disastrous. There was a strong case for an energy conservation programme, if only on psychological grounds.

Roy [Jenkins] ruminated: 'Your memory is better than mine, Prime Minister, but I believe it is ten years ago to this very day that we sat in this room discussing the Defence Review. The world has changed out of all recognition since then.' He then talked about the changes in the power blocs, adding that those like himself who had expected the coherence of Europe to develop strongly had found the reality 'disappointing'. The Middle East situation was full of menace and he believed a pre-emptive strike by the USA was possible. Eric [Varley] talked about energy extremely competently, though he insisted that looking for major energy savings was likely to be 'extremely disappointing'. He was 'very opposed' to petrol rationing and maintained that rota cuts, organised systematically, would be the only effective method – and they were out of the question. The only hope was to move to energy self-sufficiency. But the miners' attitude was frightening. He had been speaking only a day or two ago to a miners' meeting attended by what he called the 'Scargill Mafia'. When he told them that the Government could have used more oil at the power stations this summer and so built up coal stocks for the winter against a possible strike, but hadn't, they merely retored, 'More fool you' and thanked him for letting them know how strong their position was. He concluded sadly: 'Don't let us frighten the oil companies away.' We needed their investment.

Wedgie [Tony Benn] then made what I found a very effective speech, pointing out that we had got to look at the problem in domestic as well as international terms. A devolution of power had also been going on at home and all our policy must take account of it. 'We cannot win consent to a technocratic solution. We must redistribute power in this country by peaceful means. Beyond the slump must be the perspective of a better society.' He did not believe the solution lay in bigger and bigger units: he had been immensely struck by the emphasis which Jim [Callaghan] laid on devolution in his paper. 'We must show what sort of Government we are.' Were we going to go for impersonal macro-solutions, or were we going to realise that the people were looking for us as their leaders to provide an answer to their difficulties? To them their leaders seemed utterly remote. 'Without consent no solution we work out round this table will have a chance.' Mike [Foot] said wryly that if, as Harold Lever said, we had only a 50 per cent chance of avoiding catastrophe, we had better work out a contingency plan in case that chance did not come off. Roy [Mason] made a fluent contribution about the added danger of war in the Middle East.

The gathering gloom was compounded by Jim [Callaghan] acting Cassandra as usual. 'When I am shaving in the morning I say to myself that if I were a young man I would emigrate. By the time I am sitting down to breakfast I ask myself, "Where would I go"?' (Laughter).[220] Mike had talked about contingency plans for catastrophe, he continued. If we ever got to a siege economy he, Jim, dreaded the effect on our democracy. He didn't think that the US would do a Suez in the Middle East. The more likely prospect was our declining influence. 'One prospect is that we shall lose our seat on the Security Council.' Jim concluded gloomily that in his view we should go on sliding downhill for the next few years. 'Nothing in these papers makes me believe anything to the contrary. I haven't got any solution. As I said, if I were a young man, I should emigrate.'

By this time faces were getting pretty long. I hadn't intended to speak on the external affairs section, but the discussion had widened so much that I came in with the attached remarks.

Mrs Castle's contribution to this cornucopia of political wisdom and strategic insight was that policies had to be put in their philosophical context to win consent. Presentation was the key. It must be demonstrated to the ordinary worker what he gained from public expenditure, the so-called 'social wage'.[221] At this point, Denis Healey, Chancellor of the Exchequer and the Cabinet's intellectual heavyweight, weighed in:

Denis rallied the defeatists with a robust speech: what everyone had said showed how pretentious were some of the demands made by the party for us to interfere here, there and everywhere. 'It is no good ceasing to be the world's policeman in order to become the world's parson instead.' But he would have nothing of Jim's gloom. 'If we do join the Third World it will be as a member of OPEC.' He wasn't as pessimistic as Harold L. (who by this time had gone home, pleading that he was suffering from gastric flu). We could not sensibly plan ahead for a doomsday-type catastrophe. He agreed with Wedgie about the dissolution of the power blocs. He rejected the conspiracy theory of foreign affairs. 'International Communism has as much or as little significance as the Commonwealth.' by this time it was nearly 1.00 pm. Harold summed up by saying the discussion had been first-class: 'the best I have ever heard in this type of gathering'.

Wilson's last remark is truly chilling. He had been Prime Minister for nearly seven years in all when he produced that judgement. What can the 'second-class' discussions of his Cabinets have been like? This was not some throwaway line intended to perk them up before lunch after a morning of incoherent doomwatching. He took the opportunity of his first book after leaving No. 10 to state, 'I was not exaggerating when I called the 1974 Cabinet the most experienced and talented Cabinet this century, transcending even the Campbell-Bannerman Administration of 1905.'[222]

Matters did not improve in the afternoon when Tony Crosland, a man of immense intellectual curiosity and an adornment of the Oxford

Economics Faculty in the immediate post-war period, added his dose of wisdom and hope: '"There was", he said, "no surefire recipe for economic growth." (He can say that again!) There was a role for general incentives and also one for selective assistance. We needed to find a balance between them and help the regions to help themselves.' We did not know, continued Crosland, how our relative decline had taken place. He added what could, with a slight dose of exaggeration, serve as the epitaph of modern Cabinet government: 'All we can do is press every button we've got. We do not know which, if any, of them will have the desired results.'[223]

Lord Wilson found nothing untoward about the quality of that Chequers discussion when I reminded him of it in conversation more than ten years later. 'It meant that I'd got through all my policies . . . [they] all had a little bit of fun and expression and there was no change in policy. I was quite pleased with it.'[224]

On minor matters, too, Cabinet drift was evident. Joel Barnett, a new boy to Cabinet-committee life, was suitably shocked by what he found. 'On complex issues, Cabinet committees are just about the worst possible way of arriving at sensible decisions. . . . In most cases, the ministers not directly involved had either read the brief late the previous night, or started to do so as the argument proceeded.'[225] He quickly learned the tricks. The Cabinet committee on a new Government Conference Centre to be built on the Storey's Gate site ruled out the investment on grounds of cost (it was subsequently given the go-ahead and, as of Autumn 1985, has almost been completed). Playing it long became second nature. Barnett wanted to defer the building of a new British Library next to St Pancras Station. 'I was once told of a favourite phrase of Harold Wilson's: "A decision deferred is a decision made." Well, we deferred many difficult decisions, and this was just one of them.'[226]

But Wilson remained supreme at one aspect of Cabinet management and control: the art of isolating his more turbulent opponents within the government. For example, Tony Benn, his Industry Secretary, was wedded, in a fashion the Prime Minister found highly inconvenient, to the manifesto pledges on greater public ownership and planning. Wilson used both his Policy Unit, which contained a special 'Benn-watcher', the economist Richard Graham, and the Cabinet machinery to geld Benn's favoured strategy. Industrial policy was effectively hijacked from the Department of Industry to No. 10 and the Cabinet's Public Enterprise Committee, which produced the 1974 White Paper on the Regeneration of Industry with its watered-down National Enterprise Board and voluntary planning agreements.[227] The diluting of the industrial strategy was a classic Wilsonian operation, as Bernard Donoughue remembers: 'I'm sure that Tony Benn felt himself betrayed by his Prime Minister because the moment the word got around, as it rapidly did in Whitehall – and the Cabinet Office made sure that it got around – that the Prime Minister was not giving his support to Tony Benn, then the civil servants began to back off from their minister. Although in this case Mr Benn had backed off from them in the beginning.'[228]

But in another area Benn had a fairly dramatic if temporary impact on the conduct of Cabinet government. In successfully pressing for a referendum on the Common Market, he obliged Wilson to suspend the doctrine of collective Cabinet responsibility, an event without precedent since the National Government had done the same on the free-trade issue in the early thirties. Neither Lord Wilson nor Peter Shore, reflecting on the suspension ten years later, remembered it causing any difficulties inside the Cabinet Room. 'I think we managed to keep our personal relations reasonably good', said Shore, a strong anti-Marketeer.[229] And Lord Wilson, who was in favour of continued EEC membership, said, 'I made it very clear, that as soon as this was all over, we would revert to strict Cabinet rules and collective views and all that kind of thing.'[230] Prime ministers go to great lengths to preserve public appearances over collective responsibility. For example, it was quite a story in December 1985 when Mrs Thatcher briefly appeared to have allowed Michael Heseltine, Secretary of State for Defence, to campaign publicly against the Cabinet's position that the Westland helicopter company could do a deal with the American firm Sikorsky if its shareholders so wished. Political correspondents were told initially that the Prime Minister believed his activities to be 'unorthodox but in order'.[231] The day after that smoke signal was released, the same non-attributable sources let it be known that Heseltine had been rebuked in Cabinet for busting the collective line.[232] And the rest, as the saying goes, is history.

Wilson Mark II contributed two innovations to the practice of Cabinet government, both on the public-expenditure side. He sanctioned the use of cash limits as a means of control.[233] And he established the principle that any decision which drew on the contingency reserve of public money should go to full Cabinet and not be taken in Cabinet committee, where the Chancellor and the Chief

Secretary could all too easily fall prey to ambushes set by cabals of spending ministers.[234]

James Callaghan, who succeeded Wilson in April 1976, was the sweatiest of old political sweats. He had held all three great offices of state – the Exchequer, the Home Office and the Foreign Office – before succeeding to the premiership. His style was emollient. He was a great fixer. He was discriminating in his use of advisers and the techniques of advice. He retained both the Downing Street Policy Unit and the CPRS, regarding them as complementary. But Programme Analysis and Review, which had not flourished since the early Heath era, effectively died under Callaghan, though it was not formally buried until Mrs Thatcher was in No. 10. Callaghan tinkered very little with the machinery of government apart from breaking off a chunk of the Department of the Environment and re-creating a separate Transport Ministry in his ministerial reshuffle of September 1976. After the sterling crisis of autumn–winter 1976, he did toy with the idea of splitting the Treasury into a finance ministry and a department of management and budget, which would have combined the Treasury's spending-divisions with the manpower work of the Civil Service Department. He postponed a decision until the 1979 election and, had he won it, a reshaping of the central departments was a strong possibility.[235]

Callaghan was a superb manager of Cabinet, as Peter Shore recalls:

I didn't support Mr Callaghan as successor to Harold Wilson. [There were] several reasons for it: one of them was I thought they were too much alike. But their styles were really very dissimilar and that became very plain from the moment really that Mr Callaghan took over. There was a much more, if you like, restful quality about him. He inspired, I think, a great deal of confidence in the country and indeed among his colleagues, and deservedly so. And looking back on it, when you think about his own experience – he'd been Home Secretary, Chancellor of the Exchequer and Foreign Secretary – I think most of his Cabinet colleagues who served under him would say he was a better prime minister than he was a secretary of state in either of these three roles. In other words he was a successful prime minister, successful in his personal relationships in Cabinet, successful in getting the business of government done, again in the extremely difficult circumstances of having no majority in the House of Commons.[236]

In terms of Cabinet conventions, Callaghan was an arch-traditionalist. After the leak of Cabinet minutes on child benefit in 1976 he decided it was time, once more, to have a secrecy law under whose rubric juries were likely to convict. He established and chaired a Cabinet committee on reform of the discredited section 2 of the Official Secrets Act, 1911. He stacked the membership of GEN 29 to ensure that freedom of information did not get a look-in, despite a pledge in the October 1974 Labour manifesto to introduce an open-government statute.[237] In February 1978 he circulated a Prime Minister's personal minute on 'Disclosure of Cabinet Committees'. It contained not a trace of the spirit of openness, and its timeless tone will be familiar to all connoisseurs of *Questions of Procedure for Ministers*:

Consistently with the practice of all former Prime Ministers I have always refused to publish details of Cabinet Committees or to answer Questions in the House about them. Hitherto this has led to some allegations in the Press about Whitehall obscurantism but little interest or pressure in Parliament itself. There is however now some evidence that Select Committees would like to interest themselves in the Committee system and may be seeking to erode the present convention. I have therefore been considering the case for taking the initiative and disclosing details of the Committee structure.

I accept that the present convention has certain disadvantages for us. In particular non-disclosure makes it difficult to answer charges that the government's policies are not properly coordinated. For example the Select Committee on Overseas Development has recommended the establishment of a Cabinet Committee to coordinate political, trade and aid policies towards the developing world largely because the ODM were not able to disclose that such a Committee (RD) already exists. It is also arguable that non-disclosure is inconsistent with a policy of greater openness. In any case some parts of the Committee structure are quite widely known about outside Government; in these cases what is at issue therefore is a refusal to admit publicly what a lot of people know about privately.

It is important therefore to understand the reasons for the current practice of non-disclosure. They are as follows: the Cabinet Committee system grew up as the load on the Cabinet itself became too great. It allows matters of lesser importance to be decided without troubling the whole Cabinet; and major issues to be clarified in order to save the time of the Cabinet. The method adopted by Ministers for discussing policy questions is however essentially a domestic matter; and a decision by a Cabinet Committee, unless referred to the Cabinet, engages the collective responsibility of all Ministers and has exactly the same authority as a decision by the Cabinet itself. Disclosure that a particular Committee had dealt with a matter might lead to argument about the status of the decision or demands that it should be endorsed by the whole Cabinet. Furthermore publishing details of the

Committees would be both misleading and counter-productive. The existence of some could not be disclosed on security grounds; others are set up to do a particular job and then wound up. The absence of a Committee on a particular subject (for example, agriculture or poverty) does not mean that the Government do not attach importance to it; and the fact that a particular Minister is not on a Committee does not mean that he does not attend when his interests are affected. Publication would almost inevitably lead to pressures for both more and larger Committees, and for disclosure of information about their activities.

I do not believe that we could in any event disclose the existence of the GEN groups. This is partly because of their ephemeral nature and partly because disclosure would often reveal either that very sensitive subjects were under consideration or that we had something in train about which we were not ready to make an announcement. Disclosure of the main standing Committees would thus give a partial picture only. Moreover having gone as far as this I do not believe that it would be possible for me to hold the line and refuse to answer any further questions about the composition and activities of the Committees. At the minimum we would be under pressure to reveal the names of the Chairman. This would make it harder for me to make changes; and it would have implications for the responsibilities of Departmental Ministers since Select Committees would try to summon the Chairman of Cabinet Committees to give evidence in addition to the responsible Minister. I should also be under continuing pressure to say that a Committee was considering a particular subject (and often it would be a GEN group); and there would be questions about when Committees were meeting, the work they were doing, whether particular Ministers are on them, the details of under-pinning Official Committees, etc.

I have therefore decided that we should not change our stance on this matter. The present convention is long established and provides a basis on which we can stand. Any departure from it would be more likely to whet appetites than to satisfy them. I ask my colleagues therefore to rest on the position that the way in which we coordinate our decision is a matter internal to Government and not to answer questions about the Cabinet Committee system.

LJC February 1978[238]

Callaghan's secretive instincts had been strongly reinforced by the leaks which poured out of the Cabinet Room in the autumn of 1976, the first of the two great crises of his premiership. The collapse of sterling in September and October 1976 forced the government to seek a loan from the International Monetary Fund. Managing his colleagues and steering them to a compromise between the Fund's tough conditions for a loan and those on the Left who favoured a siege economy as an alternative to rescue by the international banking community obliged Callaghan to practise traditional Cabinet government in the classic mould. It took twenty-six separate Cabinet meetings to resolve the issue.[239] Callaghan carried the day early in December 1976 without a single resignation. But it had been a very close-run thing. As one very senior official put it, 'The IMF was real Cabinet government but it was very unusual. Even there it was Cabinet government because everything else was swept up in one issue.'[240] Peter Shore agrees with the 'classical cabinet government' interpretation of the 1976 crisis:

HENNESSY   It seems to me that it was the high-water mark of collective Cabinet government [of] the traditional type in recent times. One got the impression that Mr Callaghan felt that he had to put on one side the normal practice of consulting only a small group of inner ministers on economic issues, and had to carry all the colleagues, all twenty-two, if he was to have a hope of carrying the party in the country clearly out of the crisis. Is that a fair assessment of it?

SHORE   Yes, it is. I haven't heard it put like that, but I think it's a very accurate and perceptive one. The Cabinet did behave as a Cabinet and although I said earlier about the Treasury being forced to disgorge information when the DEA existed, that wasn't the case to the same extent in 1976. But sitting round the Cabinet table were at least three ex-Chancellors, about four ex-Presidents of the Board of Trade, one ex-Secretary of State for Economic Affairs and all of us, I suppose, had our different advisers on economic policy whom we contacted. And we did require and demand and obtain from the Treasury a great deal of information before we would allow, as it were, any decision to be made. And there were times indeed, I think, that the effect of the very strong resistance to public-expenditure cuts and then the promulgation of an alternative economic strategy, which I myself was much concerned with, did have a very considerable effect.

Callaghan took great pains inside the Cabinet to be seen to let the notion of an alternative strategy have a fair run. But he managed very effectively to isolate Benn and others who leaned towards a siege economy. Tony Benn, who acknowledges that 'Jim Callaghan . . . ran the Cabinet with considerable skill',[241] brought to the 1976 Cabinet a set of Cabinet minutes from August 1931 'in which exactly the same discussion took place . . . to remind them that there was a history in this matter'.[242] Benn was invited by Callaghan to prepare a Cabinet paper containing the alternative strategy of planned growth and industrial reconstruction behind a tariff wall. Callaghan also invited the CPRS to prepare two papers – one putting flesh on the siege-economy option, the other assuming Britain's continued engagement in open trading. The exercise was called 'Fortress Britain'. The CPRS's view, after surveying the evidence, was strongly in favour of the open economy.[243] Meanwhile, Callaghan primed sympathetic colleagues to counter Benn, as Bill Rodgers, then Transport Secretary, remembers: 'Jim Callaghan tipped off a number of people to have their questions ready and [Benn's paper] was completely massacred. . . . Callaghan was brilliant . . . one of the great achievements of his period in Cabinet as Prime Minister was isolating Benn.'[244] The middle ground, personified by the sceptical Tony Crosland, swung into line, and Callaghan, after twenty-six Cabinets, was home and dry.

Successful he may have been in October–December 1976 at using the full Cabinet as a forum for crisis management, but Callaghan was not tempted to extend the practice in more tranquil times. As a member of his Policy Unit, the economist Gavyn Davies, revealed in a private paper for a Fabian Society inquiry in 1980, Callaghan withdrew effective decision-taking on sensitive market-related issues into a highly secret 'economic seminar' which was not even given the status of a formal Cabinet committee.[245] The 'seminar' included Denis Healey, Chancellor of the Exchequer; Harold Lever, Chancellor of the Duchy of Lancaster; Gordon Richardson, Governor of the Bank of England; Sir Douglas Wass, Permanent Secretary to the Treasury; Sir Kenneth Berrill of the CPRS; Sir John Hunt, Cabinet Secretary; Kenneth Stowe, Callaghan's Principal Private Secretary; plus a supporting cast from the Treasury and the Bank of England. Ministers were outnumbered about three or four to one by officials. As Davies told the Fabians, 'collective responsibility under these circumstances was a sham':[246] 'The Cabinet was not informed of the existence of this group, or of its critical decisions. The Prime Minister is able to operate a system of "divide and rule" mainly because of the tradition of secrecy which permeates the entire system of British government.'[247]

And, as his administration staggered through its winter of discontent in the first two months of 1979, Callaghan's famed skills as a crisis-manager seemed to desert him. He vacillated over the lorry-drivers' strike, shrinking in the end from declaring a state of emergency and ruling out the use of troops to move medical supplies from the docks.[248] There was the daily undignified spectacle of Sir Clive Rose of the Civil Contingencies Unit meeting with Alex Kitson of the Transport and

General Workers' Union to discuss breaches of the union's voluntary code on picketing during the lorry-driver's dispute.[249] Macabre humour broke out inside the Unit, as Joel Barnett recalled:

We leafed through the various contingency plans in the Home Secretary's committee but none seemed satisfactory. It was made clear to us that Operation 'Brisket' for the road haulage dispute, 'Bittern' for the rapidly growing ambulance drivers' dispute, and 'Nimrod' in the case of the water workers' action, were all long on detailed planning, but short on how much could actually be done in a major dispute. (Gerald Kaufman, later appointed to assist the hard-pressed Merlyn Rees [Home Secretary], said the next plan would be called 'Loony'.)[250]

Barnett's account of the Cabinet meeting of 1 February shows that matters had improved little in the command and control post of the British system of government since that awful day at Chequers in November 1974 when gloom descended:

The Prime Minister summed up what many of us wanted to say when he put a question to Tony Benn: 'what do you say about the thuggish act of a walk-out, without notice, from a Children's Hospital?' [The hospital ancillary workers were also taking industrial action against Callaghan's 5 per cent pay norm.] Tony replied that: 'When decent people become irrational, something must be wrong if they are driven to such desperate acts.' Jim Callaghan's response was that he 'had never in fifty years been so depressed as a trade unionist'.[251]

Three months later a very different Prime Minister took over and established a very different command and control post in No. 10.

3

Conviction Cabinet, 1979–86

It must be a conviction government. As Prime Minister I could not waste time having any internal arguments. *Mrs Margaret Thatcher, February 1979*[1]

She cannot see an institution without hitting it with her handbag. *Julian Critchley, MP, on Mrs Thatcher, 1982*[2]

I take your point about frankness! That's what Cabinets are for, and lively discussions usually lead to good decisions. *Mrs Thatcher to James Prior, August 1984*[3]

A brilliant tyrant surrounded by mediocrities. *A view of the Thatcher Cabinet attributed to Harold Macmillan, Earl of Stockton, 1985*[4]

I had not expected to find it necessary to leave the Cabinet. But when I did so, the words I uttered for the record were that I could not accept that the proper constitutional practices, as I understood them, were being observed. *Michael Heseltine, 1986*[5]

My eyes light up at the sight of her even though she's hitting me about the head, so to speak. *Sir Keith Joseph, Secretary of State for Education, on Mrs Thatcher, 1985*[6]

There are only two ways of getting into the Cabinet. One way is to crawl up the staircase of preferment on your belly; the other way is to kick them in the teeth. *Aneurin Bevan, undated*[7]

In one area, Mrs Thatcher has proved to be a Keynesian on a scale unmatched by her predecessors in the recent past. Her style of government has turned out to be a marvellous make-work scheme for political scientists, contemporary historians and political commentators. She is, as one permanent secretary put it, the 'most commanding prime minister of recent times'.[8] Once the Cabinet purges of 1980 and 1981 had been completed, a large proportion of the Cabinet were what Nye Bevan would have called 'staircase' men, who owed their high office entirely to her patronage rather than any independent standing in the Conservative Party. Commenting on the effect of the September 1981 reshuffle in an interview with Jeremy Mayhew, James Prior said of the Cabinet,

I don't think it was ever as good a debating forum again. There was more and more control by the Prime Minister. To that extent there was greater cohesion in Cabinet, because there were a lot of new faces who owed their promotion much more to her than to their record in the party. I don't think it was as good a Cabinet and certainly the debates on economic policy really ceased to exist.[9]

A fairly convincing case for an imperious premiership could be assembled even before Heseltine's 'grand remonstrance of protest', as the *Observer* called it.[10] After all we had been warned. Three months before defeating Callaghan at the polls she announced publicly her intention of running a 'conviction Cabinet'. An argument-free zone was to be established in the Cabinet Room. Her homage to frankness in her letter to Jim Prior more than five years later caused a great deal of ironic laughter in Whitehall.[11] There was no shortage of evidence from her Cabinet purges about the disagreeable qualities of life in the Thatcher Cabinet Room. As one senior figure put it, 'She was not really running a team. Every time you have a Prime Minister who wants to take all the decisions, it mainly leads to bad results. Attlee didn't. That's why he was so damn good. Macmillan didn't. The nearest parallel to Maggie is Ted.'[12]

David Howell spoke openly about it:

HENNESSY   Mrs Thatcher has the great virtue of candour, and just before she became Prime Minister she announced in a newspaper interview how she was going to run her Cabinet and she said it must be a 'conviction' government. 'As Prime Minister, I couldn't waste time having any internal arguments.' Now this remark implied that she was going to mount a substantial assault on the traditional nature of Cabinet government, which is collective discussion – free-ranging before decisions are reached. Did it turn out like that? You were Secretary of State for Energy in '79 weren't you, when the Government was first formed. Was it actually like that in the Cabinet Room?
HOWELL   Well, it's very hard to say. On some issues there was a good deal of discussion, but if by 'conviction government' it is meant that certain

slogans were going to be elevated and written in tablets of stone and used as the put-down at the end of every argument, then, of course, that is indeed what happened. Certain things were asserted beyond peradventure: namely, that we had to get the public-sector borrowing-requirement down, because if it went up or stayed up it would keep interest rates up. Now, it happens that is a very controversial and highly questionable economic proposition. But as a political shibboleth it was raised to all-powerful heights and was used as a battering-ram to silence any suggestion by anybody that one might ever spend more on anything even if the aim of spending more immediately was to spend less later.

HENNESSY   That rather vitiates the traditional nature of Cabinet government if you have a strong-minded figure ending discussions in this way. Presumably it meant that after a while you ceased to bring things to the Cabinet that you knew would produce a put-down?

HOWELL   Of course there is a deterring-effect if one knows that one's going to go not into a discussion where various points of view will be weighed and gradually a view may be achieved, but into a huge argument where tremendous battle lines will be drawn up and everyone who doesn't fall in line will be hit on the head. Of course it deters you, and I think that element of deterrence did take place. I don't want to exaggerate it, because on the complex issues, however determined or single-minded a Prime Minister is, they have to discuss things with an inner group of colleagues. You're talking now to someone who certainly worked very closely with Mrs Thatcher and was a member of the Cabinet. But I wasn't of the seniority to be one of the inner group of ministers which all prime ministers tend to work most closely with. This country really since the sixteenth century has basically been run by five or six people. I don't think it's very different today: five or six is what you need and that's what any prime minister tends to form around them.[13]

Howell was alluding, among other things, to Mrs Thatcher's equivalent of Callaghan's 'Economic Seminar', the significance of which will be considered shortly. It all seemed a far cry from his and Heath's attempts, through those seventies acronyms, the CPRS and PAR, to inject a dose of reason and analysis into the policy-making process.

HENNESSY   You mentioned that there's a great degree of toughness since 1979 on Treasury targets and public expenditure, and the word goes down the line and there's no argument. And yet the process for fixing expenditure allocations seems to be as much of a shambles as ever it was when you and Mr Heath were so concerned about it in the late 1960s. Every September we have the small ad hoc Cabinet committee known as the 'Star Chamber' [MISC 62] in which Lord Whitelaw sits down and tries to bang heads together, and then the Prime Minister comes in at the last minute and bangs heads together even more. And it seems that the money, in so far as it emerges in budgets that clearly, is determined by crude political muscle and nothing to do with reason and analysis – all the things that you stood for in the sixties and seventies. Don't you find that depressing?

HOWELL   A bit depressing but not entirely. Because even in a more refined system there is going to be a stage where issues cannot be resolved by analysis or delicate agreement and can only be resolved by crude political battering. So I'm not totally depressed. If I'm depressed at all it is that I think that you could make this process slightly less obtrusive and violent and spark-generating if there was more systematic analysis and discussion beforehand, going back a long way. You've got to start back a long way before you get to the final decisions on costs and budgets. So more programme analysis and discussion and less argument and assertion, I think, would make the whole thing less fraught on the one side. On the other side, the fraught quality is greatly heightened and increased by the feeling I've already described that the Treasury's figures are there and absolute and that to transgress beyond them will be the end of civilization as we know it, and interest rates will go sky high and hyperinflation will return. And, therefore, the argument is of people whose backs are pinned to the wall before they're questioned as it were, and that doesn't make for a sober and calm discussion, especially as there is some doubt, I suspect, in the mind of ministers, but certainly in the mind of many people in the Conservative Party, about whether these great absolutes, this wall against which ministers and departments are nailed, really need exist in quite the form it's being constructed or whether the whole issue couldn't be handled in a rather more sensitive and relaxed way.

HENNESSY   Mrs Thatcher wrote a letter in 1984 accepting Mr James Prior's resignation from the Northern Ireland Office and she said in it, 'I take your point about frankness! That's what Cabinets are for, and lively discussions usually lead to good decisions.' How did that remark strike you?

HOWELL   It struck me with some foreboding because I feel that 'lively discussion' is a code word for argument and I don't regard high-pitched argument as the best means of reaching decisions. I think there's got to be plenty of discussion. I like a discursive approach. Now this happens not to be the style of other people, but it's mine. In the end you may get a nitty-gritty point where there has to be an argument because there are two different points of view both supported by substantial analysis and objective study. All right, but I don't think one should argue right from the start, and, if lively discussion means that the whole of government decision-making should be conducted from entrenched, opinionated positions with heavy mortar fire of argument right the way through, I query whether that's the best way to get things done. I think in the end the tortoise does better than the hare. The quiet discursive approach actually delivers the goods in terms of reforming this nation and increasing our prosperity more effectively than carrying on everything as a flat-out argument.

HENNESSY   So what you're saying is that Cabinet government in the eighties has been a matter of trench warfare with exchanges conducted in the shape of mortar fire.

HOWELL   Well, now you're putting in my words grand judgements which I'm not equipped to make and it would be impudent for me to make. I'm saying that in my experience there is too much argument and not enough discussion in processes of government generally, and I believe we would make more progress by a more discursive approach. I think it was once said that the mark of an undergraduate is someone who turns every discussion into an argument. I think sometimes that we have a shade of the undergraduate in our government which we could well do without to strengthen and consolidate this nation.

HENNESSY   Is it fun being a Cabinet minister?

HOWELL   It has good moments and very bad moments. I enjoyed some parts of it. I must confess I didn't enjoy others at all. I don't think I was on the same wavelength as the Prime Minister almost from the start, although I did work for her beforehand and try to pull together some of the policies. I preferred discussion to argument. So, I think, if you are asking me I can only speak of my personal experience. Yes, I enjoyed certain moments very much indeed but other moments were most certainly not fun. And Parliament can be a very demanding mistress indeed. And there we are: Parliament a demanding mistress; the Prime Minister a demanding mistress. How much fun can you have with so many demanding mistresses?[14]

There is plenty of lore and legend from Whitehall and Westminster to buttress the case for an imperious premiership. Take three scenes from life at the top in 1984.

(1)   Senior civil servants called to policy sessions in No. 10, says one insider, have their own four-minute warning-system. If asked by your secretary of state to speak on the departmental paper, you have four minutes to explain it, however complicated the subject matter, to present the choices and to add a touch of heterodoxy. Beyond that point, unless her interest is awakened, Mrs Thatcher's eyes glaze over. To continue is to jeopardize future promotion.[15]

(2) It is January 1984. The place is No. 10. The forum is the Cabinet's Oversea and Defence Committee. The subject is the possibility of an attempt to normalize relations with Argentina, *not* the sovereignty of the Falklands, which is the 'Great Unmentionable' of mid-eighties Whitehall. Sir Geoffrey Howe is four minutes into the Foreign Office paper on the need to open exploratory talks with the Alfonsín Government. Mrs Thatcher cuts in, 'Geoffrey, I know what you're going to recommend. And the answer is "No!"' End of item: nobody argues with the boss.[16]

(3) Seasoned Cabinet minister walks into the Commons tea room late on a Thursday morning. 'What are you doing here?' asks a Tory backbencher. 'I thought you'd still be in Cabinet.' 'Cabinet?' replied the Minister. 'Oh, we don't have those any more. We have a lecture by Madam. Its government-by-Cabinet-committee now. Half the decisions I read about in the newspapers.'[17]

One experienced Whitehall figure reckons that 'temporarily we don't have Cabinet government. . . . We have a form of presidential government in which she operates like a sovereign in her court',[18] which is just about the most toughly worded formulation of the case for Mrs Thatcher as Queen Boadicea driving a chariot of conviction politics through the conventions of collective Cabinet government.

What evidence can be gleaned for the 'Queen Margaret' school, or for the counter-argument that such changes are largely a matter of style rather than substance, by examining the procedure and mechanics of government since 1979? Take first the raw statistics of Cabinet business. It is rare for Mrs Thatcher to have more than one meeting of the full Cabinet per week.[19] Allowing for parliamentary recesses, that adds up to between forty and forty-five Cabinet meetings a year – not a particularly significant statistic if more business is being taken in committees, of which more in a moment. Attlee and Churchill, however, logged twice that figure (see table 2). The flow of Cabinet papers is well down, moreover. The CP (84) series, as the 1984 collection will be classified in the Cabinet Office's Confidential Library, includes only sixty to seventy papers, about one sixth of the annual totals accumulated in the late forties and early fifties (see table 2). Sir Robert Armstrong, incidentally, for all his protestations about open government, refused to release under Section 5(1) of the Public Records Act, 1958 (which permits declassification ahead of the thirty-year rule),

Table 2　Cabinet government, 1946–54: volume of business reaching full cabinet

Prime Minister	Year	Cabinet meetings	Cabinet papers
Attlee	1946	108	468
Attlee	1947	96	343
Attlee	1948	82	309
Attlee	1949	72	252
Attlee	1950	87	326
Attlee until 26 October, thereafter Churchill	1951	82	329[a]
Churchill	1952	108	455
Churchill	1953	81	366
Churchill	1954	92	402

[a]Up to and including 27 September 1951, Attlee held 60 Cabinet meetings, for which 267 Cabinet papers were prepared. From 30 October until the end of 1951, Churchill held 22 Cabinet meetings, for which 62 Cabinet papers were prepared.
Source: Public Record Office.

statistics on the number of Cabinet meetings and papers since 1955. He argued that 'It would be entirely contrary to longstanding conventions in these matters to publish this sort of information.'[20]

Judged by the frequency of meetings and the flow of formal Cabinet papers, full Cabinet activity under Mrs Thatcher is at an historical low. So, too, is the workload being devolved to Cabinet committees. On entering No. 10 in May 1979, Mrs Thatcher made it clear to the Whitehall machine that she was not a Cabinet-committee person. She would do business with her fellow ministers free of the curse of committees. 'Events', as one insider put it, 'soon took care of that.'[21] As we have seen from the blueprint of Mrs Thatcher's Engine Room in table 1, she now presides over some 160 of the hated things, though not, naturally, in the literal sense of chairing the lot.

Yet, she is running the slimmest Cabinet machine since before the Second World War. As we have seen, Attlee accumulated 148 standing and 313 ad hoc groups in six and quarter years, and Churchill 137 and 109 respectively in three and a half years. The figures for Eden are incomplete, and those for Macmillan and Home remain a mystery which the current Cabinet Secretary refuses to resolve. Thanks to Mrs Castle's Diary, we have some intelligence on Wilson Mark I. Elected in October 1964, he had by early 1969 (i.e. after four and a quarter years) reached his 236th ad hoc group. The Heath era is another unknown. Wilson Mark II, between March 1974 and March 1976, ran up a total of somewhere around 120 ad hoc groups.[22] Callaghan in the three years between April 1976 and April 1979 commissioned about 160 ad hoc committees, a similar growth rate to Attlee's.[23] Judging by the Cabinet-committee criterion, Mrs Thatcher has done exceedingly well. Under her, there have been 30–35 standing-committees and just over 120 ad hocs in six and a half years. So Cabinet *and* Cabinet-committee discussion is down.

Does that indicate that the load has diminished in parallel? Has Britain against the odds re-entered a period of small government? In philosophical terms the answer is probably 'Yes'; in practical terms 'No.' The reason has been stated frequently by Sir John Hoskyns. In the short run, disengaging from state activity is just as difficult and time-consuming as getting into it – if not more so. Privatization, like nationalization, imposes a stiff workload and absorbs a great deal of parliamentary time.

So, where is the business being done? A fair amount is conducted by ministerial correspondence, a perfectly acceptable method in constitutional terms. The Franks Report on the Falklands gives an indication of just how much this goes on. One reason, for example, why the Falklands issue figured so infrequently on the agenda of the Cabinet's Oversea and Defence Committee before the Argentine invasion of April 1982 is that Lord Carrington, then Foreign and Commonwealth Secretary, disliked bringing Foreign Office business before committee meetings of his colleagues.[24] Another swathe of high-level business is tackled by Mrs Thatcher in ad hoc groups which fall outside Sir Robert Armstrong's Cabinet Committee Book.

The most important of these is her version of Mr Callaghan's 'Economic Seminar', though it no longer has that name. It handles similar subjects to his – monetary policy, delicate decisions affecting the money markets. Early in her first premiership it caused her a moment of acute embarrassment. One Cabinet minister, a member of the Economic Strategy Committee but not of this most secret inner group, which was meeting straight afterwards, was a bit slow to gather his papers. As he was about to leave, Sir Geoffrey Howe, then Chancellor of the Exchequer, launched into his paper on the plan to abolish exchange controls. 'Oh', says the laggardly minister, 'are we going to do that? How very interesting.' Embarrassed silence. Then

Sir Geoffrey says, 'X, I'm afraid you should not be here.' X departs Cabinet door left.[25]

Under Mrs Thatcher the 'Economic Seminar' remains highly important. But it is a flexible, amoeba-like group whose composition changes according to circumstances. 'It's a habit of working, not an approach', explains an insider. 'If there is a problem or a proposal, she'll call a meeting involving those immediately concerned. She may also invite someone who will be important when it comes to selling it in Cabinet – someone like Willie Whitelaw.'[26]

Other ad hoc groups beyond the reach of the MISC series can have a considerable impact, even though they may only meet once or twice. For example, Mrs Thatcher convened a meeting of ministers to consider the now legendary minute entitled 'It Took a Riot' prepared for her by Michael Heseltine, then Secretary of State for the Environment, based on his experiences in Merseyside following the inner-city riots of July 1981. It proposed an ambitious programme of investment and the designation of Cabinet colleagues as ministers for various decaying areas. Mr Heseltine had evangelized Whitehall on behalf of his cause like a latter-day John the Baptist. He held a secret dinner at Locket's restaurant in Westminster for several influential permanent secretaries, including Sir Robert Armstrong. They were impressed.

The Prime Minister, however, prevailed. In September 1981 she convened an ad hoc group on inner cities and stacked it against Heseltine. It consisted of herself, Heseltine, Sir Geoffrey Howe, Chancellor of the Exchequer, Sir Keith Joseph, Secretary of State for Industry, and William Whitelaw, then Home Secretary. Whitelaw, concerned as ever to be the mediator, strove to find a middle way between Heseltine and those who did not want a penny extra for the cities for fear of being seen to reward rioters. Heseltine was isolated. There was an increase in the urban programme but on nothing like the scale he wanted.[27] On this occasion, he succumbed to the verdict of a loaded ministerial group.

Mrs Thatcher conducts a great deal of business in gatherings such as that. The pattern varies but is often along these lines. Mrs Thatcher will ask a particular Cabinet colleague to prepare a paper on a particular issue just for her, not for the Cabinet or a Cabinet committee. This explains why the tally of Cabinet papers is so low. The Minister is summoned to No. 10 with his back-up team. He sits across the table from Mrs Thatcher and her team, which can be a mixture of people from the Downing Street Private Office, the Policy Unit and the Cabinet

Office, with one or two personal advisers and sometimes a Treasury minister. She then, in the words of one insider, proceeds to 'act as judge and jury in her own cause'.[28] It is this practice more than anything else which causes those on the inside to speak of 'a devaluation of Cabinet government' and her 'presidential style'.[29] The build-up of leaks and stories from such occasions created a cumulative impression of a truly over-mighty premiership long before Heseltine's departure.

But is that impression accurate? A case can be made for both its constitutional propriety and its administrative efficiency. Take first Mrs Thatcher's version of the 'Economic Seminar'. David Howell is a critic of the Thatcher style but he sees nothing wrong in it:

HOWELL   I don't think one would have expected, not being in the Treasury, to be involved. One would have assumed that – indeed, I think it was generally known – that the Prime Minister and Treasury ministers and her Chancellor kept in very close touch with the financial authorities and the central monetary authorities, which means the Bank of England among other people, and that all that would go on. I don't think one would assume anything else. If it had a name, or a code word, well that sounds like civil servants playing games. Ministers would assume that went on. Occasionally other ministers might be called into those discussions. But of course the nexus of any government in this country is No. 10 and the Treasury, with the Bank of England as the Treasury's appendage, which unfortunately it is. I say 'unfortunately' because I would like to see a more detached monetary authority myself. Therefore one assumes they're very hugger-mugger all the time. Under this government and under the regime that emerged after '79, which wasn't quite the one we planned for before '79 . . . the nexus between No. 10 and the Treasury is decisive, it overrules, it's everything. The Treasury always knows they can win. That is why they're able to go for these very precise figures of public spending, scientific precision about estimates for the years ahead and then say, 'All argument hereafter ceases. Anyone who wants to change anything will have to somehow change it without altering the figures because they're settled and we know that if we ever go back to No. 10 or the Cabinet we'll always get the backing of the Prime Minister and the appellant will always be overturned.'

HENNESSY   Going back to the 'Economic Seminar', you seem to accept these things are bound to exist, these small inner groups. Doesn't it rather vitiate the nature of Cabinet government, though, if a decision, like the one to remove all exchange control, a very fundamental one for any economy, is in fact worked up, although it goes to full Cabinet in the end, in such a body? Doesn't it mean that you're presented with a set of *faits accomplis*?

You're meant to be collectively the highest strategic decision-making body in the land and here are all these great slices of crucial economic decisions done in a group in which ministers are outnumbered three or four to one by officials.

HOWELL   Yes, well, you say 'meant to be' and you're right to say 'meant to be', because, of course, Cabinet government is only a layer of the Government and there is a kind of inner Cabinet government, whether it's called that or not, under different prime ministers – it always tends to develop. On top of that there must be an even more inner kind of government concerned with very, very sensitive issues, of which exchange control is one. It would have been inconceivable for exchange control to be tossed around and knocked around in Cabinet.

HENNESSY   Why?

HOWELL   Because of the numbers of people involved and because of, well, I suppose I have to say it, the inevitability of leaks.[30]

Senior civil servants, the privileged connoisseurs of prime-ministerial style and procedure, tend not to be purist about the operational implications of Cabinet conventions, except when routinely deploying them in the occasional public lecture or dismissing requests for the early declassification of harmless material. They seem, in practice, to treat Cabinet government as a chunk of modelling-clay to be pummelled and fashioned by the prime minister of the hour. This is the kind of reasoning you hear when senior men think aloud in private about the theme of Cabinet government:

The Cabinet system has been different for Heath, Wilson and Mrs Thatcher. There's a reaction, which we can get in our constitution, to suit the PM of the day and his or her working relationships. The decisions get taken in the way in which people want to take them.

Mrs Thatcher is very clear about her views, very much a leader. Because of that she doesn't need or want to resolve things by collective discussion. She knows what she wants to do about almost everything. But it *is* a collective machine because they all sink or swim with her. She uses the Cabinet as a sort of sounding-board. It restrains her when restraint is necessary. She has her own instinct when she cannot carry her colleagues with her. She lets them know what she thinks. Then they try and adapt and mould it. She has very acute antennae. She's very quick to take the signals if she can't carry it.[31]

Sir Frank Cooper is happy to speak publicly about the Thatcher Cabinet style, of which he approves:

HENNESSY Do you think . . . that she has, in fact, put severe dents into the traditional model of collective Cabinet government?

COOPER No, I don't . . . I think she's changed a number of things. She certainly leads from the front. No one would argue about that and she believes it's the duty of any prime minister to lead from the front. And I would have a great deal of sympathy with that view, quite frankly. . . . We do actually need leadership of the right kind in the right areas. . . . I don't think I've got any difficulty with that.[32]

Other Whitehall insiders caution against the view that the Thatcher Cabinet is largely characterized by deferential 'staircase' men: 'Ministers report to Cabinet pretty freely and frankly. She has a passion for knowing what is going on and will be extremely cross if she isn't told.'[33]

But the Thatcher Cabinet does not behave like 'a bunch of chums', as previous Tory Cabinets tended to do, according to an experienced figure. Conservative Cabinets used to present a strong contrast to Labour ones, as 'Labour governments are very much more used to the idea of people being mandated to do things. They have tended to have fierce debates leading to some kind of resolution.'[34] But Mrs Thatcher's Cabinets have seen 'positive forces ranged against her'.[35] Michael Heseltine, Peter Walker and Jim Prior have all pressed their reservations much more explicitly in the Cabinet Room than any minister did in the Heath years. Lord Whitelaw and John Biffen come into the category of influential ministers whose views cannot be taken for granted. And, since the casualty list of the Westland Affair, there have been signs that the Thatcher Cabinet may function more collectively for a time at least.

The crucial question, however, is how much opportunity critical ministers are afforded in full Cabinet when it comes to reshaping or even reopening decisions reached in Cabinet committees, those ad hoc meetings or the Prime Minister's 'judge and jury' sessions. Sir Geoffrey Howe was surprisingly candid on this point in an interview with the *Daily Mail* in February 1984. 'There are', he said, 'very few discussions of Government decisions by full Cabinet.'[36] Sir Geoffrey was referring to the decision to ban trade unions at GCHQ, a decision taken by a small group of ministers (himself, the Prime Minister, Lord Whitelaw, Mr Heseltine, then Secretary of State for Defence, with a bit of advice on likely union reactions from Tom King, then Secretary of State for Employment).[37] Cabinet under Mrs Thatcher is 'not used so much as a formal forum where there are papers saying we have this problem and here are the options for what we can do about it. Earlier Cabinets *were* much more like that', said one senior official shortly before Michael Heseltine converted semi-covert insider objections to the Thatcher style into a glowing neon sign.[38]

The Heseltine affair was, on the face of it, about Government involvement in the financial restructuring of Westland, Britain's sole manufacturer of helicopters. The pros and cons of which financial saviour should be favoured – a bid led by the American company Sikorsky, or a European consortium including British Aerospace – need not concern us here, because to dwell unduly upon them would be like treating the assassination of an archduke in Sarajevo as the cause rather than the trigger for the First World War. In his dramatic resignation statement before a huge press conference in the Ministry of Defence on the afternoon of Thursday 9 January 1986, Heseltine explained his sudden walkout at that morning's Cabinet meeting in terms which raised it high above a small, troubled helicopter manufacturer in the West Country. His chosen battleground with Mrs Thatcher was nothing less than that sludgy amalgam, the British Constitution. The manner in which the Prime Minister had handled the Westland issue within the Cabinet system, Mr Heseltine told the world's press, was 'not a proper way to carry on government and ultimately not an approach for which I can share responsibility'.[39] This remained the leitmotif of a torrent of radio, television and newspaper interviews Heseltine gave in the days following his resignation. In an interview with Fred Emery on BBC's *Panorama* on 13 January, for example, he put the point in no fewer than three ways: 'I resigned on my judgement of a breakdown of constitutional procedures'; 'I believe there was an affront to the Constitution'; 'I decided there was a setting-aside of the Constitution and I resigned.'[40] On the same programme, John Biffen, Leader of the House of Commons, challenged Heseltine's strictures on improper breaches of Cabinet procedure. The day after the resignation, Sir Geoffrey Howe, the Foreign Secretary, accused Heseltine of presenting 'a wholly exaggerated and misleading picture' of the Prime Minister's conduct of the Westland issue.[41]

The story began to gain dramatic content deep in the entrails of the Thatcher-style Cabinet system early in December 1985. Heseltine, in his resignation statement, concentrated on 'three ministerial meetings chaired by the Prime Minister at the beginning of December'.[42] The first two, on 4 and 5 December, were ad hoc groups consisting of the Prime Minister, Heseltine, Leon Brittan, Secretary of State for Trade and Industry, John MacGregor, Chief Secretary to the Treasury, Sir Geoffrey Howe, Foreign Secretary and Sir Patrick Mayhew, Solicitor-General. They were not formal ad hoc Cabinet committees in the sense of belonging to the MISC series.[43] They were bodies whose chemistry accorded closely with the Thatcher style, like the ministerial group Mrs Thatcher had convened and stacked against Heseltine in the aftermath of the 1981 riots. They were rancorous in tone. 'One hostile critic' was quoted in the *Observer* as saying, 'she ranted and raved. It was typical of the way she conducts Cabinet Government.'[44]

At this point, disagreement about the truth of the matter intrudes into the tale. Heseltine claimed that the Prime Minister failed at these ad hoc groups to get her way, which was to 'close-off the European option' for the Westland rescue.[45] By the following Monday 'Downing Street sources' were telling journalists that the records of those two ad hoc meetings showed 'that a majority of those present were probably prepared to repudiate or reject' the course followed by the national armaments directors of Western Europe, the basis of the European consortium's bid.[46] 'A source close to Mr Heseltine' swiftly countered with 'That is a lie.' Anthony Bevins's account in *The Times* continued, 'Mr Heseltine's friends said last night that ad hoc meetings were a Downing Street device to kill internal Cabinet dissent. They were known as "the club".'[47] Short of Mrs Thatcher releasing the 'club' minutes for 4 and 5 December 1985, of which there was no sign at the time of writing, it will be impossible to ascertain who is telling the truth about the tides of opinion within those gatherings.

The Prime Minister then shifted the Westland issue to a formal meeting of EA, the Cabinet's Economic Strategy Committee, on Monday 9 December.[48] This, as *Economist* journalists discovered, proved to be a highly unorthodox meeting, as two outsiders, neither of whom were bound by the Privy Counsellor's oath of confidentiality, were in attendance: 'Chaired by Mrs Thatcher, [the meeting] was attended, unusually, for part of the time, by two outsiders: Sir John Cuckney, Westland's chairman . . . and Mr Marcus Agius, a director of Lazard's, Westland's financial advisers.'[49] According to Heseltine, 'virtually every colleague who attended the enlarged meeting and thus came fresh to the arguments supported me, despite the fact that Sir John Cuckney had been invited to put his views to the meeting'.[50] Again according to Heseltine, it was decided at EA that the ad hoc group should meet again on Friday 13 December, after the Stock Exchange had closed. That meeting was cancelled. At the meeting of the full Cabinet on Thursday 12 December, the Prime Minister, said Heseltine, 'refused to allow a discussion. . . . I insisted that the Cabinet Secretary should record my protest in the Cabinet minutes.'[51] At this point, yet another mystery, unresolved at the time of writing, arose. 'When the minutes were circulated', Heseltine continued,

> there was no reference to any discussion about Westland and consequently no record of my protest. Before the next meeting I complained to the Secretary of the Cabinet. He explained that the item had been omitted from the minutes as the result of an error and he subsequently circulated an addendum in the form of a brief note of the discussion. Such an error and correction was unprecedented in my experience. The minutes, as finally issued, still did not record my protest and I have since informed the Secretary of the Cabinet that I am still not content with the way in which this discussion was recorded.[52]

The accepted convention is that, if a minister specifically requests that his or her dissent be recorded, it is so recorded. There has been a tradition too, evident in the lengthy confidential annexes containing the Cabinet discussion of Sir Winston Churchill's highly personal diplomacy in seeking a meeting with the Russians in July 1954, that when a resignation is threatened an unusually full record is created of the proceedings.[53] The mystery of the disappearing note of Heseltine's dissent remains. According to Lord Wilson, the most recent premier to go on the record about the conventions of minute-taking, 'the writing of the Conclusions is the unique responsibility of the Secretary of the Cabinet. . . . The Conclusions are circulated very promptly after Cabinet, and up to that time, no minister, certainly not the prime minister, asks to see them or conditions them in any way.'[54] It is not known if Mrs Thatcher continues to practise this self-denying ordinance. Unless Sir Robert Armstrong takes the unprecedented step of issuing a statement, this will have to remain one of what he has called 'the marvels and mysteries of Cabinet government'.[55]

Whatever the ins and outs, it was the abandonment of that third ad hoc meeting which prepared Heseltine for take-off. As he told Fred Emery on *Panorama*, 'from the moment that decision was taken to cancel the opportunity for a collective judgement to be taken, I knew that something very wrong had happened.'[56]

What finally propelled him from his Cabinet seat on 9 January was the promulgation of a new and improvised Cabinet convention by Mrs Thatcher – that all future ministerial statements on the future of Westland would have to be cleared by the Cabinet Office.[57] As Heseltine wrote in the *Observer* the following Sunday,

I told the Cabinet that I could not accept that the traditional basis for collective responsibility had been established. In these circumstances, on a constitutional matter, I was obliged to leave the Cabinet. . . .

Of course, Westland and all the associated issues about the harmonisation and rationalisation of the European defence industrial base are important, but I doubt that one specific case would in itself have been enough to become a resigning issue.

What was much more important to me was the emergence of what I consider to be the breakdown of constitutional government. That was something I could not live with. There was, therefore, no option for me but to resign.[58]

But, as Heseltine's private secretary, the highly regarded Ministry of Defence official Richard Mottram, put it during the trial of Clive Ponting, 'In highly-charged political matters, one person's ambiguity may be another person's truth.'[59] John Biffen, a very straight character and very much his own man, said of Mrs Thatcher's handling of Westland, 'I thought the Cabinet discussion . . . was reasonable enough. It wasn't obviously a particularly long discussion . . . you are dealing with a company of a modest size. . . . I don't feel the discussion of it was particularly skimpy.' And, as for the cancellation of the ad hoc ministerial meeting due on 13 December, Biffen said, 'I don't think there was any question of constitutional impropriety.'[60]

But for Heseltine it brought a kettleful of resentment, accumulated over more than six years, to boiling-point. Quite apart from the memory of the treatment Mrs Thatcher had dealt out to 'It Took a Riot', around the time of the 1983 general election Heseltine was telling friends he was very concerned about an accretion of power to the premiership[61] (this was the period when the possibility of a prime minister's department or, at the very least, a beefed-up Downing Street Policy Unit was being floated). But, in terms of the written conventions, in his very public championing of the European-consortium option prior to his resignation, Heseltine himself was bending the rules. Take the section in *Questions of Procedure for Ministers* dealing with collective responsibility, which reads,

Decisions reached by the Cabinet or Cabinet committee are normally announced and defended by the minister concerned as his own decisions. There may be rare occasions when it is desirable to emphasise the importance of some decisions by stating specifically that it is the decision of Her Majesty's Government. This, however, should be the exception rather than the rule. The growth of any general practice whereby decisions of the Cabinet or of Cabinet committee were announced as such would lead to the embarrassing result that some decisions of government would be regarded as less authoritative than others. Critics of a decision reached by a particular committee could press for its review by some other committee or by the Cabinet, and the constitutional right of individual ministers to speak in the name of the government as a whole would be impaired.[62]

Since the EA meeting on 9 December, Heseltine had succeeded in making the decision to let Westland seek succour from whom it wished look distinctly 'less authoritative than others'. He himself had not ceased to 'press for its review by the full Cabinet', pressure which eventually brought about his downfall.[63] There had not been anything to match the Westland affair as an example of competitive leaking since the 'display of histrionic talents', as Edmund Dell put it,[64] which accompanied Callaghan's Cabinets on the terms of a loan from the International Monetary Fund.

By resigning and going public, Heseltine stimulated a crescendo of complaint about the Thatcher style of Cabinet government. Sir Ian Gilmour, sacked from the Cabinet in September 1981, was on both main television news bulletins on 10 January, telling viewers that being a good listener was not one of Mrs Thatcher's virtues,[65] and that there had been 'a downgrading of Cabinet government'; Cabinet meetings were something to be got through, not the place where views were to be aired and decisions reached.[66] For Dr David Owen, Leader of the Social Democratic Party, the whole Westland affair was 'damning evidence of a total contempt for democratic Cabinet government'.[67]

Even more remarkable was the manner in which the resignation of Leon Brittan, after the Prime Minister's revelation in the Commons that he had authorized the leak of a confidential letter from Sir Patrick Mayhew, the Solicitor-General to Heseltine, stimulated Mrs Thatcher and her Home Secretary, Douglas Hurd, to deliver in public disquisitions on Cabinet management. At lunchtime on Sunday 26 January 1986 Hurd told Brian Walden in a television interview:

I think it is very important that people should see that we are under Cabinet government. I think that is what people prefer and want to know about . . . they want to see that it is Cabinet government.[68]

Speaking almost simultaneously on Tyne-Tees Television's *Face the Press*, Mrs Thatcher showed an acute awareness of criticisms of her Cabinet style and used it as an explanation for not confronting Heseltine earlier in the Westland debate:

There was a period when the Cabinet did not seem and, in fact, was not acting with collective responsibility, because one person was not playing as a member of a team. The press were very critical of me in many ways before that. Some said that I should, in fact, have dealt with it and asked Mr Heseltine to go earlier. I can only tell you that had I done that . . . I know exactly what the press would have said: 'There you are, old bossy-boots at it again.'[69]

But was the Heseltine resignation proof positive of the Queen Boadicea or 'bossy-boots' interpretation of Cabinet government since 1979? Not really. Thatcher diktats do not simply slide down the Cabinet table like castor oil. Anticipation of Cabinet resistance does prevent Mrs Thatcher from establishing ministerial groups skewed in favour of policies she might favour but which will not run in full Cabinet. Instances given by insiders include the total abolition of the closed shop; the radical breaking-up of the National Health Service; student loans; rates; vouchers for schools; and, in earlier, pre-Hillsborough days, the restoration of what she and the late Airey Neave used, according to insiders, to refer to in private as the restoration of good local government in Northern Ireland.[70] She may have siphoned much of the collective spirit from the Cabinet Room in the way meetings are conducted, but more than a shadow remains. Her style is not collegiate. But to call it 'presidential' is both to go too far and to dignify it.

Her fervent anti-collectivist impulse is a strong shaper of the kind of policy advice she wants and the way it is served up. Mrs Thatcher is very much alive to new ideas, 'ideas that support and implement her view of the world', as somebody inside her ideas market put it. 'That's why her style is better suited to a Policy Unit that is hers rather than to a CPRS which serves the Cabinet.'[71] Yet, when the think-tank was wound up at the first Cabinet meeting after the 1983 general election, not a single minister spoke up in its defence.[72] Certainly, compared to the Rothschild days, it had run out of steam. As one of Mrs Thatcher's own people put it, 'The CPRS was not delivering the goods. The conclusion in No. 10 was, therefore, that it had become part of the Cabinet Office and was politically starved . . . on anything that had a political dimension, the tank found itself rather isolated.'[73] For Professor John Ashworth, the CPRS Chief Scientist in the late seventies and early eighties, it was quite simple. Margaret Thatcher and the kind of neutral policy analysis the tank produced simply do not mix: 'Of its very existence it sort of encapsulated a view about government for which she had no great sympathy. She was what she called a conviction politician. There is a difference between being a conviction politician and being a rationally guided politician.'[74] Even David Howell, one of the tank's progenitors, dances, albeit regretfully, on its grave:

By the time we got back in 1979 the CPRS had already changed beyond recognition. It had become a sort of trouble-shooting body that had been put in to try and dish the Foreign Office and got a bloody nose. It had been asked to do strange one-off affairs and its reports had been leaked and bandied about in Parliament and any role it was originally supposed to have, as a systematic, regular bringing-together of reports of programme analysis throughout Whitehall to present an overall strategic picture to the Prime Minister and the Cabinet, had long since disappeared. It had become a sort of one-off adventurer and then after '79 it took on another role again.

The head of the CPRS had a seat at the table of ministers and ministerial committees, which is a very significant thing. And he was always there and really was another voice, not a bad role actually. But, of course, if you're going to be another voice you really need to know what you're talking about and you need to have vast access to information at least as good as all the departments who are putting forward their voices, and you need to have the time and the staff and I don't think they always had that. So as a result papers would fly round of, I'm afraid, rather a shallow kind – a last minute dash by some bright brain on a subject which very able people in departments and outside advisers might have worked on for months and months and months. And that created a slight sort of canary-hopping attitude to policy-making which I don't think was very good and in the end I think Mrs Thatcher felt the same. 'What's the point of having this body?' she must have felt. She much rather wanted a real policy-research unit, which of course is what she's now got.[75]

Her craving for advice with a Thatcherite spin on it does not mean that the Prime Minister will automatically diminish Civil Service contributions as flowing from a tainted source. One well-placed career official does not accept the 'four-minute warning' principle. 'It can be fifteen seconds or ten minutes. It depends on whether you interest her. There are people in the Civil Service who can talk in a way that fascinates her.'[76] And even Mrs Thatcher's detractors in the senior bureaucracy do accept that her anti-collectivist, commanding style is one way of tackling the overload problem, temporarily at least. 'The number of Cabinet meetings is not necessarily an index of efficiency', said one who believes her brand of Cabinet government ('a president within a monarchy') is a more effective way of shifting business than the traditional collective model.[77] Another, more sympathetic figure reckoned that a slimmer committee system and under fifty Cabinet meetings a year 'doesn't indicate overload – she manages to get through the business in a different way'.[78]

We shall return to the overload theme in the final chapter. But, before leaving the Thatcher phenomenon, a glance at the Falklands War and what preceded it is a must. For it shows modern Cabinet government at its best and at its worst. And, in the Franks Report on ministerial handling of the conflict, we have an archive which not only shortens dramatically the interval before the normal release of classified information but goes considerably further than any disclosures at the end of the statutory thirty years in the amount of intelligence material displayed.[79]

For one seasoned Whitehall figure involved in the build-up to the Falklands War, in the conflict itself and its aftermath, among the starkest lessons of the greatest trauma of the Thatcher period was the way in which the shortcomings of contemporary Cabinet government were thrown into sharp relief. 'The biggest gap we had', he said, 'was trying to get the Falklands put before some kind of Cabinet committee. The whole thing went undiscussed throughout 1982, though people had been trying to have it discussed since they came back from their holidays in 1981.'[80]

Why was it so difficult to get ministers to meet (a judgement, incidentally, buttressed by a careful reading of the Franks Report)? The problem is particularly acute for the key ministerial group concerned, the Oversea and Defence Committee. Its members are very often dispersed at summits, EEC meetings and foreign visits of various kinds. There is an aversion to holding meetings at short notice with a diminished complement. Many secretaries of state are not particular admirers of their junior ministers and do not care for the department to be represented by them at OD. Lord Carrington, Foreign Secretary in the crucial period, disliked meetings of ministers and preferred to do as much business as possible through ministerial correspondence.[81] And probably the most important factor of all, until the beginning of March 1982 (the Argentine invasion of the islands took place on 2 April), the Falklands was very much a 'backburner' issue compared to the EEC budget, the Middle East, pressure on defence-spending, the NATO decision to deploy cruise missiles, and a host of other apparently more pressing concerns, as the Franks Report makes clear:

Government policy towards Argentina and the Falkland Islands was never formally discussed outside the Foreign and Commonwealth Office after January 1981. Thereafter the time was never judged to be ripe although we were told in oral evidence that, subject to the availability of Ministers, a Defence Committee [i.e. OD] meeting could have been held at any time, if necessary at short notice. There was no meeting of the Defence Committee to discuss the Falklands until 1 April 1982; and there was no reference to the Falklands, in Cabinet, even after the New York talks of 26 and 27 February [with the Argentine government], until Lord Carrington reported on events in South Georgia on 25 March, 1982.[82]

In their understated way, Lord Franks and his fellow privy counsellors commented,

We cannot say what the outcome of a meeting of the Defence Committee might have been, or whether the course of events would have been altered if it had met in September 1981; but, in our view, it could have been advantageous, and fully in line with Whitehall practice, for Ministers to have reviewed collectively at that time, or in the months immediately ahead, the current negotiating position; the implications of the conflict between the attitudes of the Islanders and the aims of the Junta; and the longer-term policy options in relation to the dispute.[83]

Ministers are busy people. They cannot be expected to read every piece of intelligence that pours into Whitehall. They pay clever people to do that for them – people who, collectively, go under the name of the Cabinet Office Assessments Staff. The system works like this. Each Monday, current intelligence groups for various parts of the world meet in the Cabinet Office, bringing together line men from all the intelligence-gathering agencies and their customer departments. They filter and assess new material. Every Wednesday morning, their bosses gather in the Cabinet Office for a meeting of the Joint Intelligence

Committee. They do a quality-control exercise on the product of the current intelligence groups and compile a 'Red Book' of summaries which, the following day, is circulated to ministers on the OD Committee on a strictly 'need to know' basis. There is a current intelligence group on Latin America. In military terms, it has two preoccupations: Belize in the north and the Falklands in the south.

The most chilling sentence in the Franks Report is this one: 'We were told in evidence that the Latin America Current Intelligence Group met 18 times between July 1981 and March 1982, but did not discuss the Falkland Islands on those occasions.'[84] The Cabinet's watchdog on the Falklands had failed to bark. One insider explained how difficult it was, with the cuts in secret budgets, to run a proper intelligence operation in Argentina, certainly compared to the late forties and early fifties (when Churchill sent *his* task force). Wartime concerns with the pro-fascist inclinations of the government in Buenos Aires had bequeathed a large intelligence operation to the peace. But in the early eighties it was very different, and, as the same observer comments, Argentina then 'was a very hermetic society. Actually to go and take pictures of a dockyard would have been very difficult.'[85] Another insider said, 'I think there *was* an invasion plan. But I don't think we had it or that it would have made any difference if we had.'[86] At the time of writing, it has been disclosed at the trial of the former military junta in Buenos Aires that on 5 January 1982 it 'set up a working group to analyse the possibility of taking the islands'. On 6 March the junta ordered the chiefs of staff to make detailed preparations. On 26 March the junta decided that the invasion would take place on one of the first three days in April.[87]

Sir Frank Cooper was Permanent Secretary at the Ministry of Defence during the Falklands crisis. I asked him how he read the lessons of the Franks Report:

HENNESSY   We're lucky, outsiders like me, in that we've got the Franks Report on the origins of the war, which covers the seventeen-year build-up, the era of non-decision-taking almost, which led to the Argentine invasion of 1982. And I've always thought it [the Report] did for foreign and defence policy-making and intelligence . . . what the Crossman and Castle diaries did for economic and domestic policy-making. It seems to show it's a shambles with more or less benign intent. Do you think there are lessons for the wider public in the Franks Report? Was it in fact such a creaking system as all that?

COOPER I'm not sure I'd wholly agree with what you've just said. But I think what the Franks Report illustrates to me very, very clearly indeed is that, within a parliamentary democratic system of government, there are some issues which are insoluble in that the government of the day . . . are incapable of delivering through the House of Commons. And the question to me is that, where you have got a parliamentary system and where essentially you're dealing with the backbenchers of the . . . government in power, can you deliver them? And the British government in some ways is very much more effective at delivering what it decides to do than many other governments – it's much more effective than the American government. And this was what happened in the Falklands. Neither the Labour government nor the Tory government was able to deliver its party.

HENNESSY I accept that. But if you look inward, inside the Cabinet system itself, in the way that Franks allows one to, you'll see, will you not, that it was very difficult to get the relevant Cabinet committee – the Oversea and Defence Policy Cabinet committee, which the Prime Minister chairs – to discuss this issue? It was also exceedingly difficult to get the Joint Intelligence Committee and its Assessments Staff to update the intelligence assessments. So that's the bit that alarms people like me. The mechanics, the in-house mechanics, which are nothing to do with the backbenchers, which they know nothing of and understand even less.

COOPER I think one of the things that is necessary is that you do need quite a strong centre within government at the moment, and, as we deal with all these complicated issues, whether they are . . . political or intelligence issues [such] as . . . the Falklands Isles or whether it's something highly controversial such as nuclear power or defence or even road systems, you need a much stronger centre than we have got at the moment.

HENNESSY What worried me in looking at the Franks Report is that it was the same group of ministers on the same committee that were dealing with the big issues of war and peace in Middle Europe, with the procurement of nuclear weapons systems. Was the Falklands element in that committee and its back-up staff so peripheral, so much of a backburner issue, that in fact it gives a false impression of it? Or are they as incompetent as that across the whole waterfront?

COOPER No, I don't think they're as incompetent as that even if I accept that they were as incompetent as you imply. What I think was true was that the Falklands was not regarded as a front-line issue for some period of time, and indeed the forecast was that it wouldn't really boil up again until August or thereabouts in 1982. But, having said that, it is not or was not an issue at the forefront of British politics and in a sense you can say the whole nation was guilty in that way. It's part of the price you do pay for democracy.

HENNESSY   I as a taxpayer pay money for clever chaps like you to be the production engineers of the Cabinet system of government. Once a week ministers will get their intelligence summary in the 'Red Book', all the trouble spots in the world, and one pays clever people like you to actually sit there and be plugged in as best one can to the trouble spots, with much better sources of information than the poor old chap in the street, to alert ministers on our behalf of potential disasters. That's your job and the Franks Report shows that the function was not being carried out at all.

COOPER   No. I personally do believe that it would have been much better if ministers had had a number of discussions about the Falkland Islands in the period preceding the invasion of the Falklands by the Argentinians. But, having said that, there is no system in the world, whether it be in government, outside it, public-sector, private-sector, wherever it may be, which is going to get everything right the whole time. And one of the difficulties . . . is that [private citizens] have an innate belief that the government should get everything right all the time. They're just like other men and women. They're going to get some things wrong every now and then. The price that's paid tends to be higher in government than it does elsewhere.

HENNESSY   . . . If . . . one prescient soul at your level, say, early in 1982, . . . really had thought ministers should be forced to meet on this issue and they kept postponing discussions on the Falklands, could you as Permanent Secretary of Defence have ensured that relevant Cabinet ministers did get together and look at the problem rationally and seriously, in so far as it's possible, in time? Could you have shifted it as an individual in the right direction?

COOPER   I don't honestly know the answer to that. I think it is possible. It might have been. But it would depend very much on you getting hold of the relevant minister–it would probably almost inevitably be your own secretary of state–and saying, 'Look we really must have a situation where there is a discussion about the Falklands.'

HENNESSY   And presumably you didn't do that with Mr Nott, the Secretary of State of the day?

COOPER   I think there was great anxiety about should there or should there not be a discussion about the Falklands within the Cabinet-committee system. But we also, I think, all took the view, because that was what all the signs were showing at the time, that the crunch would come later than it did, and I think that was the perceived view of anybody working in Whitehall at that stage.

HENNESSY   You mentioned that we need a stronger centre in government. On the intelligence assessment of possible trouble with the Argentines in the South Atlantic, you say the intelligence assessments were it might boil up in . . . August . . . 1982. Well, by April 1982, surely the Cabinet should have been thinking about it. It was leaving it a little bit late, even if there was the possibility of serious trouble in the summer, not to be talking about it.

COOPER   I didn't actually talk about the intelligence assessments at all. I was talking much more about the political assessment. And the political assessment was that there would be another round of talks in the summer. But that if they did not make progress we were going to be in a really difficult situation which might have military overtones as well. And that was, I think, the essential issue at stake in those days.

The engine room, the Cabinet-committee structure, may have seriously under-performed in the six-month build-up to the Argentine invasion of the Falklands, but its command post, the full Cabinet, according to one senior minister not of the Thatcherite persuasion, performed its classic function once the crisis had broken: 'She had to carry the Cabinet on every major decision', he said. 'That task force would never have sailed without Cabinet approval. There is no question of that.'[88]

Intriguingly, the Falklands made Mrs Thatcher turn to a pair of old statesmen for assistance: Lord Franks, probably the most distinguished Ambassador to Washington since 1945, to sort out the origins of the affair once the war was over; and Harold Macmillan, now the Earl of Stockton, at the outset. Lord Stockton has revealed, in a television interview with Ludovic Kennedy, the substance of his conversation with Mrs Thatcher in Downing Street in the fraught days immediately following the seizure of the islands:

MACMILLAN   I did try and help her about how to run a war because it's such a long time since anybody's run a war – I mean the technical methods of running a war – which she did very well.

KENNEDY   What were you able to draw on there in your own experience?

MACMILLAN   Well, I mean that you have to have a War Cabinet, you have to have a Committee of Chiefs of Staff, that the Secretary of the Committee of Chiefs musn't be the Secretary of the War Cabinet. It must be the nearest thing you could get to Lord Ismay . . . it was just the tip how to run it, how to manage it from the Government point of view. All of which I'd learnt from Churchill, of course.[89]

Mrs Thatcher followed his advice. She commissioned a War Cabinet of five: herself; her deputy, William Whitelaw; Francis Pym, Foreign Secretary; John Nott, Defence Secretary; and Cecil Parkinson, Paymaster General and Chairman of the Conservative Party, to liaise with the party and press and, according to Whitehall talk, to ensure she had a majority in the War Cabinet's deliberations. Officially, the War Cabinet was a sub-group of OD. It was known as OD(SA) – Oversea and Defence (South Atlantic). The 'nearest thing she could get' to a Lord Ismay was Sir Michael Palliser, who had just retired from the headship of the Diplomatic Service. Sir Michael was installed in a new Falklands Unit in the Cabinet Office and attended meetings of OD(SA), though not as its secretary. That job was performed by Sir Robert Armstrong.[90]

During the Falklands War, Mrs Thatcher was punctilious about keeping full Cabinet informed about major developments, and consulted them before implementing the bigger decisions. Under duress from external events, she practised collective Cabinet government in something approaching the traditional form, though David Howell, at that time Secretary of State for Transport, cautions against being carried away by the collective theme:

HENNESSY   Some observers have thought that the Falklands crisis of 1982 actually saw a revival, albeit briefly, of classic Cabinet government. I know you weren't in the War Cabinet, the small group that ran it operationally, but you were in the full Cabinet. In fact this small War Cabinet had to consult the full Cabinet at all the big decisions, like sending the task force, the landing at San Carlos, before they could actually take any decisions to move in, and . . . this was a restoration of almost nineteenth-century Cabinet government. Do you think that's right?

HOWELL   Well, I can't discuss that. It would not be proper or right for me to discuss what went on on the specific issues in the Cabinet and I don't wish to do so. But I think it is reasonable to observe that the major issues of the Falklands War were more or less written in the stars. There wasn't actually a great sense of option or choice. It was clear the task force had to go. Having gone, it was clear that, if it reached there before any kind of serious and sensible peace proposal could be offered, . . . the task force then had to do something. It was clear that . . . fudge proposals from the Argentinians which amounted to saying 'We've done what we've done now let's negotiate from here' were quite unacceptable and it was clear that the task force had to land and do its bit. So I think, of course, it was right and proper that these things came to Cabinet. But I think it would be glorifying things a bit to say that re-created Cabinet government in its full glory, if it ever existed in its full glory in the nineteenth century, which I frankly rather doubt.[91]

The aftermath of the war did oblige Mrs Thatcher to engage in a piece of Cabinet reform on a small but important scale. The Franks

Report was critical of the operation of the Joint Intelligence Committee and its assessment machinery. Its one recommendation was confined to this area:

> We are concerned here with defects in the Joint Intelligence machinery as we have seen it working in an area of low priority. As we have seen only the papers relevant to the subject of our review, we are not able to judge how the assessment machinery deals with areas of higher priority, but we believe that, in dealing with Argentina and the Falkland Islands, it was too passive in operation to respond quickly and critically to a rapidly changing situation which demanded urgent attention.
>
> We consider that the assessment machinery should be reviewed. We cannot say what the scope of such a review should be in respect of the machinery's wider preoccupations, but we think that it should look at two aspects in particular. The first . . . is the arrangement for bringing to the Joint Intelligence Organisation's attention information other than intelligence reports.[92] The second is the composition of the Joint Intelligence Committee. On this, consideration should be given to the position of the Chairman of the Committee: to the desirability that he or she should be full-time, with a more critical and independent role; and, in recognition of the Committee's independence in operation from the Government Departments principally constituting it, to the Chairman's being appointed by the Prime Minister and being a member of the Cabinet Office.[93]

As a result of the Franks recommendation, the JIC was reviewed. The Foreign Office lost the chairmanship. It moved to the then co-ordinator of security and intelligence in the Cabinet Office, Sir Antony Duff, who was given the right of direct access to Mrs Thatcher and encouraged to override the JIC's supporting machinery and voice his concerns at the highest level when a potential emergency was sensed.[94] It is immensely difficult for outsiders to begin to assess the efficiency of the secret world. But, one year later, some experienced figures reckoned the post-Franks changes had been pretty superficial. 'Falklands is now on the agenda', said one. 'But how do people know that things are not the same today? How often is Hong Kong discussed? Belize? Gibraltar? The Caribbean?'[93] For one participant, the lesson of the Franks Report was the dangerous degree to which civil servants run policy on the intelligence side: 'Ministers should meet and say "we have heard what you think but our view is . . .".'[96] The shortcomings of the JIC and the secret agencies tend only to be exposed after the kind of failure they exist to prevent. In 1984 Sir Antony Duff was moved to the directorship of MI5, the Security Service, to clean it up after the Security Commission had criticized it as part of its investigation of the Bettaney affair. In 1985 Duff was succeeded as JIC 'overlord' and Cabinet Office co-ordinator by Sir Colin Figures, the former Director-General of the Secret Intelligence Service, MI6.[97]

Given the record of her 'conviction Cabinets' between 1979 and 1985, where, in a spectrum stretching from collective decision-taking to 'presidential' command, does Mrs Thatcher's handling of Cabinet place her? The public rhetoric tends to point firmly in one direction. Three quick examples give what is a fairly consistent flavour. First, Nicholas Budgen, the somewhat maverick right-wing Tory MP, said on 5 December 1984 when receiving the *Spectator* Backbencher-of-the-Year Award, 'My hope is that this Parliament will see a restoration of Cabinet government.' I telephoned him and asked him to explain. He did so: 'I wasn't surprised by what has happened. After all, before the 1979 election she said the Cabinet was going to be a place for handing down the orders of Great Britain Limited and was, no doubt, applauded for it in Rotary Clubs throughout the land.'[98]

Next, Peter Jenkins, the respected political commentator of *The Sunday Times*, writing on the possible impact of such men as Kenneth Baker and Kenneth Clarke brought into the Cabinet in the September 1985 reshuffle (in alliance with existing Cabinet members such as Douglas Hurd and Norman Fowler): 'It is not easy to reassert Cabinet government in the face of determined prime ministerial power but the new Cabinet contains a group of capable and ambitious men of political middle age who are not eager to sacrifice the best years of their careers for the sake of someone else's "conviction politics".'[99]

Finally, let us take a pre-Heseltine witness from the inside track. In the autumn of 1985, Peter Walker, Secretary of State for Energy, had taken to making the following joke in after-lunch speeches: he would quote the Duke of Wellington's reaction to his first Cabinet meeting as Prime Minister: 'An extraordinary affair. I gave them their orders and they wanted to stay and discuss them.' Then he would pause and say, 'I'm so glad we don't have Prime Ministers like that today.'[100] The broadside of Mr Walker's friend and colleague Michael Heseltine has already been examined.

The implication of the Heseltine resignation, assorted other speeches, asides and articles can be made to seem too strong. For a start, no prime minister's exposition of Cabinet government is consistent. The Falklands obliged Mrs Thatcher to behave more collectively for a time, as did the unexpectedly hostile reaction across the political spectrum to her handling of the trade-union issue at GCHQ, where policy-making by cabal truly backfired.[101] And after the resignations of Heseltine and Brittan there were signs of a revival of collegiality in the Cabinet Room. Her sensitivity at all times to what will run in Cabinet is genuine, even though she always lets colleagues know what she wants at the outset of any discussion. There genuinely is a contrast between her rhetoric and assertion of personality and the reality of the decision-making process.

Having acknowledged that, Cabinet does meet less frequently, it discusses fewer formal papers, it is presented with more virtual *faits accomplis* at the last moment, and she does prefer to work in ad hoc groups – many of the most important ones remaining outside the Cabinet-committee structure. Collective deliberation on the basis of choices served up by the official machine go against Mrs Thatcher's personal grain. She likes advice with her kind of spin on it and brisk meetings with those most closely involved. She has certainly flouted the spirit of traditional Cabinet government. But she has not handbagged it, to use Julian Critchley's metaphor, beyond recognition. She has certainly not privatized it from the Constitution, for all Michael Heseltine's complaints. At worst she has put Cabinet government temporarily on ice. In a political and administrative system as riddled with tradition as the British, the old model could, and probably will, be restored in the few minutes it takes a new prime minister to travel from Buckingham Palace to Downing Street.

4

Cabinets and the Bomb

I thought that some of them were not fit to be trusted with secrets of this kind. *Lord Attlee, 1958, recalling the decision to build an atomic bomb in 1947*[1]

The Prime Minister [Sir Winston Churchill] said that he would like to invite the Cabinet at an early date to decide in principle that hydrogen bombs should be made in the United Kingdom. *Minute of a meeting of GEN 464, April 1954*[2]

It isn't a question of not trusting. It's a question that the more people you have, the more people can be got at. *Lord Wilson, 1985, on nuclear-weapons policy-making 1964–70, 1974–6*[3]

The Government's perfectly entitled to take decisions in any way it wants. *Sir Frank Cooper, 1985, on the taking of the Trident decision in Cabinet committee*[4]

Attlee's failure to take to full Cabinet the decision to build the first British atomic bomb has been a staple item in the phenomenology of opponents of the British nuclear-weapons programme *and* students of Cabinet government since the appearance of Mackintosh's *British Cabinet Government* in 1962. For Mackintosh, the A-bomb decision was a touchstone of Attlee's firm management of his Cabinet:

He controlled the agenda and if he so desired, kept matters to himself or discussed them with one or two others. All questions connected with the manufacture of atomic and hydrogen bombs by Britain he considered unsuitable for the full Cabinet. This matter was discussed in the Defence Committee and though its decision was circulated to the Cabinet, the references to such a momentous conclusion were studiously kept minimal and technical and no attempt was made to draw the Cabinet's attention to these items.

This was quite deliberate on Mr Attlee's part as he thought that the fewer people who were aware of what was happening, the better. It is not surprising, therefore, that after the existence of a British H-bomb was announced, several members of the Cabinet said they had no knowledge that work of this kind was being done. Had the matter not been discussed formally in the Defence Committee of the Cabinet or had it decided to record no minutes there would not even have been the saving clause of an inadvertent acquiescence by the Cabinet.[5]

Mackintosh's account needs amending in several ways. For example, the Attlee administration took the decision to build a fission bomb, an atomic *not* a fusion or thermonuclear weapon. The 'hydrogen bomb', as the latter type is commonly known, belonged to the next generation of nuclear technology, and it was the Churchill Administration which took the decision to manufacture it. But the Mackintosh version requires updating in other important respects in the light of Professor Gowing's official histories published in 1974[6] and the papers which began to reach the Public Record Office in 1978. Office in 1978.

The story is best told by tracing the origins of the British bomb project to the pioneering days at the beginning of the Second World War. Professor Gowing describes Britain as the 'midwife'[7] of the American weapons dropped on Hiroshima and Nagasaki in August 1985:

If it had not been for the brilliant scientific work done in Britain in the early part of the war, by refugee scientists, the Second World War would almost certainly have ended before an atomic bomb was dropped. It had been the cogency and clarity of the British Maud Report in 1941 which had persuaded the Americans of the practical possibility of an atomic bomb and the urgency of making one.[8]

The cost (some $2000 million) of developing and building the bomb was beyond Britain alone. The United States took over as the leading partner, and British scientists travelled to New Mexico to work with the Americans on research and development. The Quebec Agreement, struck between Churchill and Roosevelt in August 1943, and refined by the Hyde Parke *aide-mémoire* of September 1944, guaranteed that Anglo-American collaboration in the development of atomic power for military and civilian purposes would continue after the defeat of Germany and Japan unless terminated by joint agreement. The

McMahon Act, passed by the United States Congress in August 1946, made the sharing of America's atomic secrets illegal. There were no exceptions, not even for Britain, the midwife of the new technology, despite the Quebec Agreement.

In 1945 the newly elected Attlee Government protested in vain. It was clear Britain would have to go it alone. Work was quickly under way. On 18 December 1945 Attlee's highly secret Cabinet committee on atomic energy, GEN 75, authorized the construction of an atomic pile to produce plutonium, the fissile material for the bomb. At the same meeting it was decided that 'The Chiefs of Staff would submit a report on our requirements for atomic bombs and the possibility of making consequential reductions in other forms of armament production.'[9] An Air Ministry file of November 1946 contains the specification for a new long-range bomber. It mentions a capacity for carrying a single 'special bomb' of 10,000 pounds 'to a target 2000 nautical miles from a base which may be anywhere in the world'.[10] The Royal Air Force was on the way towards acquiring, in what became the Vulcan bomber, a delivery system for atomic weapons.

But it was not until 8 January 1947, that a specially convened Cabinet committee, GEN 163, met specifically to authorize the manufacture of a British atomic bomb. The impetus for the taking of a formal decision came from Lord Portal, the former Second World War Chief of the Air Staff, whom Attlee appointed Controller of Production, Atomic Energy, inside the Ministry of Supply, Whitehall's department for procuring weaponry. Portal opened the discussion in the Cabinet Room that January afternoon by saying, in the recorded language of the minutes,

that so far as he was aware, no decision had yet been taken to proceed with the development of atomic weapons. He had discussed the matter with the Chiefs of Staff who were naturally anxious that we should not be without this weapon if others possess it. About three years' work would be needed to solve the problems of nuclear physics and engineering involved in the bomb mechanism.[11]

A senior Ministry of Defence official, recalling from the perspective of the early 1980s the outcome of the first and last meeting of GEN 163, described it as an 'of course' decision.[12] A similar view is held by Professor George Jones, who believes 'there was no point in having a Cabinet session on a matter on which they were all agreed'.[13] But, the evidence suggests, the bomb question was not quite that cut and dried. If it was so routine a piece of business, why did Attlee feel the need to reconstitute GEN 75, the Cabinet committee which had done the preparatory work, as a one-off group, GEN 163, summoned for the purpose of taking a formal decision on the bomb?

The answer can be found in the composition of the two committees: GEN 163 was GEN 75 *minus* the two leading ministers concerned with economics – Hugh Dalton, Chancellor of the Exchequer, and Sir Stafford Cripps, President of the Board of Trade – and *plus* A. V. Alexander, the Minister of Defence. At a meeting of GEN 75 on 25 October 1946, Dalton and Cripps resisted, on the grounds that the economy could not afford it, a proposal to spend between £30 million and £40 million over four to five years to build a gaseous diffusion plant for the production of Uranium 235.

The minutes do not attribute views, but the gist of the Cripps–Dalton argument is recorded in the passionless prose favoured by the Cabinet secretariat:

In discussion it was urged that we must consider seriously whether we could afford to divert from civilian consumption and the restoration of our balance of payments, the economic resources required for a project on this scale. Unless present trends were reversed we might find ourselves faced with an extremely serious financial situation in two to three years time.[14]

Dalton and Cripps doubted whether the country needed an atomic bomb and looked like winning the argument.

According to the recollections of survivors who talked to researchers for a BBC *Timewatch* television programme broadcast on 29 September 1982 (the minutes of GEN 75 are, as is customary, free of personality and nuance), Portal and other Ministry of Supply officials working on the bomb became increasingly jumpy. Where was their patron, Ernest Bevin, Foreign Secretary and strong man of the Attlee Cabinet? At last he waddled in, apologizing for his late arrival, explaining that he had enjoyed a heavy lunch and had fallen asleep. (Attlee had opened the meeting at 2.15.) Sensing what was about to happen, he wielded that raw power and personality for which he was famous and routed Dalton and Cripps.

According to Sir Michael Perrin, one of the surviving officials, Bevin said, 'That won't do at all . . . we've got to have this. . . . I don't mind for myself, but I don't want any other Foreign Secretary of this country to be talked to or at by a Secretary of State in the United States as I have just had in my discussions with Mr Byrnes. We have got to have this thing over here whatever it costs.' Sir Michael remembers Bevin adding, 'We've got to have the bloody Union Jack on top of it.' In the car on the way back to the Ministry of Supply, Portal turned to Perrin and said, 'You know, if Bevin hadn't come in then, we wouldn't have had that bomb, Michael.'[15]

GEN 163 consisted of Attlee plus five ministers: Bevin; Herbert Morrison, Lord President of the Council; A. V. Alexander; Lord Addison, Secretary of State for Dominion Affairs; and John Wilmot, Minister of Supply. The absence of the leading financial minister, Dalton, and the leading industrial minister, Cripps, can only be explained by Attlee's determination that the decision should go through on the nod, which it did after Bevin made what could be construed as an anti-American contribution: 'We could not afford to acquiesce in an American monopoly of this new development. Other countries also might well develop atomic weapons. Unless therefore an effective international system could be developed under which the production and use of the weapon would be prohibited, we must develop it ourselves.'[16]

GEN 163 was faced with further decisions about the degree of secrecy which should surround the British atomic-weapons programme. Portal's note circulated ahead of the meeting argued 'that a decision is required about the development of atomic weapons in this country' on the grounds that 'The Service Departments are beginning to move in the matter and certain sections of the Press are showing interest in it.'[17] He suggested three choices:

(a) Not to develop the atomic weapon at all.
(b) To develop the weapon by means of the ordinary agencies in the Ministry of Supply and the Service Departments.
(c) To develop the weapon under special arrangements conducive to the utmost secrecy.[18]

Portal's reasoning is worth contemplating in full, as the ministers on GEN 163, by accepting his advocacy of the 'utmost secrecy' option, effectively precluded a wider involvement of the full Cabinet. In addition, they set a pattern which thirty-four years later caused Sir Frank Cooper, at a House of Commons Public Accounts Committee inquiry into the Chevaline improvement to the Polaris strategic nuclear force, to tell MPs that the concealment of the true cost of Chevaline from Parliament

was an inheritance of the early days of nuclear work. It was kept for a very long period of time within an exceptionally limited circle of people who were privy to the innermost details of nuclear thinking and nuclear technology. As long as I can remember – which goes right back to the start – there was a somewhat similar arrangement to this when there was going to be a nuclear development.[19]

At the time when the tradition of nuclear secrecy was set in official concrete, Portal swiftly dismissed the no-bomb option, as he imagined it 'would not be favoured by H. M. Government in the absence of an international agreement on the subject'.[20] He clearly did not favour the second possibility of using the usual organizations of weapons supply, as it would

be impossible to conceal for long the fact that this development is taking place. Many interests are involved, and the need for constant consultation with my organisation (which is the sole repository of the knowledge of atomic energy and atomic weapons derived from our wartime collaboration with the United States) would result in very many people, including scientists, knowing what was going on.[21]

Portal was also worried that the American authorities would hear that Britain was developing its bomb and be spurred into still greater reticence on atomic matters. The Americans, post McMahon Act, appear to have been the bogy for Portal as for Bevin. The Russians do not seem to have featured in the deliberations of GEN 163. Portal weighted his evidence in favour of the third option, of utmost secrecy:

If for *national or international* [Emphasis added] reasons, the special arrangements . . . are thought desirable, we are at present well placed to make them. The Chief Superintendent of Armament Research (Dr Penney) has been intimately concerned in the recent American trials and knows more than any other British scientist about the secrets of the American bomb. He has the facilities for the necessary research and development which could be 'camouflaged' as 'Basic High Explosive Research' (a subject for which he is actually responsible but on which no work is in fact being done) . . . he could be made responsible . . . to me for this particular work and I would arrange the necessary contacts with my organisation in such a way as to secure the maximum secrecy. Only about five or six senior officials outside my own organisation need know of this arrangement.[22]

As a clinching ploy, Portal added that the Chiefs of Staff strongly recommended the third option. GEN 163 bowed to their combined opinion.

The 'maximum secrecy' approach did not prevent the Soviet Union from discovering the secrets of the British bomb project. Klaus Fuchs, who had worked on the bomb in the United States returned to Britain to lead the Theoretical Physics Division at Harwell in June 1946. By the time he was exposed in 1950, he had achieved a place in history as 'probably the most dangerous spy of all, since it was he who gave the Russians the secret of the bomb'.[23] But it did keep atomic decision-taking away from the full Cabinet *and* its Defence Committee.

The true picture was very different from that painted by Mackintosh, as Professor Gowing, who had access to the complete set of files, showed in 1974:

It [the Cabinet] took no part in the decisions to establish a research establishment, to build piles to produce plutonium, or, later, to build gaseous diffusion plants to separate uranium-235; no part in the decisions to make and then test an atomic bomb, and about the planned place of atomic bombs in British strategy; in the decisions about priorities; in the decisions concerning atomic relations with other countries, including the important atomic negotiations with America after 1945.

It was usual, during and after the Second World War, for many other policy questions to be formulated and settled within Cabinet Committees and small groups of Ministers. The difference in the case of atomic energy was that major decisions were not reported to the full Cabinet but were, even at that level, shrouded in secrecy.[24]

Professor Gowing reckons 'It is possible that Cabinet Ministers not attending GEN 75 meetings did not even know of its existence.'[25]

Now that the minutes of the full Cabinet and its Defence Committee are open, a check on the files shows the agenda of both completely bereft of anything to do with the atomic-bomb decision, though it is possible that full Cabinet was alerted on Thursday 6 May 1948 of the intention to announce, in a planted parliamentary question the following Wednesday, that Britain was developing atomic weapons. Item 1 on the agenda for 6 May was the standard subject of the coming week's business in the Commons. The minute, as is customary, consisted of a single sparse sentence: 'The Cabinet were informed of the business to be taken in the House of Commons in the following week.'[26] One indicator that the bomb announcement was included would have been the presence of the Minister of Supply, a non-Cabinet minister, for the item. George Strauss, who had replaced Wilmot in the post, attended the 6 May Cabinet for items 3–6 but *not* for the first. The parliamentary answer was in the name of Alexander, the Minister of Defence, rather than Strauss. But Strauss's absence does suggest that the Cabinet did not even receive warning of the momentous announcement.

'Momentous' is the right adjective, because a country is changed when it becomes a nuclear power. Dreadful responsibilities instantly fall upon its government. This became immediately obvious in August 1945, when the United States dropped the two atomic bombs that have been used in anger. The mushroom cloud that rose above Hiroshima on 6 August became a symbol of the most frightening leap ever achieved in weapons technology. Each time another nation has demonstrated the ability to manufacture and detonate an atomic device, it has been a major international development. From a narrower domestic point of view, the decision to undertake a nuclear-weapons programme is costly and can have a substantial distorting-effect on the conventional elements of a country's defence budget and a considerable impact on the national economy as a whole, as it absorbs not only finance but also an important slice of scientific brain-power. In short, going nuclear is one of the most important decisions a government can take.

Why was Attlee so determined to proceed through small, concealed Cabinet committees? Why did nobody question Portal's advice that the 'utmost secrecy' option should be picked? (This was changed in May 1948 not for reasons of open government but because excessive secrecy was delaying progress, since it was difficult for those engaged in aspects of the bomb project to comprehend its urgency, high priority and importance, when they were prohibited from knowing the wider picture. The 'high explosive' cover story was proving too successful.[27])

There were a number of reasons for what Professor Gowing called the decision to proceed in 'the darkest secrecy'.[28] Churchill had set the precedent for keeping the Cabinet uninformed about atomic weapons. Attlee was confirming existing policy. The Prime Minister and his inner atomic group also 'wanted the public to know as little as possible lest an enemy learn even more'.[29] As we have seen, Bevin was particularly sensitive about the US Government discovering Britain's atomic plans. And Attlee said later of his ministers that he 'thought that some of them were not fit to be trusted with secrets of this kind'.[30] It is probably unfair to apply this remark to Cripps and Dalton, the dissenters within GEN 75 (though Dalton was a notoriously indiscreet gossip). GEN 75 in its original composition continued to meet after GEN 163 had decided to make the bomb. Dalton and Cripps knew the project was going ahead. Indeed Cripps, by this time Chancellor of the Exchequer, urged in the spring of 1948 that an announcement be made, as it was widely assumed that Britain was making atomic bombs and there was little point in trying to keep the fact secret.[31]

Cripps's remark reinforces the point of that senior civil servant in the early 1980s: the 1947 conclusion was an 'of course decision'. There was no Campaign for Nuclear Disarmament in existence. Apart from Cripps and Dalton, it is most unlikely that other ministers would have dissented if the issue had reached the agenda of the full Cabinet in the winter of 1946–7. Dissenters generally were few, though their number included a pair of famous names: Professor P. M. S. Blackett and Sir Henry Tizard.

Blackett, the Professor of Physics at Manchester University, had sat on the original Maud Committee. Now he was serving on Sir John Anderson's Advisory Committee on Atomic Energy, which was invited by Attlee to feed independent advice to GEN 75. Blackett, a Labour supporter, struck a note more attuned to the party's stance on nuclear weapons in the early 1980s than to the views held on atomic energy by most of the inner group of ministers in the late 1940s. His note 'On the Formulation of British Policy in Regard to Atomic Energy' is undated. But it was circulated to the membership of GEN 75 on 8 February 1947, just a month after GEN 163 had taken the decision to proceed.

Whether or not the United Kingdom became allied to the United States (NATO was more then two years away) for the purposes of a preventive war or a defensive war against Russia, Blackett argued,

Britain would clearly need a military machine closely integrated with that of America and would herself be compelled to make as many atomic bombs as possible and to prepare Britain to be a base for American atomic bombs.

This eventuality would clearly be disastrous for Britain, for it is widely agreed . . . that in a war between Russia and America, Russian forces are likely initially, at any rate, to overrun Western Europe. Then London and the South of England could be destroyed slowly e.g. by rockets.

Blackett sketched his alternative: first-class home and sea defence; a mobile force for limited overseas operations; and a garrison force for occupation purposes:

We would . . . not make in quantity long range heavy bombers or rockets, atomic bombs, BW [biological weapons] or gas. But we would retain the right to make prototypes of these weapons in certain cases.

In the field of atomic energy, we would announce that we were not going to make any bombs. . . . We would appeal to other countries which had interests similar to our own to likewise renounce weapons of mass destruction and to admit inspection.[32]

The big man on both GEN 75 and GEN 163 was not impressed. Bevin said of Blackett, 'he should stick to science'.[33]

More than two years later, after the Soviet Union had exploded its first atomic bomb, Sir Henry Tizard, Chief Scientific Adviser to the Ministry of Defence, warned against a continuing great-power illusion and his views were greeted 'with the kind of horror one would expect if one made a disrespectful remark about the King'.[34]

Tizard's heresy – like Blackett's, expressed privately in Whitehall – is not shocking to hindsight-laden eyes

We persist in regarding ourselves as a Great Power, capable of everything and only temporarily handicapped by economic difficulties. We are not a Great Power and never will be again. We are a great nation, but if we continue to behave like a Great Power we shall soon cease to be a great nation. Let us take warning from the fate of the Great Powers of the past and not burst ourselves with pride (see Aesop's fable of the frog).[35]

Such thinking would have found scant sympathy in political or public thinking. Cripps was right in claiming it was widely assumed Britain was making a bomb. Few questioned the country's great-power status. Britain, after all, had stood alone in 1940–1 and held Hitler back until a war-winning Grand Alliance had been built around her. She was, like America and Russia, one of the Big Three. And great powers needed the latest weapons. A. V. Alexander announced the bomb's manufacture on 12 May 1948. Most newspapers merely reported his low-key answer verbatim:

Armed Forces
(Modern Weapons)

Mr George Jeger asked the Minister of Defence whether he is satisfied that adequate progress is being made in the development of the most modern types of weapon?

The Minister of Defence (Mr A. V. Alexander): Yes, sir. As was made clear in the Statement Relating to Defence, 1948 (Command 7327), research and developments continue to receive the highest priority in the defence field, and all types of modern weapons, including atomic weapons, are being developed.

Mr Jeger: Can the Minister give any further information on the development of atomic weapons?

Mr Alexander: No. I do not think it would be in the public interest to do that.[36]

In no paper was this the lead item on the front page. The *Financial Times* and the *Daily Mirror* did not bother to report it at all.

It is difficult to recapture over a gap of forty years the picture of the world, and of Britain's place in it, carried inside the heads of policy-makers in the late 1940s. The magnitude of the problems on defence and foreign policy as the Grand Alliance of the Second World War withered and fell apart, and the exposed position occupied by Britain until NATO was created in 1949, can best be appreciated by reading Lord Bullock's masterly survey, in his biography of Bevin, of 'The World in the Summer of 1945'.[37] Without such an appreciation, the decision taken by GEN 163 cannot be set in its place. That same senior official in the early 1980s said, 'If we were trying to enter the game now, there would not be any point. But in 1947, it was different. And whether we should give it up now is an entirely different question.'[38]

Lord Bullock's defence of Bevin against the criticism that he sustained great-power illusions across a range of issues, concerning Europe, the Middle East, the Far East and the bomb, is that he kept options and opportunities open for his successors:

Whether they made the best use of them is another matter. To take only one example: in failing to take Britain into Europe in 1955–6 when the opportunity was renewed, I am sure they did not.

The same argument applies to nuclear weapons. After sharing with the Americans in the development of the A-bomb Bevin and Attlee were faced with having to accept their exclusion from further co-operation and under American pressure having to abandon the idea of producing one of their own. The decision will always remain a controversial one. But what Bevin was doing when he backed the proposal to continue was to prevent an option being closed off which, once abandoned, could never be re-opened.[39]

Attlee's immediate successor in No. 10 was a firm admirer of Bevin. But Churchill seemed confused by the details and the implications of the atomic programme on his return to power in October 1951. As Professor Gowing has noted, by this time

the pioneering or heroic period of the atomic energy project . . . was almost over. . . . Penney's team had almost finished working out the bomb design and bomb mechanics. The first military stage of the project was almost complete and the Government had simply to wait for the programme to reach its terrifying pyrotechnic culmination. . . . Thus the new Conservative Government's immediate atomic problems were tidying-up ones.[40]

Churchill's first reaction was puzzling. He seemed to believe a deal was possible which would restore wartime atomic collaboration with the United States and avoid the need for a weapon with a Union Jack on it, as Bevin put it. On 15 November 1951 he wrote in a personal minute to Lord Cherwell, Paymaster General and the minister responsible for atomic matters:

I have never wished, since our decision during the war, that England should start the manufacture of atomic bombs. Research, however, must be energetically pursued. We should have the art rather than the article. A large sum of money will have to be provided for this. There is, however, no point in our going into bulk production even if we were able to. When we go to Washington in January we can, I have no doubt, arrange to be allocated a reasonable share of what they have made so largely on our initiative and substantial scientific contribution.[41]

Attlee would have harboured no such illusions about the possibility of restoring the position to that which held before Congress passed the McMahon Act. In another most un-Attlee-like intervention the following month, Churchill sent a minute to Sir Edward Bridges, Permanent Secretary to the Treasury, asking 'How was it that the £100 millions for atomic research and manufacture was provided without Parliament being informed? How was this very large sum accounted for?'[42] Churchill, according to Professor Gowing, felt a trace of envy for Attlee's ability to conceal such a huge weapons programme and 'felt he would have been branded as a warmonger for a similar feat'.[43] Professor Gowing believes Churchill's minutes on atomic matters in the first months after his return to office bear witness to the deterioration of his powers.[44]

Cherwell was a firm believer in Britain having her own bomb – the article as well as the art. His chief came round to the same view. The talks with President Truman did not restore wartime collaboration. The British bomb was successfully detonated at Monte Bello off the north-west coast of Australia on 3 October 1952. Bevin posthumously had his wish fulfilled: there was a Union Jack on it. Britain was the third power to join the nuclear club, after the United States (1945) and the Soviet Union (1949). In 1985 that club has seven members. In short, Churchill continued Attlee's policy even to the extent of concealing the money from Parliament. Cherwell and Duncan Sandys, the new Minister of Supply, did not favour disclosing the cost to Parliament, on the grounds that they might give information the Russians would find useful while not impressing the Americans one bit. Churchill commented, 'There are also the British. But I agree to the answer.'[45]

Where Churchill did differ from Attlee was over the handling of *his* nuclear decision: whether or not to proceed to the second generation of nuclear weapons with the manufacture of a British hydrogen bomb. The decision-taking process began as usual deep in the Cabinet committees. The sequence of meetings began in April 1954 and ended with no fewer than three discussions in full Cabinet, the last of which, on 26 July 1954, authorized the production of a hydrogen bomb – the first and last time that a British Cabinet has been allowed to take the decision on a new generation of nuclear weapons.

Ironically, the spring round of ministerial meetings on the bomb began with yet another attempt to ensure that Parliament had no inkling of the true cost of the existing atomic-weapons programme. The issue had rearisen because responsibility for maintaining the programme was passing from the Ministry of Supply to a new Department of Atomic Energy (now known as the United Kingdom Atomic Energy Authority). A special Cabinet committee under Churchill's chairmanship, GEN 458, was convened to consider a paper from

Sandys.[46] 'I feel it my duty', wrote Sandys, 'to draw attention to the fact that, if the Estimates of the new Department of Atomic Energy are published in the form at present proposed, they will disclose to the world the level of our expenditure on atomic weapons.' The problem, it emerged, when the Cabinet committee met in No. 10 the next day, was that just how *little* Britain was spending on its atomic arsenal – 'substantially less than £14 million a year on the production of atomic bombs' – could be deduced from the detailed estimates of monies received by the Ministry of Supply. 'Apart from giving gratuitous information to a potential enemy,' said Sandys, 'this disclosure was bound to weaken our foreign policy and reduce our influence for world peace.'[47] At this stage, Britain's atomic stockpile probably consisted of fewer than ten bombs.[48] GEN 458 authorized Sandys to account for bomb expenditure in other totals and avoid disclosing information about the size of the British atomic stockpile.

It was at a meeting in Churchill's room in the House of Commons on the evening of 13 April 1954 that ministers set in motion the process leading to a British hydrogen bomb. At the first meeting of Churchill's Cabinet committee on atomic-energy development, GEN 464, five other ministers (the same number as in Attlee's GEN 163) were present: Sir Anthony Eden, Foreign Secretary; R. A. Butler, Chancellor of the Exchequer; Lord Alexander of Tunis, Minister of Defence; (*not* to be confused with A. V. Alexander, Attlee's Minister of Defence); Lord Swinton, Secretary of State for Commonwealth Relations; and Lord Salisbury, Lord President of the Council, who had assumed responsibility for atomic-energy matters when Cherwell retired in 1953.[49]

Salisbury opened by saying he was not seeking at this stage authority to start research and development on the hydrogen bomb:

If, however, it were decided that we should make hydrogen bombs, we should need additional supplies of thorium and heavy water. Therefore, without pre-judging the major decision of policy, he was seeking authority to take two steps which would put us in a position to go forward with this project, if it were eventually decided that we should do so.

The problem with thorium supplies was that the United States was placing such large orders that they would be exhausted if Britain did not make a swift claim. On heavy water, Salisbury wished to revive a scheme to build a plant in New Zealand. Butler said the Treasury would allow the money needed – between £1 million and £7 million over three years for thorium, and £1.8 million over two years for the heavy-water plant.

At this point Churchill broke with tradition (though, if the Cabinet conventions were observed, he did not know how Attlee had proceeded), and said he would 'like to invite the Cabinet at an early date to decide in principle that hydrogen bombs should be made in the United Kingdom'. GEN 464 concurred.[50] On 16 June the Cabinet's Defence Committee decided to build the hydrogen bomb. It is not possible to assess the discussion, as the minutes are retained in the Cabinet Office under Section 3(4) of the Public Records Act, 1958, presumably because they contain still-sensitive material. The issue reached full Cabinet the following month.

It appeared on the agenda for the Cabinet meeting in No. 10 on the morning of 7 July 1954 as item 5, 'Atomic Energy, Weapons Programme'. Present for it were sixteen Cabinet ministers, plus Sandys and Cherwell, who was there in a personal capacity. Churchill opened by informing the Cabinet that

the Defence Policy Committee had approved, on 16th June, a proposal that our atomic weapons programme should be so adjusted as to allow for the production of hydrogen bombs in this country. His recent discussions in Washington and Ottawa had been conducted on the basis that we should produce hydrogen bombs. He therefore suggested that the Cabinet should now formally approve that hydrogen bombs should be produced in this country, and should endorse the preliminary action which had already been taken to this end.[51]

Churchill then launched into his version of deterrence theory. No trace here of his autumn 1951 thinking about Britain possessing 'the art rather than the article':

The Prime Minister said that we could not expect to maintain our influence as a World Power unless we possessed the most up-to-date nuclear weapons. The primary aim of our policy was to prevent major war; and the possession of these weapons was now the main deterrent to a potential aggressor. He had no doubt that the best hope of preserving world peace was to make it clear to potential aggressors that they had no hope of shielding themselves from a crushing retaliatory use of atomic power.

For this purpose the Western Powers must provide themselves, not only with a sufficient supply of up-to-date nuclear weapons, but also with a multiplicity of bases from which a retaliatory attack could be launched. They must put themselves in a position to ensure that no surprise attack, however large, could wholly destroy their power of effective retaliation. These considerations, in his view, made it essential that we should manufacture hydrogen bombs in the United Kingdom so as to be able to make our contribution to this deterrent influence.[52]

When Churchill had finished what even from the sparse language of Sir Norman Brook's minute sounds like one of his classic Cabinet *tours d'horizon*, Salisbury spoke in support of 'the strategic argument' outlined by his chief. He revealed to ministers not on the Defence Committee that 'plans were now in preparation for the production of hydrogen bombs' in Britain. Provided additional scientists could be recruited, the H-bomb programme could be mounted 'without serious disruption of the existing programme for the manufacture of atomic weapons'. The Defence Committee had already approved the preliminary steps towards a thermo-nuclear programme.

True to tradition, Cabinet ministers not on GEN 464 or the Defence Committee had no idea that the Government had reached the brink of such a momentous decision. Harry Crookshank, the Lord Privy Seal, an independent-minded man who was not averse to criticizing Churchill in the privacy of the Cabinet Room, 'said that the Cabinet had had no notice that this question was to be raised and he hoped they would not be asked to take a final decision on it until they had had more time to consider it'.[53] A decision was duly postponed.

In fact, it took two more meetings before the Cabinet authorized Salisbury to proceed. The next day, ministers undertook a detailed discussion of the cost, the international implications *and* the morality of nuclear weapons – the first time, almost certainly, that the spiritual dimension had intruded at the highest political level. The trigger for this was the Methodist Conference in London, which had passed resolutions on the matter.[54] Unbeknown to the good nonconformists, their initiative had inspired a first in the history of British Cabinet government.

On the question of cost, the Cabinet was told, presumably by Salisbury though the minute does not specify, that the net additional cost to the existing atomic programme 'would not be very substantial. The capital cost should not exceed £10 millions, and the thermonuclear bombs would be made in lieu of atomic bombs at a relatively small additional production cost.' Much of the material needed would have been required anyway for the existing atomic programme. Atomic bombs could be converted into hydrogen bombs, and, in terms of explosive power, the thermo-nuclear weapon was more economical.

At this point, the issue of non-proliferation was raised. Would it not be easier to prevent other Western nations, particularly West Germany, from making thermo-nuclear weapons if Britain refrained? Other defence preparations were based on the assumption that Britain would not engage in a major war except as an ally of the United States. Could the country not continue to rely on America to match Russia in hydrogen bombs?

Again, the minutes do not specify, but it looks as if it was Churchill who countered by playing down the difference between atomic bombs and the hydrogen weapon: 'In reply it was pointed out that the strength of these arguments was weakened by the fact that we had already embarked on the production of atomic weapons. There was no sharp distinction in kind between atomic and thermo-nuclear weapons.'[55] Why should Britain deny herself the advantage of having the most up-to-date weapons? Sir Anthony Eden, the Foreign Secretary, added his authority to the pro-H-bomb argument by claiming that Britain's power to control the manufacture of the weapon in Western Europe would not be weakened by the fact that she was making it.

In contradiction to the claim that there was 'no sharp distinction' between an atomic and a thermo-nuclear capability, it was recognized that 'with this vast destructive power . . . there was no doubt that a decision to make hydrogen bombs would offend the conscience of substantial numbers of people in this country'. Here, evidence from the recent Methodist Conference was cited. Once more, responsibility was sloughed off to Attlee and GEN 163:

In reply, the point was again made that there was no difference in kind between atomic and thermo-nuclear weapons; *and that, in so far as any moral principle was involved, it had already been breached by the decision of the Labour Government to make the atomic bomb.*

It was also argued that the moral issue would arise, not so much on the production of these weapons, but on the decision to use them; and that the resolution of the Methodist Conference was directed mainly against the use of atomic weapons. The further point was made that, if we were ready to accept the protection offered by the United States' use of thermo-nuclear weapons, no greater moral wrong was involved in making them ourselves. [Emphasis added.][56]

At this stage, the great-power argument was expressed in a simple direct fashion – 'unless we possessed thermo-nuclear weapons, we should lose our influence and standing in world affairs' – and the American bogy was raised (again, almost certainly by Churchill, though the minute is non-attributable) in a fashion that would have won Bevin's approval:

It was at least possible that the development of the hydrogen bomb would have the effect of reducing the risk of major war. At present some people thought that the greatest risk was that the United States might plunge the world into war, either through a misjudged intervention in Asia or in order to forestall an attack by Russia. Our best chance of preventing this was to maintain our influence with the United States Government; and they would certainly feel more respect for our views if we continued to play an effective part in building up the strength necessary to deter aggression than if we left it entirely to them to match and counter Russia's strength in thermo-nuclear weapons.[58]

Doubt was expressed about the possibility of keeping secret a decision to proceed. Thought would be needed about how best to justify a British H-Bomb to opinion at home and overseas. What seems to have been a Churchillian peroration on the requirements of a great power and a lofty dismissal of the moral counter-arguments clearly did the trick. Going thermo-nuclear seems to have as much an 'of course decision' as going atomic seven and a half years earlier:

It emerged from the discussion that there was general support in the Cabinet for the proposal that thermo-nuclear bombs should be manufactured in this country. Some Ministers asked, however, that there should be a further opportunity for reflection before a final decision was taken. Meanwhile, it was agreed that there should be no interruption of the preliminary planning which had already been put in hand.[58]

The Cabinet finally reached the moment of decision on the British H-bomb on 26 July 1954. The argument conducted at length on 8 July was briefly reprised. Then 'The Cabinet agreed that in order to preserve our position as a leading military Power and to maintain our influence in world affairs it was necessary that we should possess a stock of the most up-to-date thermo-nuclear weapons. This would enable us to play our part in deterring a potential aggressor from embarking on major war.'[59]

Ministers immediately began to consider 'the publicity aspects of this decision' and wondered how long the news that an H-bomb was to be developed could be kept secret. They need not have feared. In those relatively uninquisitive mid-fifties, the press rarely did its job of informing the electorate of the big decisions that were being taken secretly on its behalf. The news did not leak. The Government was able to announce the building of the hydrogen bomb at a moment of its own choosing, with the annual Defence White Paper on 17 February 1955, more than six months after the decision had been taken.[60] Churchill may not have come clean with Parliament or the public on the true cost of the British nuclear-weapons programme or the precise timing of decision-taking, but he did almost triple the number of ministers involved in the decision-making process by raising the issue from the hidden depths of the Cabinet-committee structure to full Cabinet itself – the only time this has happened in the forty-year history of Cabinets and the bomb.

For the Churchill Cabinet, the building of a hydrogen bomb with a Union Jack on it was an 'of course decision'. Conservative ministers were even less likely than Labour ministers to contemplate Tizard's contention that Britain was a great nation but no longer a great power. As Sir Frank Cooper, at that time private secretary to the Chief of the Air Staff, recalled more than thirty years later, 'We still thought of ourselves as world leaders in science, you know, which it is arguable that we were until the fifties, quite frankly. . . . I think an H-bomb was simply a manifestation of that.'[61]

In contrast to the relatively smooth passage of the H-bomb decision through the Cabinet Room, with caveats on costs, morality and the enormous leap in destructive force from the fission to the fusion weapon easily brushed aside, there was disquiet on the Labour side when the intention of manufacturing the thermo-nuclear weapon was imparted to the House of Commons in February 1955. Attlee, though, gave it his general endorsement.[62] If Labour had won the general election of April 1955, which followed Churchill's retirement and Eden's assumption of the premiership, there would have been no question of a new Attlee Cabinet abandoning the project.

The task of announcing the decision in the Commons fell to the Minister of Defence, Harold Macmillan, who had been Minister of Housing and Local Government when the issue reached Cabinet stage the previous summer. Macmillan succeeded Eden as Prime Minister in January 1957, shortly before the V-bomber force became fully operational and four months ahead of the successful Christmas Island test which made Britain the third power, after the United States and the Soviet Union, to acquire the hydrogen weapon.

Macmillan's six-and-a-half-year tenure in No. 10 was very much a nuclear premiership. He put a great deal of effort into it. And, with the near-disaster of Skybolt as a glaring exception, he was highly successful in draining the special relationship with Washington of every drop of nuclear advantage. His first achievement was the restoration of that special relationship on atomic matters that had been ruptured so severely by the McMahon Act. The position had eased slightly with the passage of a new US Atomic Energy Act in 1954 which permitted a limited exchange of information. But it was the explosion at Christmas Island which enabled President Eisenhower to propose an amendment to the 1954 measure which would allow a more intimate nuclear relationship with nations that had 'made substantial progress in the development of atomic weapons'.[63] In July 1958 Congress passed the necessary legislation. The special atomic relationship was restored. It was not an act of altruism on the Americans' part. Nor was it a belated recognition of the injustice of the McMahon Act twelve years earlier. As Professor Freedman has made clear, there was something substantial to be gained by the nuclear super-power:

The United States accepted . . . the virtues of a division of labour in an area where talents and resources remained scarce. Information on British techniques would provide a useful check on the adequacy of its own, and on occasion might allow for important innovations. British nuclear materials might also be used to make up for shortfalls in American supplies. In return Britain would receive details on all components of a military nuclear capability, including delivery vehicles, as well as nuclear submarine fuels.[64]

The all-encompassing nature of the Macmillan–Eisenhower deal proved a godsend when the Skybolt missile, the delivery system on which the British Government was relying to keep the V-force effective into the 1970s, was suddenly cancelled by the US Government on 7 November 1962 (the British Government was informed privately the next day). Skybolt was a stand-off rocket which could be fired from a bomber a considerable distance from its eventual target. Rapid strides in Russian air defence were making the big British bombers – the Valiant, the Victor and the Vulcan – increasingly vulnerable as they neared Soviet territory. Skybolt, an American system with a British hydrogen bomb in its nose-cone, was to be the solution.

The decision-making process used by the Macmillan Cabinet in plumping for the Skybolt option remains unknown. Some details of the Whitehall machinery used to resolve the crisis precipitated by the Skybolt cancellation can be pieced together, however. The chief ministerial forum was the new Defence and Oversea Policy Committee of the Cabinet (DOPC), created as part of the current review of defence organization. Its existence was eventually announced in June 1963.[65] As a result of the cancellation of Skybolt in the first week of November 1962, the Cabinet Office's working-group of officials on nuclear weapons prepared a paper for the DOPC, which in early December met to consider it under Macmillan's chairmanship.[66]

The key to a possible solution was the United States Polaris missile, the first under-water deterrent, which was designed to be fired from undetectable submarines. In 1962 Polaris was the state of the art. There was an assumption in Whitehall's tight and tiny nuclear-weapons community that Polaris would replace Skybolt in due course. The question for the DOPC in December 1962 was, could a swift leap to the next generation of weapons be achieved? The problem was twofold: would the Royal Navy be prepared to take over the deterrent role from the Royal Air Force as the hydrogen weapon descended from bomber to submarine; and would the Kennedy Administration let Macmillan have Polaris now that Skybolt was no longer on offer, and provide the know-how needed to build the nuclear submarines to carry it? The 1958 agreement allowed for both. But it was an enabling-measure. It created a possibility – it did not guarantee delivery. Only the American President could do that.

On 11 December the US Government announced publicly that Skybolt had been cancelled. On 18 December Macmillan flew to Nassau to meet Kennedy. The DOPC had reached the conclusion that the answer must be Polaris. The possibility of the United Kingdom ceasing to be a nuclear power did not arise. The decision was, according to an insider, 'the maintenance of a continuous policy', stretching back through Churchill to Attlee.[67]

The problem for Polaris was dissent not in London (the Royal Navy was agreeable) but in Washington. A strong political strain in the Kennedy Administration which held that independent nuclear systems made a dangerous world more dangerous than it need be. Macmillan's ploy was to offer the V-force and, if he got it, Polaris as a component of NATO's strategic nuclear strike force, except in cases 'where Her Majesty's Government may decide that supreme national interests are at stake'.[68] It was not an easy negotiation, as Macmillan recorded in his diary entry for 23 December 1962 (the day he returned to London): 'The discussions were protracted and fiercely contested. They turned almost entirely on "independence" in national need. I had to pull out all the stops – adjourn, reconsider; refuse one draft and demand another etc., etc. Whether Parliament and the country will think we have done well or badly I cannot tell yet.'[69]

The panic after the Skybolt cancellation had involved mainly the DOPC and the Cabinet Office working-group. But Macmillan was careful to consult the Cabinet before concluding a deal with Kennedy on the spot in Nassau. The discussion had started on Tuesday 18 December. Early on the morning of Thursday the 20th, before what was clearly going to be a difficult session with the Americans on the assignment of the British nuclear force to NATO in normal times, Macmillan informed his press secretary, Harold Evans, 'that he contemplated submitting to the Cabinet overnight any formula that might be reached during the day'.[70] In so doing, Macmillan described to Evans the world-view which made the continuation of the British bomb as much an 'of course decision' for him as the initiation of the A- and H-bomb projects had been for Attlee and Churchill:

He thought we should make it clear [to the press] that switching from one weapons system to another was not like switching from one club to another, or going into a shop to buy a new shirt. As to why we attached so much importance to having an independent deterrent, it was not a question of adding to the nuclear armoury against the Russians, but *because without it we would be in no position to take an independent line on all the other issues in which we became involved round the world*. [Emphasis added.][71]

Macmillan appears to have been punctilious about beaming reports across the Atlantic to his colleagues in the Cabinet Room. He would have had keen memories of the protracted whinge which greeted Churchill on his return from Washington in July 1954 after his personal attempt to thaw the Cold War. 'Throughout the Conference', wrote Macmillan, 'we sent full reports to our colleagues in London.'[72] The Cabinet, in fact, did not altogether like what had arrived overnight on the Thursday. Recalling the Friday morning in Nassau, Harold Evans wrote, 'I tackled the PM once again before the President arrived – but with the knowledge that the Cabinet had shown unhappiness and had proposed some rewording, and also that the Chief Whip had sent a message of foreboding, suggesting that it would be better to have further consultations in London before clinching a deal.'[73]

In the end, Macmillan carried everyone – President Kennedy the Chief Whip and the Cabinet ('Their amendments were all embodied in the final texts'[74]). On 3 January 1963, the Cabinet took the final decision to build a second-generation deterrent around Polaris. Macmillan noted in his diary, 'We met again at 5pm for two hours, to discuss the Nassau agreement. After a very full and very good discussion, the Cabinet approved what we did.'[75] The submarines and warheads would be British; the missiles American. The V-force was the first and last truly home-made British deterrent, a fact of some importance when the Labour Party chose to make the independence of Polaris a major issue in their 1964 election campaign.

Away from the public exchanges between the politicians on the Nassau Agreement, a network of committees was established in the secret nuclear world to make Polaris happen. Four were crucial to the project: one ministerial, three official. Policy decisions went to the DOPC. Feeding it were the Polaris Interdepartmental Steering Committee, the Polaris Policy Committee and the Polaris Operational Planning Steering Committee.[76] In organizational terms, Polaris was an exemplary project. As Professor Freedman noted, 'the whole programme cost 13 per cent less than anticipated . . . as well as arriving on schedule, a most unusual phenomenon'.[77] The efficiency factor was to prove an important factor in saving the project when Labour returned to power in October 1964 on the defeat of Sir Alec Douglas-Home, a convinced deterrent man.

As Leader of the Opposition, Harold Wilson lost few opportunities to decry Polaris, using phrases similar to the put-down enshrined in the Labour Party's election manifesto: 'it will not be independent and it will not be British and it will not deter'.[78] The manifesto pledged a Labour government to 'the renegotiation of the Nassau Agreement', which would 'add nothing to the deterrent strength of the western alliance'. It would mean 'utter dependence on the United States' for the supply of Polaris missiles. The system, therefore, would not be an independent British deterrent.[79]

As manifesto pledges went, it was an unambiguous indication that Labour would stop the Polaris programme in its tracks. In his memoir of his first two administrations, Wilson manages to confine his *volte-face* on Polaris to a single paragraph:

In the first days of the new Government in October 1964, I had discussed with Patrick Gordon-Walker [Foreign Secretary] and Denis Healey [Defence

Secretary] the future of the Polaris project in the light of the information now available to us. It was clear that production of the submarines was well past the point of no return; there could be no question of cancelling them except at inordinate cost. We decided to go ahead with four of the projected five submarines and to ensure their deployment as a fully committed part of the NATO defence forces. There was to be no nuclear pretence or suggestion of a go-it-alone British nuclear war against the Soviet Union. This decision was endorsed by the Cabinet Defence Committee, and later by the Cabinet.[80]

For all its terseness, Wilson's Polaris paragraph is revealing. The effective political grouping on nuclear matters had been reduced to three ministers, half the number used by the Attlee Administration, and it did not even carry the status of a Cabinet committee. In fact, Wilson bounced the Cabinet on cost and the passing of the point of no return on the submarines. Denis Healey, according to Barbara Castle's diary, admitted as much three and a half years later, when the Cabinet were, yet again, discussing defence cuts in the aftermath of the devaluation of the pound. Her entry for 12 January 1968 states,

Denis admitted that it would have made economic sense to cancel Polaris when we came in, but argued that it wouldn't do so now. Ninety-five per cent of the cost was spent or committed. If we abandoned it, it wouldn't affect the spread of nuclear weapons. And to leave France now as the only nuclear power in Europe would be an 'act of stupendous irresponsibility'. I challenged his version of the facts. My recollection of the decision of 1964 (and no one challenged it) was that we had been told the cost of cancelling the four Polaris would be as great as keeping them on, so all we could do was abandon the fifth, which we readily did. Now we learned that the running costs would be £20 million a year – an economy worth making when we know we could not keep in the nuclear race without prodigious cost beyond our means.[81]

Lawrence Freedman corroborates the Healey–Castle view and, without naming him, rebuts Wilson's claim that the cost of cancellation in 1964 would have been 'inordinate':

It has been suggested that one good reason for not abandoning Polaris was the exorbitant cancellation costs written into the contracts. In fact the Treasury had been holding back on authorising new expenditure during 1964 until the election was over. By the time Labour come to power, £40 million had been spent and another £270 million had been committed on all aspects of the programme. The net cost of foreclosing would have been £35–40 million . . . this was not prohibitive.[82]

Crucial to the case Wilson and Healey put to the Cabinet for retaining Polaris was the efficiency of the programme and its relatively low cost. At their private pre-Cabinet discussion 'it soon became clear to Healey and Harold Wilson that the Polaris deal had been a good one',[83] the exact reverse of the Labour manifesto claim. A briefing for 'virtually the whole Cabinet'[84] was arranged for mid-November 1964.

Barbara Castle's recollection was accurate. Ministers were told the cost was not burdensome, the system would last a generation, that it would not become obsolete and that the programme would be completed on time and at cost. The manifesto claim that it would not deter was also turned on its head: 'To bring home the fact that, in spite of being small compared with super-powers' strategic force, the British Polaris Fleet would still be able to pack a punch, the Ministers were told that missiles from three of the submarines would be able to destroy 15 to 24 cities and up to 25 million of the Soviet population.'[85]

The saving of Polaris was a considerable if back-handed compliment to what Whitehall still regards as the exceedingly favourable terms wrested from Kennedy by Macmillan at Nassau. Polaris did not replace the V-force as the carrier of the British deterrent until the summer of 1969. As we have seen, the more unilateralist-minded ministers tried to reopen the question during the cuts round which followed devaluation in November 1967. Crossman's diary shows that Wilson either remained ambivalent about Polaris or was behaving at his most devious in the management of his left-wing Cabinet colleagues. Wilson and Roy Jenkins, his newly appointed Chancellor of the Exchequer, had impressed upon the Cabinet the need 'to slaughter some sacred cows in order to appease the bankers'.[86] Crossman saw an opening. 'My new bright idea', he recorded in his diary entry for 27 December 1967,

was that to make it fair we should add to the right-wing sacred cows the abandonment of the nuclear deterrent. Recently Harold has talked to me about this, though on the last occasion he said, 'That's not for this package'. On another occasion he remarked that this is the kind of campaign Tam ought to be prosecuting, demanding the abandonment not only of the next generation but of this generation of nuclear weapons. Several times he's mentioned the notion that the Americans buy Polaris back.[87]

'Tam' is Tam Dalyell, then Crossman's parliamentary private secretary, and a formidable exponent of backbench assaults on governments of all colours.

That episode is a vivid illustration of Wilson's technique for concealing the real world of nuclear policy-making from those ministers outside his atomic circle. In early summer 1967, his nuclear group had decided not to buy Poseidon, the multiple independently targeted warhead the United States developed to replace Polaris.[88] But on 10 October 1967, more than two months before Wilson was spinning his abandonment line to Crossman, Barbara Castle learned part of the true story of Wilson and the deterrent. Her source was Sir Solly Zuckerman, Chief Scientific Adviser to the Government and a veteran nuclear policy-maker very much on the inside track. Zuckerman invited Castle to lunch and, among other things, told her, 'there was one Cabinet committee not even mentioned in the official list – the one dealing with our nuclear policy. To his own knowledge a paper currently being circulated to this committee was advocating the direct opposite of the Party's policy and he was just off to discuss it with Harold.'[89] This was almost certainly a whiff of what become the Chevaline, or Polaris Improvement, Programme, designed to counter any anti-ballistic missile system the Russians might develop and to keep Polaris effective into the 1990s. Zuckerman was a consistent critic of Chevaline.[90] Once Wilson's secret nuclear group had decided against purchasing Poseidon, the Atomic Weapons Research Establishment at Aldermaston was instructed to investigate the possibility of a new British-designed warhead to improve Polaris's penetration power.[91]

Two decades later, Wilson was quite unrepentant about his practice of keeping nuclear policy away from full Cabinet. In an interview with him which was broadcast in the summer of 1985, I mentioned to Lord Wilson that Labour prime ministers seemed to keep nuclear-weapons decision-taking in very tiny groups of ministers and the following exchange took place:

HENNESSY   Is this wise? Isn't it counter-productive? Doesn't it produce conspiracy theories?
WILSON   It could be counter-productive. They might start to complain. On the other hand . . . the fear of leaks is of tremendous importance here

and the smaller the numbers the less chance of the leak. It also meant that a very small team of ministers – I don't think it was even recognized as an official committee of the Cabinet[92] – . . . could get on and make some progress, have the relevant civil servants, until we were ready to put it before Cabinet. And quite a lot we did put before Cabinet, if I remember rightly, more on the basis of oral explanation than circulating papers. You have to be very careful about circulating papers. There could be a mole somewhere. There are things like photostat machines these days.

HENNESSY   But it seems that you can't trust your Cabinet colleagues or your party on an issue like nuclear-weapons policy?

WILSON   It isn't a question of not trusting. It's a question of the more people you have, the more people can be got at, for example, by backbenchers, who then start to press them.[93] There's a danger they would say too much if they'd been told too much and there's a danger also that they would be, as it were, 'converted' by these very strong-minded, avid backbenchers. If you can imagine two of them who were MPs in the same city or something of that kind, it could be very difficult.[94]

Wilson went on to give a string of justifications for maintaining a British nuclear weapon, some of which are very different in kind from those advanced by Bevin, Churchill and Macmillan.

HENNESSY   You sound now, despite what you were saying in 1964, very proud that you kept the British nuclear deterrent going over your period.

WILSON   I never believed we had a really independent one. On the other hand, I didn't want to be in the position of having to subordinate ourselves to the Americans when they at a certain point would say, 'Oh, we're going to use it', something of that kind. And, in fact, I mean I doubt if anyone expected it ever to be used.

HENNESSY   But you went to enormous pains to keep it going over those years, didn't you? Not least, it cost a lot of money.

WILSON   Oh yes, it wasn't that we wanted to get into a nuclear club or anything of that kind. We wanted to learn a lot about them – about the nuclear thing and so on. We might need to restrain the Americans . . . if we learnt about new things that could happen [of a] devastating character . . . where we would feel, perhaps . . . dragged along by the Americans' coat-tails. Otherwise we could just have been regarded as their stooges. And it also helped us in our general negotiations with the Americans on quite other things not in the field of foreign affairs but in economic co-operation or something of that sort you see? In order that they could get us to agree to some of the things they wanted, we got them to agree to a few of the things we wanted, like money.[95]

For Wilson, it would appear, the bomb was a way of restraining the United States from adventurism in foreign affairs and a lever to prise dollars from the US Treasury to bail out the British economy. In this long list of benefits supposedly conferred by the possession of Polaris, deterring the Soviet Union and the Warsaw Pact countries does not seem to figure.

The Conservatives were returned to power in June 1970, exactly one year after Polaris began its continuous patrol and assumed the deterrent task from the V-force. The Heath Administration reopened the question of building a fifth Polaris submarine but decided against when presented with a likely capital cost of £90 million.[96] The possibility of purchasing Poseidon was also raised. One of the reasons for its rejection was a desire to maintain an unspoken consensus between the parties on the deterrent. If the Conservatives avoided moving to a 'mirved' system (i.e. in the appalling nuclear jargon, a force of multiple independently targeted re-entry vehicles) such as Poseidon, it would make it much easier for a future Labour government to keep the enterprise going.[97] At this point, nuclear theology and practical politics fused around the Chevaline system, which, with its clutch of warheads to be scattered but *not* independently targeted, would defeat the anti-ballistic missile screen around Moscow. In 1973 the Conservatives authorized Aldermaston to move Chevaline into its development stage.[98]

Edward Heath's machinery of government for matters nuclear remains unknown, though a great deal of the spadework was done by a group under Sir Hermann Bondi, Chief Scientific Adviser at the Ministry of Defence, commissioned in 1972 to review longer-term nuclear-weapons policy.[99] But, thanks to the electoral lottery, it fell to yet another tiny, super-secret group of Labour ministers to make the decision to put Chevaline into production.

Within weeks of regaining office in March 1974, Wilson summoned a group of five to decide. There was an air of urgency. The first British underground nuclear test for nine years was scheduled for the Nevada desert in May 1974. The Conservatives' self-restraint on forgoing Poseidon paid off. Wilson, Denis Healey (Chancellor of the Exchequer), James Callaghan (Foreign Secretary), Roy Mason (Defence Secretary) and Roy Jenkins (Home Secretary) gave the go-ahead. A sense of *déja vu* attaches to the Chevaline decision. It was almost an exact re-run of Wilson's management of the Cabinet over Polaris exactly ten years earlier. His group of five had approved Chevaline between the general elections of 1974. Labour's manifesto for the October election renounced 'any intention of moving towards a new generation of nuclear weapons'.[100] Announcing the Chevaline decision to the full Cabinet a month after winning a small working majority on the basis of that pledge (among others) required a bravura performance from the Prime Minister. Wilson was on his mettle, as Mrs Castle records in her entry for 20 November 1974:

The main rub came over nuclear policy, on which Harold was clearly expecting trouble. He needn't have worried: Mike [Foot]'s comments were to be so muted as to be almost token. Harold prepared the way carefully by saying that, though we would keep Polaris and carry out certain improvements at a cost of £24 millions, there would be no 'Poseidonization and no MIRV'. The nuclear element represented less than 2 per cent of the defence budget but it gave us a 'unique entrée to US thinking' and it was important for our diplomatic influence for us to remain a nuclear power. Germany, for instance, would not like it if France were the only nuclear power in Europe. And he stressed that the policy was in line with the Manifesto and that the decision on it in the Defence and Overseas Policy Committee of the Cabinet[101] had been unanimous.[102]

The decision did not go through without a token Cabinet debate. Callaghan backed Wilson playing the 'world influence' card. But there were dissenters:

Mike [Foot] came in almost hesitantly. He admitted Harold was trying to keep within the compromise of the Manifesto on this though we were committed to getting rid of the [American] nuclear bases [in Britain]. 'We shall proceed to negotiate this within the overall disarmament talks', Harold countered promptly. Mike then said that he remained of the view that we should rid ourselves of nuclear weapons, but recognised that he was in a minority and so would not press the matter. Peter [Shore] and Wedgie [Tony Benn] said nothing.[103]

Mrs Castle herself was not so restrained:

I was more emphatic than Mike. It was not only that I was a nuclear disarmer, I said, but I thought the decision was self-contradictory within the context of our own defence strategy. What we were saying was that we needed nuclear weapons in order to exercise influence, yet intended to let them diminish in credibility by refusing to keep them up to date. This exercise in defence futility was not cheap: £24 million a year over ten years meant £240 million. . . .

The debate then died away. Harold summed up cheerfully, saying that Cabinet, with a few of us expressing dissent, had endorsed the policy and he added unctuously that he was extremely grateful for the constructive spirit in which those who disagreed with the policy had put their views. He then took himself off, looking pleased with himself, as well he might. The fact is that the spirit of the Campaign for Nuclear Disarmament no longer walks the land.[104]

An even more uncanny echo from the 1960s occurred when Denis Healey argued retrospectively that cancelling Chevaline had been the best option. On Tyne Tees Television's programme *Face the Press* on 19 December 1982, Healey said he very much regretted that as Chancellor of the Exchequer he had not killed Chevaline, as it had been designed to penetrate a Russian anti-missile system which was not eventually deployed. 'I blame myself as Chancellor for not investigating the project more seriously during that period', he said.[105]

Chevaline left a scar on the Healey Treasury. For its cost, as John Nott, a future Conservative Defence Secretary, was to remark, had 'gone bananas'.[106] But Chevaline was not merely an example of the Treasury slipping up on its task as spending-watchdog. It represents a classic case of failure in the Cabinet system itself. For in November 1974 the Cabinet was not offered, nor did it ask for, the kind of detail needed to assess the requirement for such a huge enterprise or to make a judgement about the possibility of cost escalation.

In fact, in 1974–5 Chevaline went into metaphorical orbit in expenditure terms. Only seven years later did the story emerge after the Commons Public Accounts Committee, prodded by a campaign in *The Times*,[107] investigated the project. The 1972 project definition for Chevaline envisaged a five-year development programme to be followed by a production programme at a total estimated cost of £175 million measured at autumn 1972 prices. In its report of April 1982, the Public Accounts Committee took up the story:

However Chevaline proved more complex than expected and between 1972 and March 1976 the estimated costs increased to £595 million (£388 million at 1972 prices). In 1977 the estimate was again revised to £810 million (£494 million at 1972 prices). [The Ministry of Defence] told us that since 1977, apart from an increase to £35 million in the contingency allowance, there has been no further real increase in the project cost estimate which is now £1000 million (£530 million at 1972 prices).[108]

Chevaline was Wilson's last contribution to the sustenance of the British deterrent he had so derided as Leader of the Opposition in 1963–4. The mantle then fell on his successor, James Callaghan, who became Prime Minister in April 1976. Callaghan, as we have seen, was a convinced deterrent man, though as Chancellor of the Exchequer in 1964–5 he had floated the idea that the Polaris force might be cut down to three submarines.[109] Callaghan, like Wilson, had to contend with Labour's October 1974 manifesto pledge renouncing the intention of proceeding to a new generation of nuclear weapons. Yet he knew in the late seventies that, if Polaris was to be replaced in the 1990s, the time-frame for decision-taking was approaching, as it takes ten years to design and manufacture a modern strategic nuclear force, particularly if submarines are involved.

In January 1978, the Ministry of Defence and the Foreign and Commonwealth Office sought ministerial approval for the preparation of studies on possible successor systems to Polaris.[110] Callaghan decided to proceed despite the manifesto commitment. He kept the issue away from his DOPC, on which sat one or two disarmament-minded sticklers for the manifesto, most notably Michael Foot – by this time Lord President of the Council and the number-two figure in the Callaghan administration. Instead, Callaghan convened a group of four which did not even carry a number in the GEN series, so secret was its task. Callaghan's nuclear group had one less member than Wilson's 1974–6 team and one more than the trio which decided to keep Polaris in October 1964. One man sat in all three – Denis Healey, who carried on as Chancellor when Callaghan replaced Wilson. The others were Dr David Owen, Foreign Secretary, and Fred Mulley, Secretary of State for Defence. The labours of the committee of four spanned fifteen months.[111]

Once Callaghan had given the go-ahead to the Ministry of Defence and the Foreign Office in January 1978, two Whitehall working-parties were established to prepare material for the committee of four. The first was chaired by Sir Antony Duff, then a Foreign Office deputy secretary, now (1985) Director General of the Security Service, MI5. The Duff group examined the political and military implications of a third-generation British nuclear deterrent. The second group, chaired by Professor Sir Ronald Mason, Chief Scientific Adviser to the Ministry of Defence, drew up a list of possible delivery systems. The driving force on both groups was Michael Quinlan (now Sir Michael), then

Deputy Secretary (Policy and Programmes) at the Ministry of Defence, where he was known as the 'high priest of deterrence'.[112]

Callaghan's committee of four were presented with a document which came to be called the Duff–Mason Report. Callaghan and Owen were convinced of the need to proceed to a new generation of weapons. Healey was too, but as Chancellor he was worried about the cost. Mulley was agnostic. As Secretary of State for Defence, he was institutionally in favour; intellectually he was against.[113] By the time the Callaghan Government fell in March 1979, the committee of four had agreed to proceed to a third generation. They had also agreed that it should be submarine-borne. There was to be no new V-force.[114] Callaghan favoured the Trident system, the state-of-the-art technology under development in the United States as the successor to Poseidon.[115] Owen, strongly influenced by the thinking of Lord Zuckerman,[116] who still retained a room in the Cabinet Office eight years after his retirement as Chief Scientific Adviser to the Government and saw all the papers, pressed the case for the far cheaper 'minimum credible deterrent': cruise missiles to be launched from the torpedo tubes of the Royal Navy's existing 'hunter killer' submarines.[117] The Trident/cruise choice had not been resolved by the time of the 1979 general election.

As Callaghan prepared for the polls, the only visible sign of the secret life of his nuclear committee was the compromise wording which he managed to insert in the manifesto:

In 1974, we renounced any intention of moving towards the production of a new generation of nuclear weapons or a successor to the Polaris nuclear force; we reiterate our belief that this is the best course for Britain. But many great issues affecting our allies and the world are involved, and a new round of strategic arms limitation negotiations will soon begin. We think it is essential that there must be full and informed debate about these issues in the country before any decision is taken.[118]

It was an admirable expression of the case for open decision-taking on matters nuclear. But Callaghan had refrained from practising it in the Cabinet Room. The question of replacing Polaris was one of the most pressing issues facing the new prime minister in May 1979. She quickly established a Cabinet committee, MISC 7, with herself in the chair, to examine it.[119] Mrs Thatcher expanded the inner ring of nuclear ministers to five, one more than Callaghan's group. They were, in addition to herself, William Whitelaw, Home Secretary and Deputy Prime Minister; Lord Carrington, Foreign Secretary; Sir Geoffrey Howe, Chancellor of the Exchequer; and Francis Pym, Secretary of State for Defence.[120] It must have seemed very familiar to Carrington. As First Lord of the Admiralty from 1959 to 1963, he had been intimately involved in the initial decision-taking on Polaris.

The spirit of the Campaign for Nuclear Disarmament, as Mrs Castle put it, was once more walking the land as MISC 7 set to work. But, for the inner circle of Conservative ministers, the choice of Trident was an 'of course decision'. Mrs Thatcher was highly impressed with Michael Quinlan's advocacy,[121] and, such is the bias against specialism in Whitehall, rewarded him with the permanent secretaryship at the Department of Employment in 1982. The incoming Conservative Government would, under the Whitehall convention which preserves the sanctity of a previous administration's papers, have been told nothing about Callaghan's committee of four. What cannot have escaped Mrs Thatcher's attention, however, was the amount of detailed preparatory work which officials were swiftly able to place before MISC 7. Ministers would have received the Duff–Mason Report with a new top and tail to distinguish it from the original given to the committee of four.[122]

The full Cabinet was kept away from the Trident decision. Mrs Thatcher followed Attlee rather than Churchill. However, Cabinet ministers not on MISC 7 would have known of its existence after *The Times* disclosed it on 4 December 1979. Trident did not reach the agenda of the full Cabinet until the morning of 15 July 1980, a few hours before Pym announced in the House of Commons the Government's intention to purchase it. A sense of urgency had intruded into the proceedings. Rumours had reached Whitehall that Richard Birt, national security specialist of the *New York Times*, was about to break the story in the United States.[124] The Cabinet was invited to note the decision, not to debate it, though, by way of belated compensation, the full Cabinet was treated to an informal two-hour briefing in the Cabinet Office by Cabinet Office and Ministry of Defence officials and Sir Terence Lewin, Chief of the Defence Staff, before MISC 7 took the subsequent decision to buy the bigger, fatter D5 version of the Trident missile.[125]

Five days earlier, Mrs Thatcher had written to President Carter telling him that 'the United Kingdom government attaches great importance to the maintenance of a nuclear deterrent capability' and asking that the terms of the Polaris sales agreement be extended to cover the Trident C4 missile.[126] Carter agreed. In his reply he confirmed 'that the United States attaches significant importance to the nuclear capability of the United Kingdom and to co-operation between our two Governments in maintaining and modernizing that capability.[127] The difference between 'the great importance' mentioned in Mrs Thatcher's letter and the 'significant importance' in Carter's is intriguing. Within a year MISC 7 had decided to drop the option of a fifth submarine for the Trident force and to ask the United States for the D5. The request was granted, thus meeting 'the real point of the British deterrent', which, according to one insider privy to the Trident decision, 'is to lock the United States into Europe. So long as we have a weapon that is as good as the biggest bang they can make, the Americans cannot disengage themselves',[128] the idea being that Russian air defence cannot see whether a Union Jack or Old Glory is decorating the Trident travelling in their direction. Within eighteen months Chevaline, at last, was being fitted to the Polaris force (the story had blown open in January 1980, when Pym revealed the £1000 million price-tag in the Commons).

With Trident in the bag, it looked as though, in Bevin's words, the Union Jack would remain on a British bomb until the 2020s, nearly eighty years after GEN 163 reached its decision. But in 1985, with British politics in a highly fluid state, nothing could be taken for granted on the future of the deterrent.

Dr Owen, Leader of the Social Democratic Party, continued to press the option he had favoured on Callaghan's committee of four: 'of cruise missiles on hunter killer submarines' as 'a minimum deterrent at a lower cost' than Trident.[129] He had still to persuade his Liberal allies of the need to replace Polaris with anything. A joint Liberal–SDP policy statement was promised for 1986. Labour's official policy, drawn up by a joint working-party of its National Executive Committee and Parliamentary Party and endorsed by the 1984 conference by nearly five to one, was unambiguous about the fate of Polaris: 'The Polaris system is getting older. Labour is opposed to any successor nuclear weapon system. Unlike the Tories, Labour believes that Polaris should be phased out in successful international arms negotiations in the next few years. If this is not done, Labour will, on assuming office, decommission Polaris from service.'[130]

Labour's policy attracted contumely from Mrs Thatcher in her wind-up speech at the 1985 Conservative Party Conference: 'By the end of this century it is predicted that several more countries will have acquired nuclear weapons. Labour wants Britain to give them up. At the very time when any sensible person would be renewing his insurance cover, Labour want to cancel Britain's policy altogether.'[131]

The Whitehall defence and foreign policy community was unhappy about Labour's plans. In an unprecedented move, Sir Antony Acland, Head of the Diplomatic Service and Permanent Secretary to the Foreign and Commonwealth Office, admitted as much when interviewed by Simon Jenkins for the BBC Radio documentary series *With Respect, Ambassador*:

I think that if a government were to decide to take Britain out of Europe, that would be very unsettling and worrying for a large number of members of the Foreign and Commonwealth Office, and I think that for home civil servants as well. But there are other issues to which would cause them great anxiety: I think the withdrawal from NATO, *or going wholly unilateralist*, would also create great anxieties in the minds of quite a number of us. [Emphasis added.][132]

The withdrawal from NATO or the EEC is *not* part of the Kinnock programme. But unilateral nuclear disarmament *is*. I had a chance to ask him about the Acland point shortly after the 1985 party-conference season:

HENNESSY Let me ask you whether Whitehall would actually carry out your instructions on day one to bring Polaris home, because Sir Antony Acland, Permanent Secretary to the Foreign Office, said publicly it 'would create great anxiety' in Whitehall. Can you be so sure that you'll get the Chiefs of Staff and the permanent secretaries to collaborate?

KINNOCK On the day that senior civil servants and Chiefs of Staff in Britain do not follow the elective will of government, we will live in a very different kind of society. I think you do both the Chiefs of Staff and junior officers and senior civil servants and their juniors a disservice in believing that they are so prejudiced against the ideas of government – an elected government – as to try and frustrate its will especially in an important area of activity. So I don't think they would change the habit of a lifetime, which . . . is . . . admired throughout the world, for the purpose that you suggest.[133]

Veteran nuclear policy-makers in Whitehall think any British prime minister would pause before abandoning the deterrent, for fear of never being forgiven by history if Britain found herself exposed in a future international crisis.[134] They believe the lesson of 1940 – of standing alone, with the Wehrmacht in the French Channel ports – is deeply ingrained.[135]. It is impossible for British ministers to play the anti-American card, Bevin-style, in public. But the uncertainty about the United States as an ally and the memory of 1940 tend to march in step as the most powerful motivation for keeping in the deterrent business, as David Owen revealed on Granada Television's *Under Fire* in September 1985 under questioning from Jack Straw, Labour MP for Blackburn:

STRAW   Do you envisage no circumstances in which you would use Britain's independent deterrent if the Americans disagreed?

OWEN   I think the only circumstances in which you could ever contemplate that would be if the United States pulled out completely from the defence of Europe, and you were left in Europe defenceless with an isolationist America. . . . it would be a situation . . . where the Americans were on the other side of the Atlantic and the Soviets had attacked and had engulfed Germany and were threatening France. It would be a situation rather similar to early 1940. And in those situations, even then, you would hope that the possession of the deterrent would stop the Soviets from advancing.[136]

Neil Kinnock is of a younger generation than the veterans in Whitehall, less moved, perhaps, by the image of 1940. He has been a member of the Campaign for Nuclear Disarmament since student days at Cardiff University. His commitment to bringing Polaris home to port for the last time seems deep and unequivocal. Assume he reaches No. 10 with an absolute majority and commissions a Cabinet paper from his Defence Secretary on the practical implications of a nuclear-free defence policy. Assume too a nuclear armoury roughly at present levels, which are substantial when compared to the ten or so atomic bombs and the Lincoln bombers at the disposal of Churchill in 1953.

Table 3 presents an inventory of weapons systems currently deployed. The number of delivery systems, however, is not the same as the number of weapons capable of delivery. From the beginning, Whitehall has never disclosed the size of the British nuclear armoury. But there have been unconfirmed suggestions in the press that, as in the 1950s, it is in the mid-1980s smaller than the public might think. Duncan Campbell, quoting in the *New Statesman* 'a defence

Table 3   UK weapons systems capable of delivering nuclear warheads

System	Number deployed	Nationality of warhead
Polaris	4 submarines with 16 missiles each	UK
Tornado	9 squadrons	UK
Buccaneer	2 squadrons	UK
Lance missiles	1 regiment, British Army of the Rhine	US
155mm Howitzer and 8-inch Howitzer	5 regiments, British Army of the Rhine	US
Royal Navy helicopters	5 Sea King squadrons 13 Wasp flights 44 Lynx flights	UK nuclear depth bombs
Nimrod Maritime Patrol aircraft	4 squadrons	US nuclear depth bombs
Royal Navy Sea Harriers	2 squadrons	UK

This is a version of a table first published in *The Times* in May 1981, updated in October 1985 with the help of the Ministry of Defence. For the original, see Peter Hennessy, 'How Labour Might Disarm Britain', *The Times*, 15 May 1981.

specialist who has worked inside the nuclear programme during the 1980s', gave an estimate of the weapons stockpile:

> 80 RAF tactical 'lay-down' bombs, type WE177, believed to have a variable nuclear yield between about 5 kilotons and about 200 kilotons. . . .

> 25 RN [Royal Navy] nuclear depth bombs, a low yield variation of the RAF tactical bomb, for use against submarines.

> 40 Polaris–Chevaline missile warheads type A3TK, believed now to carry three separately targeted nuclear weapons.[137]

Given the Kinnock commission, officials at the Ministry of Defence would attach to their brief for the Secretary of State to take to the first meeting of the new Cabinet a note on the health and safety aspects of unscrambling the UK-manufactured warheads. If the safety rules were followed, the intricate task of dismantling each warhead would take Aldermaston and the Royal Ordnance Factory at nearby Burghfield between three and five years.[138] Given the British genius for slow, meticulous work, not to mention restrictive practices, the task could easily stretch to five years – which just happens to be the life of a Parliament.

British governments and the bomb:
benchmarks 1941–1985

1941 Maud Report demonstrates feasibility of an atomic bomb.

1943 Quebec Agreement guarantees Anglo-American atomic collaboration in war and peace.

1945 Labour Government elected. Attlee becomes Prime Minister. US Air Force drops atomic bombs on Hiroshima and Nagasaki.
Cabinet committee, GEN 75, authorizes construction of an atomic pile to produce plutonium.
Chiefs of Staff instructed to assess British requirement for atomic weapons.

1946 McMahon Act passed by US Congress undoes Quebec Agreement. Anglo-American collaboration ceases.
GEN 75 authorizes construction of gaseous diffusion plant.
Bevin says 'bloody Union Jack' must be on the bomb.
Air Ministry draws up plans for V-bombers.

1947 GEN 163 authorizes manufacture of a British atomic bomb.

1948 Decision announced in Parliament.

1949 Soviet Union successfully tests an atomic bomb.

1950 Klaus Fuchs convicted for passing atomic secrets to the Soviet Union.

1951 Conservative victory at the polls. Churchill replaces Attlee.

1952 United States explodes a hydrogen bomb.
British Atomic bomb tested successfully off the coast of Australia.

1953 Soviet Union explodes a hydrogen bomb.

1954 Churchill Cabinet authorizes manufacture of a British hydrogen bomb.

1955 Decision announced in Parliament. Eden becomes Prime Minister.

1956 Suez. Russians threaten to use rockets on London and Paris.

1957	Macmillan succeeds Eden. V-bomber force fully operational. British hydrogen bomb tested successfully. Campaign for Nuclear Disarmament founded.
1962	Skybolt cancelled. Nassau Agreement concluded. Britain to buy Polaris from the United States.
1963	Cabinet endorses Polaris purchase. Wilson elected Labour Leader and campaigns against Nassau Agreement. Home replaces Macmillan.
1964	Labour manifesto pledges renegotiation of Nassau. Independent deterrent a central plank of Home's election campaign. New Labour government decides to keep Polaris.
1967	Labour ministers decide not to buy Poseidon. Early Chevaline studies commissioned with a view to updating Polaris.
1970	Conservative election victory. Heath becomes Prime Minister.
1972	Ministers decide not to buy Poseidon. Development of Chevaline improvement to Polaris approved.
1974	Labour election victory. Wilson Prime Minister. Ministerial group authorizes production of Chevaline. Cabinet endorses decision.
1974–5	Chevaline costs escalate dramatically.
1976	Callaghan succeeds Wilson.
1978	Callaghan commissions committee of four to consider Polaris replacement in 1990s.
1979	Callaghan group decides to replace Polaris but new system undecided when Government falls. Thatcher elected and convenes Cabinet committee, MISC 7, to ponder Polaris replacement.
1980	Trident purchase agreed by MISC 7. Cabinet informed. Decision announced in Parliament.
1981	Chevaline operational.
1983	Deep confusion over Labour defence policy in general election. Callaghan supports keeping Polaris. Conservative majority of 144. Kinnock replaces Foot as Labour Leader.
1984	Labour Party Conference adopts a non-nuclear defence policy by almost five to one.

1985   Kinnock reaffirms intention of abandoning Polaris on day
        one of future Labour government.
        Thatcher says 'any sensible person would be renewing his
        insurance cover' on nuclear weapons.

5
The Quality of Cabinet Government

Conservative Cabinet Ministers grunt, and Labour Cabinet Ministers give us out of date lectures on economics. *Senior civil servant, early 1970s*[1]

People from outside have no concept how the Cabinet generally operates, still less what is the difference between this Cabinet, that Cabinet and the rest. *Lord Wilson, 1985*

The insider–outsider divide is an often-used component in the apparatus of British secrecy: 'I was there and you were not'; 'You can have no idea what it is like to be a prime minister/Cabinet minister/junior minister/ senior official until you have been one.' Cabinet government is too important a subject to be left to the memoirs and glosses of insiders. Yet there is some truth in their claims. There is a danger of outsiders – scholars in particular – writing about people and institutions as if they were closed societies in foreign countries. Peter Riddell, Political Editor of the *Finanical Times*, told a group of political scientists in December 1983 that they sometimes wrote about Parliament as if they were Kremlinologists who had never been near the place.[3]

The Palace of Westminster, unlike the Cabinet Room, is open to the public. Any account of contemporary Cabinet government, therefore, must lean fairly heavily on the written and oral testimony of insiders, a view which led to the commissioning of the series of conversations on BBC Radio 3 in the summer of 1985 under the title *The Quality of Cabinet Government*. Insider knowledge, however, does not necessarily produce a homogeneity of evidence or interpretation even on obvious questions such as 'What is Cabinet government?', as the following comments show:[4]

LORD WILSON   I don't think there is [a conception of classic Cabinet government]. There are classic prime ministers: one can go right back to . . . Peel, Gladstone, Disraeli and the rest, and the methods of Cabinet Government obviously change as between one prime minister and another, but also they change over a period of time, so I don't think you can really talk about a classic period. Some do out of pure nostalgia, of course.

LORD HOME   Cabinet government is designed to concentrate the attention of a small number of people, rather like the board of directors of a company, on the essential business to be done. And therefore the job of prime minister, I think, is to get the agenda clear, so that only the essential business is taken. . . . That's much easier to say than to do.

DAVID HOWELL   We're now talking about Cabinet as a body of running things but Cabinet isn't that at all. Cabinet is a clearing-house, an exchange market where different interdepartmental clashes are sorted out and where also, it always used to be the theory, although that's long since gone I think, . . . that clashes between the Treasury and a department – is it right to cut something or not? – were sorted out. I say that's gone because . . . on the whole the spirit of the '79 Government and, indeed, as far as I can make out of the '83 Government, has been, 'No, don't bother me with facts, the Treasury's figures are settled. Good afternoon.' So that part of the argument hasn't come very much to Cabinet, I suspect. Although certainly it occasionally comes and there were terrific rows. But the Cabinet is not a place where decisions can be formulated. It's bound to be a place where decisions that have been formulated by smaller groups, maybe of ministers, maybe of ministers and party people together, or maybe parliamentary groups outside and then put to ministers, or maybe the Prime Minister and her advisers quite separately, are then tested and validated and argued about. And, if the implication of these decisions is that there has got to be legislation, then obviously the Cabinet's got to look at it because the people managing the government's business in Parliament are in the Cabinet.

HENNESSY   It certainly seems to have been reduced, the Cabinet, to a rather dignified body which gives an element of propriety to decisions and strategies worked out by a whole variety of people, some of whom aren't even elected.

HOWELL   I think it's more than a dignified body. I think it's a genuine part of the mechanism. You do need a coming-together of the heads of the great Whitehall departments and the people representing the parliamentary problems of interests, the people having a say in the party interests. So this coming-together at a certain layer must take place. It's a mechanism. But all I'm saying is, it isn't the originator and the fount of strategies and ideas. It is too big for that.

For a perspective spanning several administrations of different political colour, the best witnesses, for comparative purposes, are the senior civil servants most closely involved with high policy-making. Sir Frank Cooper was close to events from Attlee's time until shortly before the end of the first Thatcher administration. His tenure saw a considerable growth in the complexity of government. He is a primary witness on the 'overload' problem:

COOPER   I think the whole idea of collective responsibility, in relation to twenty-odd people, has had diminished force, quite frankly, over the years, coupled with the fact to deal with the modern world . . . with the very, very complex problems that governments have to deal with, it's inevitable that they should move into a situation where four or five are gathered together.

HENNESSY   So collective Cabinet responsibility doesn't work in the sense you can't take decisions with twenty people. It has to go to smaller groups, thereby weakening the whole?

COOPER   I think that has happened, yes.

HENNESSY   When you came in, it's regarded by historians these days – the late 1940s – as very much the apogee of government by committee. Mr Attlee ran his system with considerable efficiency and, particularly on your waterfront, foreign and defence policy, it was the period of the great post-war rethink; how to deal with the Cold War, Marshall Plan, NATO, building of British atomic weapons, and so on. Were Attlee and Ernest Bevin quite as good as all that?

COOPER   I think they had an ideal canvas on which to work, in the sense that the world was still very orderly, it was very tidy, it was very well disciplined. People believed in government. They did what government wanted them to do and we got none of the phenomena, I think, that developed very largely in the sixties. So it's not a straight basis of comparison in any sense. But you've got to add to that the fact that in the post-war world there was a lot of energy that had been conserved during the war, a lot of ideas that had been conserved during the war and a lot of thoughts that people had had they wanted to put into practice and were keen to do so.

HENNESSY   But they were big decisions and we were absolutely broke as a country.

COOPER   We didn't know that. I mean, we still had this amazing illusion for at least a decade after the war, in fact I would guess until Suez, that we were very rich, we were enormously powerful, we were arrogant and, you know, we were living on the history of our country, quite frankly.

When I asked Sir Frank about the Cabinet's remit, as the highest decision-taking body in the land, to tackle problems on behalf of the citizenry, to make use of analysis and briefing and to face up to reality, it stimulated a lengthy exchange about the unsuitability of full Cabinet as a serious forum, the inevitable drift of business into committees, the penalties of an adversary system of politics, the roles of ministers and senior officials, and that great policy intractable, Northern Ireland:

COOPER   It's amazingly difficult to discuss anything serious in a group of twenty-two, twenty-three men and women. . . . If you get twenty-two, twenty-three people round you're not going to have a free argument, and particularly when most of them are in a bargaining situation one with another – who gets the biggest share of this or that particular cake. So I think we've inevitably been driven towards a much more Cabinet-committee orientated system. What I wonder is whether we have actually supported that trend, which seems to me inevitable, with the apparatus to ensure that it does know what it's doing. But the essence of the British political system, in my view, is that you had these twenty-two, twenty-three good men and women and true and they were supposed to take . . . views whether something was good bad or indifferent. They failed to cope, I think, significantly in the post-war years with things which are highly complex and not subject to that kind of process and they've been backed up by a political system which is wholly adversary in nature. We've got a very unhealthy and in my view largely obsolescent political system.

HENNESSY   So you would say that we see this problem of the quality of Cabinet government at its most acute form on the big technical decisions, whether it be nuclear reactors, the Tornado aircraft, the big complicated science decisions with lots of money involved? Is that where you think it really bust apart?

COOPER   I think it's one of the basic areas where it bust apart. I think the other area was the continuing lack of governments communicating with the electorate and for the electorate to actually believe that the government is a sensible government – not in a political sense, but that it's actually doing the right thing. And this applies just as much to rate systems as it does to big technical decisions.

HENNESSY   Why? It's meant to be their trade. Is it because we're hyper-secretive in this country?

COOPER   No, I think the basic cause is that they've got too much involved in the nitty-gritty that they all come to work too often; that they sit at their desks and they think they know a great deal about whether you should have an inner or outer orbital London road, and the great trick I think of government is actually to take a fairly detached judgement about that without trying to argue with the surveyors about whether it should go this way or that way. All that the government needs to say about the route of a road is to say, is it politically acceptable or is it not? But so often now you get politicians of all colours sitting down and saying, why don't we veer off a hundred yards to the left, or to the right, here and there? What they want to say is, OK, we can get that through Parliament, or I'm afraid that is a non-starter. But don't get involved in the nitty-gritty.

HENNESSY   That sounds to me like a recipe for government by permanent secretary. You clever chaps do the thinking and you get your PR men, who we loosely call Cabinet ministers, to carry the weight of the flak in public.

COOPER   No, I think the last people who understand this kind of question are permanent secretaries, and, indeed, I think that one of the duties of permanent secretaries is to help the secretary of state, or whoever it may be, to take a much broader general view of the issue. You are paying people who are expert in this field. You are paying professionals to tell you which way you should go. And they'll be wrong, quite wrong; there's no doubt about that in my view. But you shouldn't try to become the stickers-in of pins on everything.

HENNESSY   I don't buy this apolitical permanent-secretary line. You were once described to me as the most successful Secretary of State for Defence we'd had since the war and nobody ever elected you to anything.

COOPER   I don't know who you talked to.

HENNESSY   You're very political people, you top permanent secretaries.

COOPER   Oh yes, of course you are. In the sense that you work in a political environment which is totally different from being political people. Obviously you must, as any kind of senior government official, be very aware of the way the elected government of the day views things and how they want to do things. In that sense you work one hundred per cent of the time in a political environment. It's equally very irritating in a management sense, because many management decisions have been delayed by political unwillingness to authorize this or authorize that. But it's working in a political environment which is the essence of it, not being a political animal yourself. You could be politically highly sensitive. But I've never claimed, nor would I wish to claim, that I was a politician.

HENNESSY   Can I ask you about one particular disaster area which you came to know intimately in the seventies – Northern Ireland. It seems to me another example of where the Cabinet system cannot cope. Maybe it's because ministers don't like thinking about it, because it's a 'no-win' set-up really. Nobody can produce any solutions. There's no glory to be gained. Nobody wants to be Secretary of State for Northern Ireland. Now, you actually saw it in a particularly nasty period in the mid-seventies when the power-sharing attempt was set up by Mr Heath and when it fell apart under the Protestant worker's strike. Do you actually think that British Cabinet government as a system was really not the right way of setting about looking at Ulster? Was there a bias against even the most minimal rational attempt to do something there?

COOPER   Well, it's not clear that what was happening in the middle part of the early seventies was an attempt to translate British democracy into an Irish environment, if I may put it in that sense. What I think it was was basically British decency at work, and it very nearly succeeded. It's always easier to say this when you look back at it, but it was a genuine attempt and a decent attempt to try and say to people, 'Look, will you kindly run yourselves, organize yourselves in a way which is for the common good.' I think it was in some ways a slightly old-fashioned way of doing it, but it very nearly came off.

HENNESSY   Wasn't it difficult, though, when you were Permanent Secretary in the Northern Ireland Office to get the troubles in Northern Ireland the political priority at Cabinet level that they in fact deserved?

COOPER   No. I think certainly in the early part of what you euphemistically call 'the troubles', successive Cabinets paid a great deal of attention to Northern Ireland. But I think it then got into the 'too difficult' category. What happens in the British Cabinet system of government, is that people will try over a period of time to deal with a particular issue. Then it gets too difficult. You're not going to have a solution. So they put it, to use an old Irish phrase, 'on the long finger' – and they don't think it's going to be soluble. They don't think it's going to be popular in terms of the votes, that it's going to cause nothing but trouble. And that's what does happen to quite a number of problems within the Cabinet system of government.

Lord Home, whose ministerial experience spanned the period from the early fifties to the mid-seventies, believes the overload problem has become much worse since the Macmillan years: 'It wasn't so bad in the early sixties. Mind you, the economic situation was so much easier then, wasn't it?' But, as Prime Minister in 1963–4, he was sufficiently exercised by the problem of overload to prepare plans to remedy it were he re-elected: 'In 1964, if I'd had longer, I would have had a shot at really pruning legislation down to the ground. But every government has failed to limit this legislation. This is a weakness in our government systems. There's far too much on ministers' plates and on Parliament's plate.' If the Conservatives had returned to power in October 1964, Lord Home would have invited Enoch Powell to rejoin the Cabinet (Powell had refused to serve under Home in 1963) and would have had a go at reforming Whitehall[5] – which would have proved, no doubt, an exquisite spectator sport as one traditional British institution took on another.

Lord Home approved strongly of the initiatives taken by his successor as Leader of the Conservative Party, Edward Heath, to tackle the deeper structural problems of central government. David Howell was one of the team of backroom boys Heath deployed on the task in Opposition in the late sixties. As Heath was the first prime minister since Lloyd George to attempt a fundamental recasting of the Cabinet system, the motivation and preliminaries to his 1970 White Paper are worth exploring at greater length than in chapter 2 above.

HENNESSY   Mr Howell, as a backroom boy, you were intimately involved in the late 1960s in a substantial rethink by the Conservative Opposition about the way the system of government in Britain works. I was interested to know if you actually looked abroad as part of that enterprise – if you looked at any foreign examples from which we might learn?

HOWELL   Yes, we most certainly did. We spent a lot of time in the United States and in Canada. Canada because we found there the blend, as it were, of the parliamentary system we run, as opposed to the American congressional system, plus a great extensive application of American methods to the organization of their decision-making in central government.

HENNESSY   Did you, in fact, set up any particular team for the purpose? Did it have a title?

HOWELL   Yes, we did. There was an organization set up called the Public Sector Research Unit which had its separate finances raised from the Conservative Research Department and that enabled a team of us to travel very extensively. I mentioned the United States. It was not just the governments, state and federal, we visited but also the various 'think-tanks' like the Rand Corporation. We invested a considerable amount of time in these organizations and they become very very interested in what we were doing as well.

HENNESSY   It seems to imply two things, this exercise: one, that Mr Heath had a tremendous personal interest in reforming the machinery of government; and, secondly, that you took a view that perhaps part of our national decline had been due to shambles inside the machinery of government that there were flaws in the system in fact. Is that a fair assessment?

HOWELL   I think it is. There was a third matter . . . which was that there was Mr Ernie Marples[6] around and he was quite a gadfly. He was in many ways a genius. He was convinced that the whole system was wrong and that you couldn't actually do things through the existing Whitehall system, and he was really quite a thorn in Ted Heath's flesh and one of the problems was what to do with Ernie Marples, so he was put nominally in charge of the Public Sector Research Unit. I say nominally: he wasn't interested in detailed work; but I must confess he did have one or two real insights into the problem which inspired us all, so I wouldn't put him on the sidelines at all. So, that said, yes, we reached the conclusion that there were fundamental weaknesses in the way that decisions were reached, policy formulated and the management of public programmes was carried out. We thought there were fundamental weaknesses in the relationship with Parliament and the control of public spending. Remember we were also caught up in a stream of thought which was much more political – namely, that we had to get a grip on the eternal growth of public spending generally, both for reasons of economic policy and for reasons of Tory political philosophy. So all these things combined together to give our work a terrific political drive, a personal drive, as I've described, and, as it were, a technical and managerial drive; and yes, Ted Heath did then become very interested when we put these ideas to him.

HENNESSY   It seems to me that the 1970 White Paper was the only attempt since Lloyd George in 1916 to actually tackle head on the problems of central-government organization, the Cabinet above all, and there's been nothing like it since. It does seem to have been a one-off thing.

HOWELL   I think it was the planting of some seeds. I agree it was very radical. We were saying not merely what we wanted to do but asking ourselves and the machine how it was to be done and that was the single new radical question. We wanted that questioning spirit to go right through the entire Whitehall system. We also wanted it to go through the nationalized-industry and local-government systems as well. But in fact the Heath government never really got round to that. Weaknesses, I think, developed because those two vast areas that are now being tackled weren't tackled then. But we did plant seeds and the more I look back on that period the more I think those seeds may not have grown very rapidly after the first few months but they were there, and later on in the seventies and certainly after '79, when, as it were, a different can of water was sprinkled on the flower bed, those seeds began to grow.

HENNESSY   It must have been a bit depressing for you, though, having put so much work into it, when the system you helped design was progressively unravelled in the 1970s. Mr Heath himself was the first person who unravelled a bit of it when he set up a separate Department of Energy and broke up the Department of Trade and Industry in the fuel crisis of '73.

HOWELL   That didn't worry me so much because, in a sense, there was a new function or set of objectives and therefore logically one could make a case for a new body structured to meet the new objectives. That didn't worry me. No, the thing that unravelled it all was something quite different. It was that after 1972 the pressure for tight control of public spending was really off. Now the whole of our thrust on administrative reform and cost-cutting, which had its roots, as I described earlier, in the political belief that we needed less and better government and could cut public spending and therefore taxation – the whole of that thrust depended upon, as it were, the other blade of the scissors: namely, a pretty mean and tight approach to public spending. It was the mean and tight approach to the money combined with the administrative reform, two blades of the scissors, which were going to cut the paper. Now, after 1972, the word came through from No. 10 and senior ministers and even from the Treasury, incredibly, that retrenchment was no longer the order of the day. On the contrary, 'expansion' was the word, so those very able civil servants who'd risen to prominence in departments as analysts saying, 'Look boys, for years I've thought we were wasting money. We could cut this out or do it different', suddenly found they were in the pending tray, got a rather smaller office, pushed down the corridor, didn't get called into the permanent secretary so often. And the whole bit of Whitehall that had been geared to this terrific, thrusting reform rather got put on a back burner. I suppose in a way I could include myself, because I was sent off to the front line in Northern Ireland.

HENNESSY   Did you protest? Did you put it to your patron, Mr Heath, that all our good work may be in vain now we've had a philosophical U-turn on the nature of economic organization?

HOWELL   I don't think I put it in those terms. I certainly said things were going very slowly and I wanted there to be more commitment from the very top. And I think, in a way, the Prime Minister was sympathetic. But he felt that his colleagues and others were getting preoccupied with other things. There was inflation coming up. There were hideous predictions that unemployment might actually rise to a million – unthinkable thought. There was Northern Ireland crowding in. There were many issues and somehow all this great thrust didn't seem so immediate and interesting. For the longer term, of course, it was valuable, and, as I said earlier, I believe it has now, over a decade later, well over a decade later, begun to produce some very substantial results.

It is possible to overdo overload. Ministers are not always and everywhere ground into political mincemeat by the Whitehall machine, as Peter Shore points out using an example from his period as Secretary of State for the Environment (1976–9).

HENNESSY   Can I ask you about stress and strain on the Cabinet system from social policy? You were very involved with inner cities – the progressive collapse of inner cities. It was after your time we had the urban riots, but the problems were growing . . . and there was a White Paper in your time. . . . It seems to me that on the front – and also on the welfare-benefits front – it has also become horrendously complicated. Implementing the Beveridge Report was a snip compared to what you have to do these days. Is that a fair impression on the social-policy side?

SHORE   If I take the inner cities one, I would say 'No.' I was struck by how much government could do when you clearly defined a new policy for the inner cities. It was a great advantage having a major spending department at the centre of it – it was my own department then, the Department of the Environment – and to be able to move resources, both people, because command of people, of civil servants, is terrifically important in getting any policy off the ground initially, and also having a big budget which one could switch money into. The fastest growing budget, although it was quite a small one to begin with, was indeed for the inner cities, even during a period of stringency. And we were able to get this new legislation through and changes in industrial-location policy, a whole range of things which you could develop and develop quite quickly. I only made my inner-city speech calling for a new inner-city policy in late 1976. We had legislation on the statute book by '77.

HENNESSY   And you had a Cabinet committee in the interim.

SHORE   Absolutely. And, although there was some departmental resistance that had to be overcome, nevertheless they were pushed–pulled into line. So it shows . . . government can move – and can move fairly swiftly to deal with what is certainly a very difficult and wide-ranging problem. Half the problems of government, as you well understand, are on the frontiers of a department, rather than centrally within it, and that co-ordination of policy . . . covering the frontiers of different departments is of course one of the great difficulties in Cabinet government. . . .

HENNESSY   Talking to an experienced veteran like yourself about the life of a Cabinet minister, it does seem to be an exceedingly grim business in recent times. I don't know why people put up with such an appalling load. It grinds people down – those endless committees, those endless reviews, the problems ever more intractable. What are the compensations for being a Cabinet minister?

SHORE   Ah, remember again Dick Crossman's book of essays, *The Joy of Politics*.[7] There's the actual challenge of new things, of events. It's endlessly stimulating. There's no question about that. And there is a kind of flow of energy that all Cabinet ministers have to have in order to deal with the workload, which is truly enormous. But, secondly, and I hope this doesn't sound too pious, there is actually the feeling that with the command of government you can do some at least of the things that you feel ought to be done for the benefit of the country and your own people and to help to carry out the ideals in which you believe. I'll willingly accept that that must be the motivation in my political opponents as much as it is in Labour governments too.

One area where Shore and his Labour colleagues have tended to suffer much more than their opponents is the suspicion and downright hostility of the international money markets when Labour attempts to implement policies distasteful to the financial community. This hostility was very important in 1964–7 and 1976, and it will be so again if a Kinnock government is elected and attempts to implement its pledge to repatriate British capital invested abroad since 1979. Shore is a fascinating witness on this, as he was deeply involved in handling the consequences of the oil-price explosion in the mid-seventies.

HENNESSY   When Wilson comes back at Prime Minister in '74, you're made Secretary of State for Trade, you're an economic minister again, and it's a Cabinet this time of very seasoned individuals. But, if you read Mrs Castle's diary day by day, you get an impression of . . . individuals being swept away on the tides of currency crisis and post-OPEC inflation. Is that how you remember those years? It seems to be a running permanent crisis in Lord Wilson's last two years?

SHORE   Yes. I think that's reasonable to say that. But then the greatest crisis that hit the Western world had occurred on Boxing Day 1973 in Tehran, when the OPEC cartel quadrupled the price of oil, and the whole post-war world, in a sense, came to an end on that day. We were formed as a government, after a three-day week and a near general strike in Britain, three months later, with the sweeping tide of balance-of-payments crisis hitting us, with oil shortage all over the world. I sat as President of the Board of Trade[8] in the first year of my responsibilities, on a trade deficit of something of the order of £3500–4000 million. We'd never had a deficit in our history anything approaching that. A crisis would have been £500 million or at most £1000 million. But that was the effect, and it was simply four times the price of the same amount of oil which was lying behind it. And, of course, the exhaustion of borrowing-power and dollar and gold reserves in the face of this huge import bill – and remember we hadn't a drop of North Sea oil at that time – was simply enormous. We knew we were riding a crisis. Furthermore, we hadn't a majority in the first few months. So Mrs Castle's reflections, in a sense of the jitteriness of it all, of having to react very swiftly, is, I think, a correct reflection of the time.

In the second great economic crisis to hit Labour in the 1970s – the collapse of sterling and the visitation of the International Monetary Fund – Peter Shore was highly active in pursuing an alternative to the deflationary measures being pressed upon a reluctant Cabinet by the IMF team.

HENNESSY   You didn't get your alternative strategy, though, which the opponents of it always dub a 'siege economy' with its import controls and building up domestic British industry behind a tariff wall, temporarily at least. Why is it so difficult to turn the system of government round in a direction of an alternative strategy, something as fundamental as that?

It's the old ocean liner image isn't it? It's exceedingly difficult even if there's a group of you . . . as persuasive collectively as the late Tony Crosland, yourself and Mr Benn and one or two others, to actually do more than place it on the agenda temporarily. Why is it?

SHORE   Partly because of inherent difficulties, to be fair about that. Partly because of the problem of assembling machinery – import controls. They didn't exist; they would have to be created. We haven't done that since the war and immediate post-war years. Partly also because, . . . to some extent, of an unsolved problem with the vast importance of financial flows. You can control physical goods and to some extent you control services in terms of your trade transactions to the rest of the world. It's much more difficult to control money. I'm not just thinking of British money, but overseas money which is deposited here or is being used here to finance international trade in one way or another. So there are genuine problems, and it's a high-risk strategy, no question about that. Nobody could argue, as I was certainly arguing, for an import-control strategy, or an import-restraint strategy at that time, who was not also aware that it was a high-risk strategy and there could be no more guarantee of success for that, or at least success in terms of avoiding unpleasant consequences, than there was involved in the orthodox strategy of going to the IMF.

HENNESSY   One could almost read into what you've been saying that a great deal of stress and strain is imposed on the British system of government in the 1970s and eighties because of external factors, the money markets and so on, which weren't there in the Labour government of the late forties, when the country was also very short of money, but you could run fairly successfully a command economy . . and you could get quite dramatic alternative strategies. Do you think that's a fair assessment: that in fact, ironically, as the country's grown relatively more prosperous it's become harder to run – both the economy and society – from the Cabinet Room?

SHORE   I think that is the case. Nobody should imagine, of course, it was easy to run Britain in the 1940s, either in war socialism or peace socialism. And remember, for a Labour government, the strong socialist commitment is always there, and that is an additional dimension of difficulty in dealing with non-socialist governments who dominate international finance and international trade. So there's always that problem. But it is true that a far larger proportion of our gross national product is now traded than was the case twenty or thirty years ago. Therefore the interplay between what's happening abroad and what is happening at home becomes much more important, much more enmeshed together . . . and therefore the reactions of others to what you do has to be a factor that you constantly have to bear in mind. Think how many multinational companies there are where previously a whole product, or a whole industry, would be based on Britain. You can see what the implications are for import controls. It is, therefore, more difficult in that sense to run the economy than it was before. What I think should have offset this is that we had this marvellous national historic opportunity from the late seventies onwards of being oil-independent and oil-rich in an energy-short world, and it is our failure to use that opportunity which I think has been the most serious disappointment of the last few years.

The performance of the Cabinet system under stress, financial and otherwise, has quite an important walk-on part in the Great Decline-of-Britain Debate. Sir Frank Cooper was blunt about that – and about the quality of the British political class which has peopled the Cabinet Room:

HENNESSY Do you think our system of Cabinet Government as it developed since 1945 has contributed at all to our national decline?

COOPER   I think the way in which it worked has contributed to that. I don't think the system itself is at the root of it. But there are two other things which strike me straightaway as having played a major part, and the first is the way that Parliament behaves, which is not very good, and the quality of people there, I think, has changed quite considerably. And the second element, of course, is that economically we've gone through nothing but vicissitudes for the last forty years.

I asked Sir Frank about one of the areas he knows best – spending on the Armed Forces:

HENNESSY   The general problem of defence expenditure never seems to have been grasped. We've had at least seven defence reviews since 1945 and each one of them was meant to be the review to end all reviews – at last our aspirations will be brought into line with our capability to pay for them. And I'm quite sure we'll have another one before too long. Why is it that British politicians seem incapable of grasping the nettle of defence expenditure?

COOPER   The reason to me is quite straightforward. The nature of economic predictions is that it's all going to get better in a few years' time, and, sadly, since the end of World War II it's consistently not got better and that's really the root cause of it. And, of course, politicians do not like pulling out of something, stopping something, because they're going to hurt somebody in the process, whoever it may be. So there's an inbuilt instinct to say 'Well, we'll carry on. We'll leave it to the last moment. Things may get better in a couple of years' time and if they do we'd be in a terrible position if we weren't ready to exploit them.' There's a whole chain of circumstances which have led to the kind of situation that you describe.

HENNESSY   How do you break that cycle of decline in terms of actually getting them to face up to reality and doing a proper damage-limitation exercise?

COOPER   Well, I don't think there is such a thing as a proper damage-limitation exercise. The only way you can actually break it is that we get into a situation where we become an economically strong country again. That's the only way it'll ever change.

HENNESSY   Do you accept anything of the school of thought which says that it's the huge burden of defence expenditure that has, in fact, prevented our taking-off in economic terms like our Western partners in the post-war period?

COOPER   No. The basic cause of many of the problems that we've had in Britain is that we actually were not destroyed in the war. We won it, and that gave us delusions of political grandeur and also weakened us, because we survived, we had old industries, they weren't all damaged or blasted out of the earth, and we went on too long finding it very difficult to know how we should change and how we should bring about change.

Earlier Sir Frank had criticized the procedure of Parliament and the quality of Westminster politicians. I invited him to elaborate:

HENNESSY   You mentioned earlier that the Parliamentary system and Parliamentary folk had vitiated the performance of Cabinet government since '45. Do you think we have a severe problem with the quality of our political class, the kind of people that the activists in constituency parties offer the electorate at election time?

COOPER   I think we've got in what I call a mid-way situation with elected members, in the sense that they are all now supposed to be activists in one way or another. They are all supposed to profess some expertise in some area or another, and yet, in my view, public confidence in them, with certain noble exceptions, has gone down consistently over the years. I think this has damaged our democracy quite considerably. We've tried, I suppose, to deal with it by having select committees in various areas. But, if you say to me quite straightly, am I impressed by the quality of our parliamentarians, the answer is, 'No, I am not impressed with them.' But I am even less impressed with the way that Parliament goes on and on, banging on, in a divisive political sense. Every time any politician whether it's on TV or the radio or in Parliament is asked a question, he doesn't actually look at the issues involved. He says the other party's wrong about this, or my party is absolutely right about this. I don't believe you can run anything in that kind of sense in the modern world. And just think what would happen in any British industrial company or any kind of other activity if you were always on two sides.

HENNESSY   When did the rot set in here, because presumably it wasn't like that when you were a bright-eyed bushy-tailed principal and assistant secretary?

COOPER   Well, I suspect it was. But one's got to remember that the issues have become so, so much more difficult. One mustn't be too beastly to politicians. They have to decide on a fresh-water reactor or gas reactor or whatever it may be. Should they put their money into the Airbus 300-and-something-or-other or should they not put their money? It's a terribly difficult decision for them to make. And one of the difficulties, of course, is that Parliament is still basically composed of people who are only interested in politics or have been in one of the non-numerate professions. All they do is to get up and argue against each other about things they know very, very little about. I think we do suffer very badly. We are a very old-fashioned democracy in many ways. We all say the Westminster model is marvellous. When you look around the world, it's not translated very well into other countries. They've all had to make adjustments which, it seems to me, they've used to leap forward in terms of time, whereas we're rather backwards in these areas.

HENNESSY   When you consider that our Cabinet is drawn from the 650 members of Parliament and one or two peers, what on earth can this country do to improve the human capital in the House of Commons, that pool of talent from which our highest strategic decision-making body is drawn?

COOPER   First of all pay them properly and secondly support them properly. It's quite ridiculous that you should be an MP and all you have is a secretary and so many free tickets for here, there and everywhere. If you look at the American system, or indeed many other countries' systems, they do actually provide their parliamentarians with the proper support organization. Ours haven't got that. I think this worries governments of the day in the sense that they do not really, in their heart of hearts, wish parliamentarians to have a proper support system. I think it would do us a great deal of good in this country if we did have a system where there was proper support.

HENNESSY   Would that actually solve the problem of the flow of partisan innumerates coming in served up by the activists?

COOPER   No. I think one of the most serious problems we're faced with in this country is, can we afford the luxury of what might be called a total adversary system? I don't believe we can. But I remember one former prime minister saying to me some years ago that the most difficult thing of all to reform in this country was Parliament. It's a great romantic illusion.

Innumeracy may be a besetting inadequacy of many politicians. Illiteracy is not such a problem. Indeed, for the guardians of Cabinet confidentiality, hyper-literacy can be the problem when the likes of Dick Crossman and Barbara Castle are around the Cabinet table. Lord Home firmly disapproves of the practice: 'I think it was pretty terrible. They went into the Cabinet and wrote their diaries in the full knowledge they were going to be published fairly soon. Very wrong. Almost unforgivable.'[9] Lord Home did not suffer from Cabinet diarists. As far as he knew, no one in his team kept one.[10] Lord Wilson, on the other hand suffered hugely. About Crossman he is scathing; about Castle, curiously indulgent:

HENNESSY   You had unique distinction as a British Prime Minister. Every hour of your premiership is covered by at least one diarist and often two – Richard Crossman and Barbara Castle. It seems to me they certainly stripped away the mystique and you can never write the standard political memoir of a very dignified progression of lofty discussion any more. It's a warts-and-all treatment of life in Cabinet. And you don't always come out of it terribly well and yet both Crossman and Castle were very close to you. Do you resent what they did?

WILSON   In the case of Dick Crossman, I was really amazed. It wasn't that I resented it. He didn't get a single fact right. Indeed, I was able to check it. I did know this that with his wife's help, and she was a very good influence on him really, he would sometimes leave the writing-up for two or three months and then he would reconstruct it as he would like to have thought of it. And it became very clear to me that he hadn't got a clue about how Cabinet government was run. He was very, very strange was Dick. Barbara was absolutely first class in my view and she's still very active.

HENNESSY   Her diaries are more accurate, you think?

WILSON   Her diary is more accurate, yes. I used to say, 'She's the best man in my Cabinet.' She was.

HENNESSY   You don't seem to resent at all that your good friend Mrs Barbara Castle got at you in this way, writing this diary and publishing it and driving a coach-and-horses through the normal conventions of Cabinet secrecy. You seem very forgiving.

WILSON   Most of these secrets got out within twenty-four hours. And do under any government. But, in her case, I thought she summarized the things extremely well and she also did it very quickly.

HENNESSY   It's very interesting hearing your relaxed attitude to the diarists in your Cabinet. But you took immense pains in 1975 to stop the first Cabinet diaries of Richard Crossman being published when you were Prime Minister again. Why was that?

WILSON   I wasn't very worried whether it was fifty, thirty, twenty-five [years] or what, but if it was going to be a question of twenty-five months or rather longer.

HENNESSY   In fact, you were the Prime Minister who liberalized the Public Records Act. You brought the rule down from a fifty-year rule down to a thirty-year rule with a specific statute.

WILSON   Having wanted twenty-five. But Ted didn't agree.

HENNESSY   Mr Heath didn't agree to that. What happened?

WILSON   He wanted fifty.[11] Then I said 'Well look, we obviously don't agree. I'm going to make this an election issue in the next election.' He then, not very happily, accepted thirty. But, as I say, the real facts are, these things leak in thirty minutes in practically any government.

Peter Shore sat along the Cabinet table from Crossman and Castle. How did he feel about their diary-keeping?

HENNESSY   You've been a prominent figure in the great diaries of the Labour years of the Sixties and Seventies. They were both great friends of yours, Dick Crossman and Barbara Castle, and you're in there in technicolor on some occasions. How do you feel about that? It's not that it was entirely favourable even though they were chums, is it? It's all there, warts and all.

SHORE   Yes. With Dick, of course, Dick Crossman's temperament largely dictated that and his moods. Dick very much reflected his own view. If you think about his diaries, he starts off in vol. I almost like a schoolboy looking at government, you know and oh, an enormous person . . . a great dame who was permanent secretary at the Ministry of Housing and Local Government.[12] And Dick is there looking at her with amazement and almost with dread. At the end of his volumes, after he'd had full experience of Cabinet government, he's a commanding figure running things at the Department of Health and Social Security, dealing with a whole range of social policies, no trouble, with civil servants doing as they were told. It's a great change that takes place there. Now Barbara Castle's diaries: I think her diaries are less reflective than Dick's. They are very much how she felt late at night, very much the world seen through those two burning blue eyes, and often very narrow in vision, although very intense in vision at the same time.

HENNESSY   It's huge institutionalized leaking actually, that business of publishing diaries. Do you resent it, that they were sitting there at the Cabinet table, and, in Mrs Castle's case, making shorthand notes because she's a good trained *Daily Mirror* reporter?

SHORE   Well, I should do, because I cannot intellectually and philosophically agree with it. I have to say that. But, in the case of Dick Crossman,

I always thought of him in terms of doing the job which I know he wanted to do. His original purpose in keeping a diary was to write a great new Bagehot on British government, and that was to be the raw material from which he drew. But things changed. His own life, of course, was measured, and he decided, I think, to publish the diaries, although he didn't complete them all, as you know, before his death. In the case of Mrs Castle, I haven't the same feeling that she had a commitment to a philosophy of government and a burning lifelong desire to describe, analyse, intellectualize about how the processes of government worked, and therefore I'm not so keen on what she has done.

6

The Reform Agenda

These days the only efficient part of the British Constitution is the monarchy. *Peregrine Worsthorne, 1984*[1]

Psychologists know that small children have a low tolerance of information; this increases in adolescence to a maximum of forty-five minutes, which is why lectures last that span. It then decreases as people get older and more important until the tolerance of information of important people in industry and of Cabinet ministers reduces to that of a six year-old. They can take no more than five minutes or three sheets of A4. *Senior civil servant, 1985*[2]

They [Cabinet Ministers] failed to cope . . . in the post-war years with things which are highly complex. . . . They have been backed up by a political system which is wholly adversary in nature. . . . We have got a very unhealthy and . . . largely obsolescent political system. *Sir Frank Cooper, 1985*[3]

I find it very odd what goes to Cabinet and what does not. *Professor Margaret Gowing, 1985*[4]

The one thing that really throws a Cabinet is a new idea. *Deputy Secretary, 1984*[5]

Cabinet government is a talisman, a symbol of proper procedure, a guarantor of continuity. Such properties contribute to its robustness. This was very evident when Sir Michael Havers, Mrs Thatcher's Attorney General, spelled out what would have happened if the Prime Minister and her senior Cabinet ministers had been killed by the IRA bomb in Brighton in October, 1984. 'He scribbled down his imagined plan of action with a red felt-tip pen' for the benefit of the readers of *The Sunday Times*:[6]

The scenario was based on the assumption that the eleven Cabinet Ministers known to have been at the Grand Hotel had died. . . . 'I am trying to be as realistic as possible', he said. 'I have assumed that by 3 am on the morning of Friday, October 12 we would have lost all the senior people in the Grand.

The Secretary of the Cabinet, Sir Robert Armstrong, would have been called at his home and he would have ordered Downing Street to contact all surviving ministers. He would have alerted, too, all the permanent secretaries.

On Friday morning, said Havers, the remnants of the Thatcher Cabinet would have gathered under tight security possibly in the offices of the Privy Council in Whitehall. 'I think everyone would be reluctant to use No. 10 on that morning. It would not seem right', said Havers.

By that evening a new prime minister would have kissed hands at Buckingham Palace. Sir Michael explained, 'The essential point is that we would, somehow, have had a new prime minister within hours, . . . if we assume the worst – that the entire Cabinet had died – then it might have taken a little longer to choose a temporary prime minister.'[7]

There are great benefits and virtues in constitutional continuity and in possessing institutions which mix symbolic properties with practical functions. In this sense the Cabinet qualifies as much as the monarchy. But, unlike the monarchy, its personnel must do much more than raise the tone on public occasions, launch ships and top out new buildings. 56 million of us depend on them to disburse £140,000 million of our money, to maintain the essentials of life and steadily to improve our lot and the condition of our society as a whole. Most of their important functions cannot be privatized or put out to international tender. The buck stops with the Downing Street twenty-two. And here a substantial problem has arisen. As Anthony King noted in his disquisition on overload, 'we yield enormous powers to government in theory even while denying them in practice'.[8] This remains true, despite Mrs Thatcher's partially successful attempts to damp down public expectations in the decade since Professor King reached that judgement. Indeed, the damage done to the confidence of the governed in their governors in the thirty years between 1945 and 1975, when King was writing, was substantial.

Paul Addison could justly write of the immediate post-war period that 'with hindsight the most striking aspect of it all was the governability of the British people'[9] despite rationing, controls and austerity. With equal justification Anthony King could write in the year of the Social Contract and hyper-inflation that 'one does not have to be a doom-monger to sense that something is wrong with our policy as well as our economy'.[10] Unbeknown to King, Tony Crosland was reaching a similar conclusion at that Chequers session with the CPRS in November 1974 when he told his Cabinet colleagues, 'All we can do is to press every button we've got. We do not know which, if any, of them will have the desired results'[11] – a pronouncement from this most capable and cultivated figure which could almost serve as the epitaph of modern Cabinet government.

A few years after Crosland's gloomy musing at Chequers and Professor King's placing of his depressing but accurate thoughts in the pages of *Political Studies*, his colleague at Essex University, the biochemist Professor John Ashworth, was 'parachuted' (his word) into the Cabinet Office as Chief Scientist in the CPRS, a body he would jovially liken to 'the casualty clearing station of the Luton and Dunstable Hospital when there has been an accident on the M1'.[12] Having a scientific background and no previous experience of government, he was shocked by what he found, as he later revealed in a lecture to the Royal Signals Institution:

Advances in technology have transformed societies within the last generation . . . but no such breakthroughs seem to me to have occurred in the
capacities of government. The telephone and the telex, those ubiquitous
instruments of modern government, are cursed as often as they are blessed
by our rulers. Thus a moment's comparison of the rather slight improvements
in the capacity to govern with the radical changes in expectation on the part
of the governed suggests that innovations are desperately needed.[13]

In fact, a fairly hefty reform agenda for the innards of Cabinet governments can be picked up by taking a vacuum cleaner to the abandoned scripts of experienced figures who have taken to the lecture halls in recent years. If you start with Lord Rothschild's Israel Sieff Memorial Lecture in 1976, you have a good decade's worth. Let's start first with the 'parachutists',[14] as Professor Ashworth, borrowing a phrase the Japanese use, calls outsiders turned temporary insiders. Several have come clean on the system once free of Whitehall. And virtually everyone has corroborated the King thesis on overload. They all pump for reform, naturally, but the point of attack varies on the conveyor belt of overload, on which sit a number of crates each containing a serious problem of its own.

The conveyor-belt starts moving in Parliament. Into the first box must go the pool of talent put there by the electorate and the way it is channelled by parliamentary procedure. In the opposition stage, what traits shown by an MP draw him to the attention of the party managers in the Whips Office and the Shadow Cabinet? How rich is the quality of policy-making in Opposition, a good deal of which will be implemented in a rush during the first six months of government?

By the time the conveyor belt has carried a politician into office, a container-load of tasks befall him: constituency duties;[15] liaison with backbenchers and the party in the country; the maintenance and improvement of his status within the party is a constant preocupation as is the burnishing of his personal image with press and public; there are the time-consuming demands of Parliamentary conventions and the peculiar and energy-sapping hours the House of Commons keeps; he must run his department as policy-maker-in-chief and, since Lord Rayner's managerial reforms, as chief executive, too; demands from overseas – NATO, EEC, foreign visits have increased substantially in recent years; how much creative energy is left for his most important function of all (in terms of the public good) as a participant at Cabinet and Cabinet committee?

Add to this terrifying list wife, family, friends, social life, pastimes to take your mind off it all, and you have a bill of goods that only a superman or a superwoman could deliver – someone with the brains of an Asquith, the drive of a Lloyd George, the heart of Churchill, the administrative temperament of an Attlee, the rhetorical gifts of Bevan and the ruthlessness of a Bevin. They don't come like that in politics or in any other walk of life. Even if they did, there is no guarantee that they would find themselves in the Cabinet given what Douglas Hurd has called the 'amazingly haphazard' way top ministerial posts are filled.[16] The job description, when packaged into parcels, is a conveyor belt to exhaustion and under-achievement all round, a predicament reflected in the final parcel which rolls off the belt – the end product, the finished policy, which is all too often defective and immensely difficult to implement. Let us look at some of the parcels our outside critics have unwrapped in the last decade.

Lord Rothschild, in his lecture 'The Best Laid Plans . . .' (1976), alluded to 'the promises and panaceas which gleam like false teeth in party manifestos'[17] and went on to say,

Something really should be done about this problem of the party's first few months in office, which are without doubt the worst. This prolonged festival, a mixture of the madness of Mardi Gras and Auto da Fé, celebrated by burning anything of a political character which is regarded as inimical, can be a great nuisance, to put it at its mildest, Governments can do dreadful things in their first heady months of office. I wish there could be a law against a new Government doing anything during its first three or so months of existence. Apart from their constituency and parliamentary duties and, of course, their ritual appearances at hospitals, new power stations, Strasbourg and the like, new ministers even if they have been in office before, should read documents, listen to expert opinion, ask questions and refrain, unless absolutely essential, from taking a positive or negative action, activities which, at the beginning of a new term of office, almost invariably create new problems. There should be a period of purging and purification, a kind of political Ramadan.[18]

Dr Tessa Blackstone, when she delivered her lecture 'Ministers, Advisers and Civil Servants',[19] had recently completed three years in the CPRS. She examined the reasons why senior ministers in Britain 'frequently work a twelve- to fourteen-hour day, six days a week', and itemized a very similar list of tasks to those parcelled on our conveyor belt of overload. She singled out Cabinet membership as 'probably the aspect of their job which they do least well, partly because of its intrinsic difficulty and partly because of the inadequate time they have to give to it'. To make matters worse, 'it is the part of their role which it is most difficult for others to take over or partly take over'. She called two political witnesses from her own specialist field, education. First, Lord Boyle of Handsworth, Minister of Education 1962–4:

any Minister who tried to get real interest in something that didn't involve a decision on expenditure, was a long-term issue but not one on the accepted agenda, at any given moment, would be more likely to meet bored acquiescence from his colleagues, rather than active agreement.[20]

. . . how often we would get on to something quite important at ten to one and would settle that by one o'clock. One or two decisions did come up which we settled in Cabinet in ten minutes, and I think somebody ought to have said 'Look, this really is rather important, and, whoever's right or wrong about this, I think we ought to give careful thought to it before reaching a conclusion.[21]

Second, Anthony Crosland, Secretary of State for Education 1965–7: 'There isn't much correlation between how important an issue is and how much time is spent on this in Cabinet. . . . The issues that take up Cabinet time are those which are controversial within the government . . . it's not their intrinsic importance, but their political context, that puts them on the Cabinet agenda.'[22]

Sir John's Hoskyns's strictures, the most trenchantly phrased material picked up by our lecture-room vacuum cleaner, were contained in two separate lectures but are best taken together, as the first ('Westminster and Whitehall: An Outsider's View', 1982[23]) was an attack on our administrative class, the second ('Conservatism is not Enough', 1983[24]) an assault on our political class. The overall theme was 'Why do governments fail?' The first Hoskyns lecture, its author fresh from three years in the Downing Street Policy Unit, set the scene depicting the shortcomings of policy-making in hard times:

Despite the oil shock of 1973 and the sterling crisis of 1976, many in government in 1979 did not seem to fully understand that we were entering uncharted waters; that we were fast approaching the point at which our problems would no longer be soluble by normal processes; or else they recognised it, but concluded that nothing could be done. . . . Instead of setting objectives for what were judged to be unattainable results, politicians and officials favoured the traditional approach: to be judged by measures taken, rather than results achieved.

Sir John has a gift for epigrammatic one-liners such as 'Politicians, even more than the rest of us, don't know what they don't know'; and 'There are broadly two types of minister: the "doer", who wants to achieve something; and the "survivor", who want to be something. . . . At a time of discontinuity the country cannot survive being ruled by survivors.' He painted a picture of overworked ministers using up their intelligence largely on self-defence, carried through each hectic day by the ritual and precedent of office, surrounded by deferential officials inducing in them feelings of infallibility which ran directly counter to reality. He concluded his first blast, delivered at the Savoy Hotel, with the contention that 'the present system of career politicians and career officials is a failed system. I don't think it is possible to look at our postwar national decline and argue that it happened in spite of high-quality policy-making.'

Sir John returned to the attack almost a year later in the Café Royal. His sacred text on this particular night was a magnificent quote from Lord Radcliffe, jurist, administrator and luminary of the post-war 'Good and Great': 'The British have formed the habit of praising their institutions, which are sometimes inept, and of ignoring the character of their race, which is often superb. In the end they will be in danger of losing their character and being left with their institutions: a result disastrous indeed.'[25] Sir John reprised his theme on the indispensability of organizational change at the heart of government: 'government is a creature without a brain. . . . Westminster and Whitehall cannot change Britain if they will not change themselves . . . there is no policy on policy-making.'

This time he was particularly cruel on the motivation of ministers (particularly Tory ones): 'They see Britain as a canvas on which a young MP . . . can paint his political self-portrait; making his way in the world until he holds one of the great offices of state, finally retiring full of honour and respectability. . . . One can still read in quite recent books of memoirs phrases like, "Charles had always wanted the Foreign Office", as though it were a 21st birthday present.' Once in office, these political romantics have, according to Sir John,

like hamsters in a treadmill, gone round and round in a strategic box too small to contain any solutions . . . ministerial and official committees all too often degenerate, into the goal-free trading of departmental views often stockpiled from previous years. . . . The crippling workload will frequently impair health and marriage, for the minister must do it all – Cabinet and its committees, the department, public appearances, attendance in the House – on top of his existing work as a constituency MP.

For Sir John, the House of Commons 'is the greatest closed shop of all. . . . For the purposes of government, a country of 55 million people is forced to depend on an overworked talent pool which could not sustain a single multinational company.'

Professor John Ashworth, in his lecture 'On the Giving and Receiving of Advice (in Whitehall and Salford)' (1982),[26] was amazed how little academic research had been conducted into the subject of advice to rulers (as compared to, say, top executives in business). Taking an approach somewhat akin to that of a women's magazine, he noted that rulers were busy people with a range of intellectual and emotional needs:

The temptation to look to wives, lovers, husbands, chauffeurs, hairdressers, old school chums and especially family relatives for advice and support in fields other than the emotional/personal is ever present and more often disastrous. The temptation for a 'ruler' to trust his intuition or instinctive 'gut' feelings is always strong because of the uncertainty inherent in the data on which he or she has to base his or her judgements.

In his second foray into the subject (his 1983 lecture 'Giving Advice to Governments'[27]), Professor Ashworth endorsed the Hoskyns emphasis on the need for a much greater capability in central government for strategic thinking and long-term planning.

Blackstone, Hoskyns and Ashworth are worth taking together because they are, in varying degrees, political people: Blackstone belongs to the Labour Party, Hoskyns to the Conservative Party, and Ashworth to the Alliance. Rothschild, though described as a Labour peer when he took over the CPRS, is rather difficult to place politically in the 1980s. Before turning to the menu of remedies the 'parachutists' offered on the basis of their diagnosis – which, in Sir John's phrase, amounted to a 'management revolution in policy work',[28] a kind of Rayner on strategy – it is necessary to assemble the lecture hall offerings of more orthodox bureaucrats. In the eighties, retired permanent secretaries trod the boards as never before, bearing dignified witness to Professor King's contention that Britain was a polity in trouble. The first to go public was Sir Kenneth Berrill, who was part 'parachutist' (he had spent the bulk of his career in the universities) but had, virtually throughout the seventies, served at permanent-secretary rank as Chairman of the University Grants Committee, Chief Economic Adviser to the Treasury and Director of the CPRS.

Sir Kenneth's theme in his 1980 lecture 'Strength at the Centre – the Case for a Prime Minister's Department'[29] was the quality of the advice to the Prime Minister, not its volume. As a firm centralist, he saw the centre of government as the troika of No. 10, the Treasury and (unusually) the Foreign Office. 'The troika is the centre and the centre has to hold.'

My thesis is a simple one. In today's world the support system for the Head of Government is a subject of increasing importance. Our competitors have, by and large, faced this issue and come to some structured solutions which have put rather more resources into the area than we have been prepared to do. We have preferred to keep a very small staff at No. 10 and rely on incremental changes in the Cabinet Office and on the flexibility of those who work there. . . . The advice is given, and very presentably too, but the depth is inevitably patchy.

Sir Kenneth may have been a bit of a Whitehall amphibian. But those who followed his trail bore the unmistakable stigmata of the Civil Service lifer. The most authoritative, *ex officio*, for the purposes of this study is Lord Hunt, the former Cabinet Secretary, who broke cover on election day 1983.

Lord Hunt, in his lecture 'Cabinet Strategy and Management',[30] took the Hoskyns–Ashworth theme of strategic capability and reached intriguingly similar conclusions:

Unless the Cabinet can provide a clear strategic oversight over the policies of getting on for 30 departments of state – let alone all the other bodies for which the government is directly or indirectly responsible – there is an inbuilt risk that decisions may be taken in an arbitrary, uncoordinated or even contradictory manner.

Cabinets are not well placed to exercise this role of continuing strategic oversight alongside the taking of specific decisions. Cabinet ministers are heavily preoccupied with their departmental work and find it difficult to make time to think about problems of other Ministers when those do not concern them directly: and . . . the more they get involved with their own work the harder it is for them to see the Cabinet strategy wood from the departmental policy trees.

After tracing the history of the Cabinet's load-bearing capability since 1916, praising the adaptability of the committee system as a work-absorber, particularly during the Attlee years, Hunt added,

Nevertheless doubts began to creep in. Governments were blown off course or simply lost their way without realising that this was happening. In the absence in our system of a Chief Executive with his own supporting staff, a 'hole in the centre' of Government was perceived which an over-worked Cabinet seemed incapable of filling.

It was widely felt that the decentralisation of so much Cabinet business to a whole lot of Cabinet committees made a coherent strategy much more difficult. It was suggested that the hard grind of a subject through the Cabinet committee system led not only to unnecessary delay but also to unsatisfactory compromises resulting from a tendency to accommodate every point of view. It was also argued that the Public Expenditure Survey did more to illustrate the inflexibility of public spending programmes than to provide ministers with clear alternative choices: and furthermore that the subsequent public expenditure arguments in Cabinet were settled by muscle rather than by relevance to the Government's strategy.

Hunt commented that 'none of these criticisms was fully justified: but in aggregate they led to a feeling in some ministers and former ministers – a feeling shared by some officials – that they were in danger of becoming prisoners of the system instead of its master'. And, after reviewing attempts to tackle these problems in the 1970s, Lord Hunt went on to make it plain that he was one of those officials sensitive to the dangers of overload: 'I have little doubt that there *is* a problem and that we have not entirely solved it yet.' When a former Cabinet Secretary comes out in this fashion, it is a very significant moment. It was almost as if the proponents of the overload thesis had received an official seal of approval. And, as if to reinforce that significance, Lord Hunt was joined later in 1983 by the BBC's Reith Lecturer, Sir Douglas Wass, in his contribution to what was becoming by the decorous standards of Britain's public-service establishment, a highly lively debate on the performance of the Cabinet system.

In his second Reith Lecture, 'Cabinet: Directorate or Directory?',[31] Sir Douglas clearly indicated that, for the purposes of formulating and implementing an overall strategy, the chemistry of the Cabinet was, in his view, all wrong:

The machinery which exists within departments to give ministers a perspective of all their activities, a set of suggested objectives and a ranking of priorities, is missing in the collective forum of the Cabinet. Ministers in Cabinet rarely look at the totality of their responsibilities, at the balance of policy, at the progress of the government towards its objectives as a whole. Apart from its ritual weekly review of foreign affairs and parliamentary business, Cabinet's staple diet consists of a selection of individually important one-off cases or of issues on which the ministers departmentally concerned are unable to agree.

The form and structure of a modern Cabinet and the diet it consumes almost oblige it to function like a group of individuals, and not as a unity. Indeed, for each minister, the test of his success in office lies in his ability to deliver his departmental goals. . . . No minister I know of has won political distinction by his performance in Cabinet or by his contribution to collective decision-taking. To the country and the House of Commons he is simply the minister for such-and-such a department and the only member of the Cabinet who is not seen in this way is the Prime Minister.

Sir Douglas saw two important consequences flowing from his analysis: first, the general thrust of policies or the need to amend strategy in view of a substantial shift in circumstances is seldom reviewed in

Cabinet; secondly, Cabinet has inadequate safeguards against an over-mighty departmental minister, who can quite easily 'railroad' it and distort overall priorities.

Finally, as if to complete a troika of the three dominant bureaucratic figures of their Whitehall generation, Sir Frank Cooper, in his 1985 lecture 'Affordable Defence: In Search of a Strategy',[32] applied the 'hole at the centre' test to his old stamping-ground of defence and foreign policy – and found it wanting. 'There is a real and continuing need', said Sir Frank, 'for Britain to have adequate machinery to look at its security in the fullest and roundest sense. Is there a defence hole at the centre of government? Do we need some kind of National Security Council with, supporting it, a properly qualified military and civil secretariat or planning staff? . . . My answer to both these questions would be very much in the affirmative.'

Taken together, this mound of criticism over ten years – with a notably accelerated rate of accumulation in the past five – is immensely sobering coming as it does from people with ringside seats in the stadium of British government. But, having depressed their listeners mightily, our critics, whether 'lifers' or 'parachutists', did not shrink from trying to cheer us up by offering remedies. Let us take first the 'lifers', the career technicians of the Whitehall machine.

Sir Kenneth Berrill advocated greater support for the Prime Minister, either through an enhanced Cabinet Office or a new Prime Minister's Department, to strengthen the centre: 'the cost of such an improved support staff would be tiny in relation to the issues involved'.

Lord Hunt told the accountants at Eastbourne, 'I am not myself strongly wedded to any particular solution', but he offered four choices: (1) a Prime Minister's Department; (2) a strengthened Cabinet Office; (3) a fusion of the CPRS with the Downing Street Policy Unit; and (4) an enhanced Prime Minister's Office.

Sir Douglas Wass toyed with the idea of an inner Cabinet of non-departmental ministers, but came down against it, citing the failure of Churchill's 'overlords'. He recommended instead the creation of 'Cabinet Review Committees' to raise departmental sights above their lobbies and to relate each area – the economy, housing, social services, and so forth – to overall Cabinet strategy. He urged, too, a new-style CPRS to serve the Cabinet as a whole. It should be tightly locked into the Public Expenditure Survey cycle, with 'a watching brief over any private deals' which might be struck.

Sir Frank Cooper wanted a 'national' security apparatus . . . right at the centre of government . . . [with a] primary remit [to] set a conceptual framework and look at our overall priorities and our ability to afford them . . . [and to] sustain a strategy which has proved extremely effective without tearing ourselves and our allies apart because of failing to face up to the realities of life'.

As for the amphibians, we have already encountered Rothschild's Law: a three-month Ramadan for new ministers. In an interview to mark the publication of his *Random Variables* in 1984, he said his first reforming-priority would be to look at ministerial workload: 'I would go through their diaries and ask them 'You are clearly ambitious and want to be Chancellor or Prime Minister. Please tell me what priority you would assign to naming this ship in Dover.'' Some of his fellow parachutists offered, by contrast, a veritable shopping-list of reforms.

Dr Tessa Blackstone recommended

(1) reduction in the amount of a minister's constituency work;
(2) reform of Parliament to avoid frequent all-night sittings;
(3) better use of junior ministers and creation of ministerial management teams in each department;
(4) that ministers should stay longer in each job;
(5) that more ministerial attention should be devoted to collective decision-taking in Cabinet and Cabinet committees;
(6) more and better political advisers, to form French-style ministerial *cabinets* (considerably expanded private offices mixing career lifers and amphibians – technically skilled, politically sensitive and working for the minister, not the department), which would blend policy specialists, advisers with close links to the party, and keepers of an overall long-term strategy;
(7) a greater say by ministers in the choice of their top civil servants; and
(8) an end to 'ministerial narcissism', i.e. the myth that ministers are the instigators of all new policies, which 'contributes most of their overwork and makes it most difficult for them to do the key parts of their job well'.

Sir John Hoskyns advocated

(1) better taxpayer support for political parties to improve policy-making in opposition and to maintain teams of 'shadow officials';

(2) replacement of 'a large number of senior civil servants with politically appointed officials on contracts at proper market rates so that experienced top quality people would be available – they might number between 10 and 20 per department';

(3) 'a small new department' to oversee and develop government's overall strategy – between 100 and 200 people, blending outsiders and career officials;

(4) that the Prime Minister should be allowed to recruit outside 'the small pool of career politicians at Westminster' when forming a government;

(5) that Whitehall should be reorganized for strategy and innovation;

(6) that the workload of ministers should be reduced;

(7) that there should be more open government, so that past failures would not be concealed, helping instead to push ministers up a learning-curve.

Sir John also raised what he called a 'larger agenda', embracing the financing of political parties, the doctrine of collective responsibility and electoral reform.

Professor John Ashworth recommended a day-release scheme for MPs to educate them in 'how the administration actually works so that it is not inevitable that if you are a professional politician you are an amateur minister'; and cabinets for each minister of Cabinet rank, with a revived CPRS at the centre pulling it all together.[34]

For the sake of completeness, one or two pieces must be added to this reform agenda. For example, two ex-Cabinet ministers from different ends of the political spectrum in the Callaghan Administration have made deliberate attempts to rupture the traditional Cabinet conventions. First, Edmund Dell insists that 'collective responsibility is a myth and one which is not believed'.[35] It should be dropped as an aid to clearer, less fudged decision-making. Second, Tony Benn, far from arguing that the centre should be strengthened, maintains that the British Prime Minister is an over-mighty figure dominating Cabinet and party through patronage and control of agendas, and needs to be cut down to size in a 'constitutional premiership',[36] a view which found partial support in a Fabian Society inquiry into the machinery of government in 1982.[37] And from certain individuals such as Norman Strauss, Sir John Hoskyns's colleague in the Downing Street Policy Unit from 1979 to 1982, there is a constant flow of criticism and ideas, the most recent in Strauss's case being 'Three reforms [which] would make for very much better government: political appointees installed alongside all permanent secretaries; full time senior inner Cabinet to adapt strategies and policies, to maintain coherence and to innovate; free access by governments to all their predecessors' papers.'[38]

Set alongside this wealth of suggestion for change – procedural, constitutional and structural – what do Mrs Thatcher's governmental reforms amount to? She has without doubt created a new *style* of government and has changed both the agenda and the language of contemporary British politics. In substantial terms her Whitehall priority has been improving the management of manpower, money and tasks through the Rayner reforms. Enhancing the management of policy has been a very poor second, because, as one well-placed insider has put it, the Prime Minister does not regard the performance of Cabinet as a problem. If there is a problem, it is the minister not the system, she has been heard to remark.[39] As we have seen, the post-Falklands inquest obliged Mrs Thatcher to change the Cabinet Office's intelligence machinery. And one other reform should not be overlooked. With the demise of the CPRS, her expanded Policy Unit (in Hoskyns's time it consisted of him, Norman Strauss, and a seconded civil servant, Andrew Duguid) has developed into a shadow Whitehall with each of its members, led currently by Professor Brian Griffiths, covering a clutch of subject areas – a distinct change from the free-ranging approach of the unit's early days or the bright-young-butterfly approach of the CPRS era.[40]

My own prejudice, evident in the pages of this study, is that a 1916-model Cabinet machine is, despite later modifications, not up to the stresses and strains of the economically and socially disturbed eighties – let alone the post-North-Sea-oil nineties; that, even if we had paragons placed around the Cabinet table instead of ordinary human beings, they would still be hobbled by the flawed instruments at their disposal; that, in short, it is time for a prime minister to do a Lloyd George on the machine and to commission, as his wartime coalition did with the Haldane Committee on the Machinery of Government of 1917–18,[41] an inquiry which tackles the system as a whole examining both the Cabinet and the departmental structure which buttresses it. Yet, even given a prime minister of energy, genius and conviction, any attempt to tackle *all* the parcels on our conveyor belt of overload would take a generation. (Just think of the swamps that lie ahead for the party-leader who wants to change the electoral system or parliamentary procedure.) Selectivity in attack is essential.

The area to go for as a priority has been identified by both our amphibian and lifer witnesses: the capability of ministers in Cabinet and Cabinet committee, the activities at which they perform least well and which, in consumer terms, matter most. Two changes are desperately needed: a reduced ministerial workload to make space for better analysis and thought, for political and policy research and development;[42] and an enhanced supply of both raw and processed food for thought. Quite how this supply-side improvement is organized by ministers and their machine-minders, the permanent secretaries, is a matter of personal taste. My own preference would be for ministerial *cabinets* linked with a revived CPRS serving the Cabinet as a collective entity. Cabinet ministers need a new enabling technology if they are consistently to do more than represent their departmental preoccupations at ministerial meetings. The constitution prescribes for them a collective function. All too often they lack the wherewithal – the briefing and the back-up – to fulfil it. It is sixteen years since one of Heath's special advisers, Mark Schreiber, accompanied by Tony Hart from the Civil Service Department, visited Paris to examine the French *cabinets ministeriels*. They came up with a tepid conclusion:

We were impressed by the enthusiasm and the vitality of the *Cabinets* we visited, and it is worth posing the question whether we now have the right balance in this part of our system – between the temporary and the permanent occupants of departments; between those who must achieve results in the lifetime of a Parliament and those who have longer; between change and stability; the new and the old; the political and the non-political. . . . If British Ministers feel the need for some personal reinforcement . . . there are features of the *Cabinet* system which could be adapted to fill the need.[43]

A reforming prime minister keen on models for fairly speedy relief of ministerial overload, which might be adapted for Whitehall use relatively easily, could find promising material across the Channel. An early updating of the Schreiber–Hart Report would make a sensible investment even for a sceptic in Downing Street. If the fairy godmother of reform were to grant me one long-term change, it would be to improve the pool of talent from which prime ministers can draw the twenty-two men and women on whom we so crucially depend. For, at the moment, very few Cabinet ministers or potential Cabinet ministers perceive a serious problem with the system. In failing to do so, they are part of the problem, not part of the solution. The sooner that position is reversed the better. For, as Sir Leo Pliatzky has put it, 'at the end of the day the decisions that matter are taken not in the Whitehall village but in the castle of No. 10 Downing Street and the Cabinet Room.'[44]

Notes

The following abbreviations are used throughout:

CIPFA   Chartered Institute of Public Finance and Accountancy
HC Deb   House of Commons Debates
HMSO   Her Majesty's Stationery Office
PRO   Public Record Office
RIPA   Royal Institute of Public Administration

Preface

1 Lord Butler interviewed by Norman Hunt, *Listener* 16 September 1965, pp. 407–11; repr. as 'Reflections on Cabinet Government' in Valentine Herman and James E. Alt (eds), *Cabinet Studies: A Reader* (Macmillan, 1975), pp. 193–209.
2 Anthony Sampson, *Anatomy of Britain Today* (Hodder, 1965).
3 Walter Bagehot, *The English Constitution*, with an introduction by R. H. S. Crossman (Fontana, 1963).
4 John P. Mackintosh, *The British Cabinet* (Stevens, 1962; University Paperback, 1968).
5 G. W. Jones, 'The Prime Minister's Power', *Parliamentary Affairs*, xviii (Spring 1965), pp. 167–85.
6 Butler, 'Reflections', in Herman and Alt, *Cabinet Studies*, p. 194.
7 Ian Gilmour, *The Body Politic* (Hutchinson, 1969), p. 206.
8 For quick and efficient access to that debate, see Anthony King (ed.), *The British Prime Minister*, 2nd edn. (Macmillan, 1985).
9 Several years later I expressed this prejudice in Michael Cockerell, Peter Hennessy and David Walker, *Sources Close to the Prime Minister* (Macmillan, 1984; Papermac, 1985), and Peter Hennessy, *What the Papers Never Said* (Portcullis, 1985).
10 The best account of the 1976 sterling crisis can be found in Stephen Fay and Hugo Young, *The Day the Pound Died* (*Sunday Times*, 1978).

11 Lord Rayner, 'The Unfinished Agenda', the Stamp Memorial Lecture, University of London, 6 November 1984.
12 Peter Riddell, 'Vacuum in the Tracks of the Think Tank's Departure', *Financial Times*, 11 January 1985.
13 See Peter Hennessy, 'Does the Elderly Cabinet Machine Need Oiling?', *Listener*, 27 June 1985, pp. 8–9.
14 Peter Hennessy, 'The Quality of Cabinet Government in Britain', *Policy Studies*, 6, 2 (October 1985), pp. 15–45.
15 Peter Hennessy, 'The Secret World of Cabinet Committees', *Social Studies Review*, 1, 2 (November 1985), pp. 7–10.

Introduction

1 Bagehot, *The English Constitution*, p. 68.
2 Colin Seymour-Ure, 'The "Disintegration" of the Cabinet and the Neglected Question of Cabinet Reform', *Parliamentary Affairs*, XXIV, 3 (1971), p. 196.
3 PRO, CAB 66/67, CP(45)100, II: 'Proceedings in Cabinet Committees'.
4 HC Deb, 8 February 1960, col. 70.
5 See Mackintosh, *The British Cabinet*, ch. 2.
6 Ibid., p. 42.
7 Patrick Gordon Walker, *The Cabinet* (Fontana, 1972), p. 10.
8 Mackintosh, *The British Cabinet*, p. 51.
9 Richard Pares, *King George III and the Politicians* (Oxford University Press, 1953), pp. 148–9.
10 Gordon Walker, *The Cabinet*, p. 13.
11 Sir Robert Armstrong, address to the Centenary Conference of the CIPFA, Brighton, 18 June 1985.
12 See Peter Hennessy, 'Whitehall Brief: Secret Life of a Public Servant', *The Times*, 22 September 1981.
13 Henry Pelling, *A Short History of the Labour Party*, (Macmillan, 1985) p. 190.
14 See Susan Crosland, *Tony Crosland* (Cape, 1982) p. 193, p. 200 and Richard Crossman, *The Diaries of a Cabinet Minister, Volume Three Secretary of State for the Social Services 1968–1970* (Hamish Hamilton and Cape, 1977), pp. 401–2.
15 N. H. Gibbs, *Keith's British Cabinet System*, 2nd edn (Stevens, 1952), p. 143.
16 Gordon Walker, *The Cabinet*, p. 91.
17 Mackintosh, *The British Cabinet*, p. 530.
18 See *Questions of Procedure*, paragraph 1, reproduced above on p. 8.
19 Mackintosh, *The British Cabinet*, p. 529.

20 Ibid., p. 414.
21 Ibid., p. 411.
22 Lord Home, interviewed in 'The Unknown Premiership', *The Quality of Cabinet Government*, BBC Radio 3, 25 July 1985.
23 Seymour-Ure, '"Disintegration" of the Cabinet', p. 196.
24 Max Nicholson, *The System* (Hodder, 1967), p. 174.
25 Seymour-Ure, '"Disintegration" of the Cabinet', p. 196.
26 Ibid., p. 203.
27 Colin Seymour-Ure to Peter Hennessy, 24 July 1985.
28 Ibid.
29 This phrase belongs to Professor George Jones.
30 Seymour-Ure, '"Disintegration" of the Cabinet', p. 203.
31 Pickthorn published his *Some Historical Principles of the Constitution* (Philip Allan) in 1925 while a Fellow of Corpus Christi College, Cambridge. St John Stevas is editor of the multi-volume collected works of Bagehot. Norman St. John Stevas (ed.), *The Collected Works of Walter Bagehot*, Vols. I–XII (Economist, 1965–74).
32 HC Deb, 26 June 1979, col. 38.
33 PRO, CAB 128/1, CM(45)18.
34 PRO, CAB 66/67, CP(45)99.
35 PRO, CAB 66/67, CP(45)100.
36 PRO, CAB 21/1624, CP(46)199: 'Cabinet Procedure. Consolidated Version of the Prime Minister's Directives'.
37 Ibid., CP(49)95.
38 Private information.
39 Tony Benn, 'The Case for a Constitutional Premiership', in King, *The British Prime Minister*, p. 229.
40 Private information.
41 King, *The British Prime Minister*, pp. 229–30.
42 Lord Hunt of Tanworth, 'Cabinet Strategy and Management', CIPFA/RIPA Conference, Eastbourne, 9 June 1983.

Chapter 1   The Cabinet Machine

1 Quoted in S. S. Wilson, *The Cabinet Office to 1945* (HMSO, 1975), p. ii.
2 Sir George Mallaby, *From my Level* (Hutchinson, 1965), pp. 16–17.
3 Peter Hennessy, 'A Magnificent Piece of Powerful Bureaucratic Machinery', *The Times*, 8 March 1976.
4 Ibid. The vans have since changed colour.
5 Dr Tessa Blackstone, 'Ministers, Advisers and Civil Servants', Gaitskell Memorial Lecture, University of Nottingham, 1979.
6 John Grigg, *Lloyd George from Peace to War 1912–1916* (Methuen, 1985), p. 488.

7 Stephen Roskill, *Hankey Man of Secrets* Vol. I: *1897–1918* (Collins, 1970); Vol. II: *1919–1931* (Collins, 1972); Vol. III: *1931–1963* (Collins, 1974). See also a slighter study, though it contains some interesting material particularly on secrecy matters: John F. Naylor, *A Man and an Institution: Sir Maurice Hankey, the Cabinet Secretariat and the Custody of Cabinet Secrecy* (Cambridge, 1984).

8 Lord Vansittart, *The Mist Procession* (Hutchinson, 1958), p. 164.

9 Mallaby, *From my Level*, p. 16.

10 Private information.

11 Sir Edward Bridges, *Portrait of a Profession*, Rede Lecture, University of Cambridge, 1950 (Cambridge, 1951).

12 Lord Ismay, *The Memoirs of Lord Ismay* (Heinemann, 1960), pp. 395–6.

13 Lord Moran, *Winston Churchill: The Struggle for Survival, 1940–65* (Sphere, 1968), pp. 795–6 (Moran's diary entry for 3 August 1959).

14 Ibid., p. 796.

15 Harold Macmillan, *At the End of the Day, 1961–63* (Macmillan, 1973), pp. 362–3.

16 Conversation with Lord Home, 5 November 1985.

17 Conversation with Sir Derek Mitchell, 14 November 1985.

18 Peter Hennessy, Susan Morrison and Richard Townsend, *Routine Punctuated by Orgies: The Central Policy Review Staff, 1970–83*, Strathclyde Papers on Government and Politics, no. 31 (1985), p. 8.

19 Edward Heath, the first Keeling Memorial Lecture, Royal Institute of Public Administration, 7 May 1980.

20 Conversation with Lord Trend quoted in Hennessy, Morrison and Townsend, *Routine Punctuated by Orgies*, pp. 8–9.

21 Conversation with Lord Trend, 13 November 1985. The article for which he was being interviewed appeared as Peter Hennessy, 'The megaphone theory of "Yes Minister"', *Listener*, 19 and 26 December 1985.

22 Conversation with Lord Home, 5 November 1985.

23 Private information.

24 Douglas Hurd, *An End to Promises: Sketch of a Government 1970–74* (Collins, 1979), pp. 117–18.

25 Keith Jeffery and Peter Hennessy, *States of Emergency: British Governments and Strikebreaking since 1919* (Routledge, 1983), pp. 237, 276.

26 Hennessy, 'Magnificent Piece of Powerful Bureaucratic Machinery'.

27 Ibid.

28 Joe Haines, *The Politics of Power* (Cape 1977), picture caption opposite p. 97.

29 Hennessy, Morrison and Townsend, *Routine Punctuated by Orgies*, p. 54.

30 Hennessy, 'Magnificent Piece of Powerful Bureaucratic Machinery'.

31 Private information.

32 Private information.
33 Peter Hennessy, 'Whitehall Brief: Thatcher's New-style Man for all Summits', *The Times*, 24 November 1981.
34 Private information.
35 Private information.
36 Private information.
37 Private information.
38 Private information.
39 Private information.
40 Private information.
41 Sir Robert Armstrong, in *Questions*, Channel Four, 1 July 1984.
42 Ibid.
43 Private information.
44 Peter Hennessy, 'Whitehall Brief: Peacemaker of Cheltenham', *The Times*, 14 February 1984.
45 Private information.
46 Linda Christmas, 'The Man who will be with the PM in 1987', *Guardian Weekly*, 22 July 1979.
47 *Questions*, Channel Four.
48 Ibid.
49 Statement by the Prime Minister to the House of Commons, 26 March 1981, *Hansard*, col. 1079 et seq. Mrs Thatcher cleared Sir Roger.
50 Christmas, 'The Man who will be with the PM'.
51 Hennessy, 'Whitehall Brief: Thatcher's New-style Man'.
52 Private information. For the possibility of a Hoskyns-led CPRS, see Hennessy, Morrison and Townsend, *Routine Punctuated by Orgies*, p. 79.
53 Private information. Details of the breakdown of the Cabinet Office into secretariats are not divulged in *The Civil Service Yearbook*.
54 Private information.
55 HC Deb, 4 July 1983, Written Answers.
56 PRO, PREM 11/952, C(53)322: memorandum on smog by the Minister of Housing and Local Government, 18 November 1953.
57 Jeffery and Hennessy, *States of Emergency*, pp. 234–8.
58 Private information.
59 Private information.
60 For an excellent comparative survey of the secretive British Cabinet system and the more open arrangements used by virtually every other nation in the Organization for Economic Co-operation and Development practising parliamentary government, see Thomas T. Mackie and Brian W. Hogwood (eds) *Unlocking the Cabinet, Cabinet Structures in Comparative Perspective*, (Sage, 1985).

Chapter 2   Overloading the Engine, 1945–79

1 Anthony King, 'Overload: Problems of Governing in the 1970s', *Political Studies*, xxii, 2–3 (June–September 1975), p. 164.
2 Hunt, 'Cabinet Strategy and Management'.
3 David Howell, interviewed in 'The Demanding Mistresses', *The Quality of Cabinet Government*, BBC Radio 3, 4 July 1985.
4 Sir Frank Cooper, interviewed in 'The Price of Division', *The Quality of Cabinet Government*, BBC Radio 3, 4 July 1985.
5 Sir John Hoskyns, 'Conservatism is not Enough', Institute of Directors Annual Lecture, 25 September 1983.
6 Paul Addison, *Now the War is Over* (Cape–BBC, 1985), pp. vi–vii. Dr Addison's earlier work was *The Road to 1945* (Cape, 1975).
7 See King, 'Overload'.
8 Ibid., p. 163.
9 McCallum is quoted in Dennis Kavanagh, 'On Writing Contemporary Electoral History', *Electoral Studies*, 1982, 1, p. 118.
10 John Colville, *The Fringes of Power: Downing Street Diaries 1939–1955* (Hodder, 1985), p. 611.
11 Ibid., p. 612.
12 Quoted in Alec Cairncross, *Years of Recovery: British Economic Policy 1945–51* (Methuen, 1985), p. 10. The best short but authoritative guide to the economic and industrial agenda facing Attlee is Sir Alec's opening chapter, 'The Post-war Situation' (pp. 3–17).
13 For an equally masterly survey of the background to foreign and defence policy, see Alan Bullock, *Ernest Bevin, Foreign Secretary* (Heinemann, 1983), 'The World in the Summer of 1945' (pp. 3–48).
14 Bullock assigns particular importance to Attlee and Bevin's active role on War Cabinet committees on post-war foreign policy (ibid., pp. 65–6).
15 Harold Wilson, *The Labour Government 1964–70* (Pelican, 1974), p. 24.
16 For an excellent sketch of the wartime Whitehall machine, see J. M. Lee, *The Churchill Coalition 1940–45* (Batsford, 1980). On pp. 98–9 he reproduces a useful chart titled 'The Central Executive Government of Great Britain', the original of which can be found in PRO, CAB 21/779.
17 This exodus and the failure to devise a peacetime equivalent of the wartime blend of regulars and irregulars is described as 'probably *the* greatest lost opportunity in the history of British public administration' in Peter Hennessy and Sir Douglas Hague, *How Adolf Hitler Reformed Whitehall*, Strathclyde Papers on Government and Politics, no. 41 (1985) p. 42.
18 Addision, *Now the War is Over*, p. 2.

19 Peter Hennessy and Andrew Arends, *Mr Attlee's Engine Room: Cabinet Committee Structure and the Labour Governments, 1945–51*, Strathclyde Papers on Government and Politics, no. 26 (1983).
20 Ibid.
21 Ibid., pp. 2–3.
22 Hunt, 'Cabinet Strategy and Management'.
23 See J. M. Lee, *Reviewing the Machinery of Government 1942–1952: An Essay on the Anderson Committee and its Successors* (1977, available from Professor J. M. Lee, Department of Politics, University of Bristol).
24 PRO, CAB 21/1701: 'Organisation of Cabinet Committees, 1946–47', Bridges to Brook, 5 July 1946.
25 Ibid.
26 PRO, CAB 21/1703: 'Cabinet Committee Book', Armstrong to Johnston, 10 July 1946.
27 PRO, CAB 21/1701.
28 PRO, CAB 21/1703.
29 PRO, CAB 21/1701.
30 Ibid.
31 Ibid.
32 Ibid.
33 Ibid., Bridges to Brook, 5 September 1946.
34 Ibid.
35 Cairncross, *Years of Recovery*, p. 49.
36 PRO, CAB 21/1701: Brook to Bridges, 13 September 1946.
37 PRO, CAB 21/1701, CP(46)357: 'Cabinet Committees', note by the Prime Minister, 26 September 1946.
38 PRO, CAB 21/1702, CP(47)280: Attlee informs the Cabinet of the new committee arrangements. For the pre-Economic Policy Committee weakness, see Cairncross, *Years of Recovery*, ch. 3.
39 PRO, CAB 21/1702: Brook's note of a conversation with Attlee which took place on 11 September 1947. In CP(47)280 Attlee informs Ministers of the abolition of fourteen Cabinet committees.
40 Cairncross, *Years of Recovery*, p. 509.
41 Ibid., p. 20.
42 Philip M. Williams (ed.), *The Diary of Hugh Gaitskell, 1945–1956* (Cape, 1983), p. 36.
43 PRO, CAB 21/1626.
44 For a fuller account, see Hennessy and Arends, *Mr Attlee's Engine Room*.
45 PRO, CAB 21/2654.
46 Ibid.
47 John Colville, *The Churchillians* (Weidenfeld, 1981), pp. 132–3.

48 PRO, CAB 21/2654: 'Composition of the Cabinet', Brook to Churchill. Undated, but it was waiting for Churchill when he resumed office on 27 October 1951.
49 Churchill's 'Caretaker' Cabinet sat from 23 May to 26 July 1945 and filled the interim between the break-up of the wartime Coalition and Attlee's assumption of power.
50 PRO, CAB 21/2654.
51 Ibid.
52 Ibid.
53 John Grigg, 'At Churchill's Court', *Listener*, 10 October 1985, p. 26.
54 Colville, *The Fringes of Power*, p. 633.
55 Once, when Lord Home travelled down from Edinburgh, where he was Minister of State at the Scottish Office, for an item of business, Churchill said 'I know what you've come down about, you've come to talk about your drains'. Lord Home explained, 'he used to look upon all our politics as drains' (Conversation with Lord Home, 6 February 1985).
56 See Lee, *The Churchill Coalition*; and Colin Seymour-Ure, 'British "War Cabinets" in Limited Wars: Korea, Suez and the Falklands', *Public Administration*, 62, 2 (Summer 1984), p. 182, and figure 1 on p. 183.
57 Anthony Seldon, *Churchill's Indian Summer: The Conservative Government, 1951–55* (Hodder, 1981), p. 102.
58 Ibid. The Treasury and Board of Trade element is mentioned on p. 543, n. 7, and attributed to Lord Plowden (then head of the Central Economic Planning Staff).
59 See below, ch. 4.
60 See Hennessy, Morrison and Townsend, *Routine Punctuated by Orgies*, p. 3 and Seldon, *Churchill's Indian Summer*, pp. 100, 103, 105, 167–8.
61 Sir Douglas Wass, *Government and the Governed* (Routledge, 1984), pp. 27–30.
62 David Felton, 'Small Business Key to Full Employment New Minister Believes', *The Times*, 12 September 1984.
63 For a delightful survey of the personality and physiognomy of members of the Churchill Cabinet at its first meeting on 31 October 1951, see Lord Kilmuir, *Political Adventure* (Weidenfeld, 1964), pp. 191–5.
64 Colville, *The Fringes of Power*, p. 633.
65 Seldon, *Churchill's Indian Summer*, p. 102.
66 Ibid., p. 103.
67 Ibid.
68 For a thorough account of the 'overlord' experiment, see Seldon, *Churchill's Indian Summer*, pp. 102–6.
69 Lord Birkenhead, *The Prof in Two Worlds* (Collins, 1961), pp. 284–94.
70 Seldon, *Churchill's Indian Summer*, p. 106.
71 Ibid.

72 Ibid., p. 85.
73 Ibid., p. 117.
74 Kilmuir, *Political Adventure*, p. 237.
75 PRO, CAB 127/27. The Cabinet meetings concerned were held in the last two weeks of July 1954.
76 Colville, *The Fringes of Power*, p. 702.
77 Seldon, *Churchill's Indian Summer*, p. 85.
78 Peter Hennessy, 'The Other Invasion Scare', *The Times*, 3 January 1983.
79 Conversation with Lord Home, 6 February 1985.
80 Colville, *The Fringes of Power*, p. 669.
81 Ibid., p. 670.
82 Ibid.
83 The Terry Coleman interview, 'A Politician as He Paints Himself', *Guardian*, 28 October 1985.
84 PRO, CAB 128/28, CC(55)28.
85 PRO, PREM 11/948.
86 PRO, CAB 130/109.
87 PRO, CAB 134/1273.
88 PRO, CAB 134/1210.
89 PRO, CAB 128/129, CM(55)45, 6 December 1955.
90 Kilmuir, *Political Adventure*, p. 257.
91 'Why Wait Thirty Years?', *The Times*, 3 January 1986. The author of the leading article was David Walker, who had filleted the 1955 files for the paper.
92 'In Eden's Day', *Economist*, 4 January 1986, p. 23.
93 The bill is contained in PRO, CAB 129/78 CP(55)166.
94 PRO, CAB 129/78, CP(55)167: Cabinet paper on colonial immigration from Lennox-Boyd, 1 November 1955.
95 PRO, CAB 128/29, CM(55)31, item 4.
96 Ibid., CM(55)30, item 7.
97 PRO, CAB 130/109–11.
98 PRO, CAB 129/78, CP(55)208.
99 David Carlton, *Anthony Eden: A Biography* (Allen Lane, 1981), p. 384.
100 PRO, CAB 129/78, CP(55)208.
101 Hugh Thomas, *The Suez Affair* (Pelican, 1970), p. 181.
102 Seymour-Ure, 'British "War Cabinets" in Limited Wars', pp. 181–2.
103 Carlton, *Eden*, p. 408.
104 Seymour-Ure, 'British "War Cabinets" in Limited Wars', pp. 183–4.
105 Ibid.
106 Ibid., p 185.
107 Ibid., p. 184.
108 PRO, CAB 129/29, CM(55)26, item 8, 28 July 1955.
109 Selwyn Lloyd, *Suez 1956* (Cape, 1978), p. 106.

110 Kilmuir, *Political Adventure*, p. 274.
111 Ibid., p. 281.
112 Ibid., p. 285.
113 Private information.
114 Anthony Sampson, *Macmillan: A Study in Ambiguity* (Allen Lane, 1967), picture caption for 'The Patrician', between pp. 261 and 263.
115 *Reflections*, Harold Macmillan talks to Ludovic Kennedy, BBC1, 20 October 1983.
116 It is reproduced in Alan Thompson, *The Day Before Yesterday: An Illustrated History of Britain from Attlee to Macmillan* (Sidgwick and Jackson, 1971), p. 163.
117 *Number 10 Downing Street*, pt I: 'The Story of a House', BBC1, 20 September 1985. The Wyndham addition was disclosed by Sir Philip de Zulueta, one of the Downing Street private secretaries in the Macmillan years.
118 Thompson, *The Day Before Yesterday*, p. 163.
119 In John Barnes's and Anthony Seldon's yet to be published study of the Conservative administrations of 1955–9. I am indebted to both of them for allowing me to see and draw upon their typescript.
120 Ibid.
121 Quoted in Barnes and Seldon, unpublished typescript.
122 *Number 10 Downing Street*, pt 1, BBC1.
123 Conversation with Lord Home, 5 November 1985.
124 Sampson, *Anatomy of Britain Today*, p. 134.
125 Barnes and Seldon, unpublished typescript.
126 Conversation with Professor George Jones, 5 May 1983.
127 Conversation with Lord Home, 13 February 1985.
128 Kilmuir, *Political Adventure*, pp. 323–4.
129 *Reflections*, BBC1.
130 David Henderson, the fifth 1985 Reith Lecture, *Listener*, 5 December 1985, p. 15. The other two were the second UK civil nuclear-power programme and the Russian equivalent of Concorde.
131 Jock Bruce-Gardyne and Nigel Lawson, *The Power Game* (Macmillan, 1976), pp. 10–11.
132 Ibid., p. 27.
133 Ibid.
134 Barnes and Seldon, unpublished typescript.
135 Bruce-Gardyne and Lawson, *The Power Game*, p. 28.
136 *Report of the Plowden Committee on Control of Public Expenditure*, Cmnd 1432 (HMSO, July 1961).
137 Harold Macmillan, *The Middle Way: A Study of the Problem of Economic and Social Progress in a Free and Democratic Society* (Macmillan, 1938; repr. with a new foreword 1966).

138 Sir Richard Clarke wrote his own authoritative account of the gestation, birth and adolescence of the PESC system. This, edited after his death by Sir Alec Cairncross, was published as *Public Expenditure, Management and Control* (Macmillan, 1978).
139 Bruce-Gardyne and Lawson, *The Power Game*, p. 26.
140 Clarke, *Public Expenditure*, p. 51.
141 Lord Home, *The Way the Wind Blows* (Collins, 1976), p. 192.
142 See J. Margach, *The Abuse of Power* (W. H. Allen, 1978), pp. 88–90, 128–9.
143 Conversation with Lord Home, 5 November 1985.
144 Conversation with Lord Home, 6 February 1985.
145 Ibid.
146 Conversation with Lord Home, 5 November 1985.
147 Conversation with Lord Home, 6 February 1985.
148 Ibid.
149 Ibid.
150 Bruce-Gardyne and Lawson, *The Power Game*, p. 99.
151 Ibid.
152 Ibid., p. 100.
153 Conversation with Lord Home, 6 February 1985.
154 Ibid.
155 Ibid.
156 S. S. Wilson, *The Cabinet Office to 1945*, p. 105.
157 Conversation with Lord Wilson, 27 February 1985.
158 Conversation with Peter Shore, 12 March 1985.
159 Ibid.
160 George Brown, *In My Way* (Penguin, 1972), p. 89.
161 *Whitehall and Beyond* (BBC, 1964), pp. 11–28.
162 Ibid., pp. 70–1.
163 Susan Crosland, *Tony Crosland*, p. 129.
164 Eric Roll, *Crowded Hours* (Faber, 1985), p. 151.
165 Lord Wilson, 27 February 1985.
166 Susan Crosland, *Tony Crosland*, p. 200.
167 R. H. S. Crossman, *Diaries of a Cabinet Minister*, vol. I (Cape, 1975) p. 29.
168 Ibid., pp. 103–4.
169 Ibid., p. 280.
170 Ibid.
171 Ibid., pp. 582–3, entry for 24 July 1966.
172 Barbara Castle, *The Castle Diaries 1964–70* (Weidenfeld, 1984), pp. 347–8.
173 Ibid., pp. 117, 129.
174 Crossman, *Diaries*, vol. III, p. 881. Crossman's 1970 Godkin Lectures at Harvard were published as R. H. S. Crossman, *Inside View* (Cape, 1972).

175 Crossman, *Diaries*, vol. III, p. 880.
176 See Roy Jenkins's characteristically elegant essay 'On Being a Minister' in Herman and Alt, *Cabinet Studies*, pp. 210–20.
177 Roy Jenkins, 'Castle Battlements', *Observer*, 4 November 1984.
178 Phillip Whitehead, *The Writing on the Wall* (Michael Joseph, 1985), p. 54.
179 Ibid., p. 52.
180 Private information.
181 Whitehead, *The Writing on the Wall*, p. 52.
182 Private information.
183 Private information.
184 Hennessy, Morrison and Townsend, *Routine Punctuated by Orgies*, p. 6.
185 Edward Heath, *My Style of Government* (Evening Standard Publications, 1972), p. 5.
186 *The Reorganisation of Central Government*, Cmnd 4506 (HMSO, 1970).
187 Ibid., p. 3.
188 Ibid., p. 4.
189 For an authoritative account of the conception, birth, development and demise of Programme Analysis and Review, see Andrew Gray and Bill Jenkins, 'Policy Analysis in British Central Government: The Experience of PAR', *Public Administration*, 60, 4 (Winter 1982), pp. 429–50.
190 For a good, clear map of departmental boundary changes, see Christopher Pollitt, *Manipulating the Machine: Changing the Pattern of Ministerial Departments, 1960–83* (Allen and Unwin, 1984).
191 *The Reorganisation of Central Government*, p. 13. For a history of the CPRS, see Hennessy, Morrison and Townsend, *Routine Punctuated by Orgies*.
192 Heath, *My Style*, p. 3.
193 See Hector Hawkins's recollection of that meeting in Hennessy, Morrison and Townsend, *Routine Punctuated by Orgies*, pp. 5–6.
194 Heath, *My Style*, p. 3.
195 David Howell, *Whose Government Works?* (Conservative Political Centre, 1968) and *A New Style of Government* (Conservative Political Centre, 1970).
196 Conversation with David Howell, 21 February 1985.
197 Private information.
198 Conversation with David Howell, 21 February 1985.
199 Private information.
200 Private information.
201 Jeffery and Hennessy, *States of Emergency*, pp. 236–7.
202 Howell was brought back from the Northern Ireland Office to be Minister of State at the Department of Energy in 1974.

203 Conversation with David Howell, 21 February 1985.
204 Quoted in Jeffery and Hennessy, *States of Emergency*, p. 240.
205 His bachelor existence at Chequers meant the Cabinet Office had to lay on teams of officials at weekends to answer the prime-ministerial queries which came off the telex machines at 70 Whitehall and in No. 10.
206 Hurd, *An End to Promises*, p. 121.
207 Whitehead, *The Writing on the Wall*, p. 110.
208 Ibid.
209 Hennessy, Morrison and Townsend, *Routine Punctuated by Orgies*, p. 25.
210 Private information.
211 Hennessy, Morrison and Townsend, *Routine Punctuated by Orgies*, p. 5.
212 Private information.
213 Private information.
214 Wilson treated the Commonwealth Prime Ministers' Conference of 1975 to a disquisition on his special-advisers scheme. It is reproduced in Harold Wilson, *The Governance of Britain* (Weidenfeld and Michael Joseph, 1976), pp. 202–5.
215 Lord Rothschild, *Random Variables* (Collins, 1984), p. 80.
216 An excellent snapshot of the Donoughue Policy Unit can be found in G. W. Jones 'The Prime Minister's Aides', in King, *The British Prime Minister*, pp. 72–87.
217 Joel Barnett, *Inside the Treasury* (André Deutsch, 1982), p. 49.
218 Quoted in Whitehead, *The Writing on the Wall*, p. 128.
219 Barbara Castle, *The Castle Diaries, 1974–76* (Weidenfeld, 1980), pp. 219–24.
220 When I published an article on the overload theme which drew on this extract from the Castle diaries – 'Does the Elderly Cabinet Machine Need Oiling?', *Listener*, 27 June 1985 – Callaghan's Westminster office contacted me to say that the former prime minister was joking when he made those remarks about emigrating.
221 Castle, *Diaries, 1974–76*, p. 221n.
222 Wilson, *The Governance of Britain*, p. 27.
223 Castle, *Diaries, 1974–76*, p. 223.
224 Conversation with Lord Wilson, 27 February 1985.
225 Barnett, *Inside the Treasury*, p. 41.
226 Ibid., p. 42.
227 See Whitehead, *The Writing on the Wall*, pp. 128–32.
228 Ibid., pp. 131–2.
229 Conversation with Peter Shore, 12 March 1985.
230 Conversation with Lord Wilson, 27 February 1985.
231 Julian Haviland, 'Heseltine Throws down Gauntlet on Westland', *The Times*, 18 December 1985.

232 James Naughtie and Michael Smith, 'Heseltine Scents Victory over Westland Rescue', *Guardian*, 20 December 1985.

233 For a full account of the cash-limits story, see Leo Pliatzky, *Getting and Spending* (Basil Blackwell, 1982), ch. 5.

234 Wilson, *The Governance of Britain*, p. 67.

235 Private information.

236 Conversation with Peter Shore, 12 March 1985.

237 This story is superbly told in James Michael, *The Politics of Secrecy* (Penguin, 1982).

238 The minute was leaked in November 1978 in the *New Statesman*, which, in the same year had begun the practice of publishing Cabinet committees, GEN numbers and all. See Bruce Page, 'The Secret Constitution', *New Statesman*, 21 July 1978.

239 Private information.

240 Private information.

241 Whitehead, *The Writing on the Wall*, p. 195.

242 Ibid.

243 Hennessy, Morrison and Townsend, *Routine Punctuated by Orgies*, pp. 54–5.

244 Whitehead, *The Writing on the Wall*, p. 196.

245 Peter Hennessy, 'Committee Decided Callaghan Economic Policy', *The Times*, 17 March 1980.

246 Ibid.

247 Ibid.

248 See Peter Hennessy, 'Whitehall Contingency Planning for Industrial Disputes', in Peter J. Rowe and Christopher J. Whelan, *Military Intervention in Democratic Societies* (Croom Helm, 1985), pp. 94–109.

249 Jeffery and Hennessy, *States of Emergency*, p. 245.

250 Barnett, *Inside the Treasury*, p. 171.

251 Ibid., p. 175.

Chapter 3   Conviction Cabinet, 1979–86

1 Interview with Kenneth Harris, *Observer*, 25 February 1979.

2 *The Times*, 21 June 1982.

3 The Prime Minister's reply to James Prior's resignation letter was reported in *The Times* on 1 September 1984.

4 'Living Legend who Rocks the Boat', anonymous profile of Lord Stockton, *Observer*, 17 November 1985.

5 Michael Heseltine, 'When I Knew I Had to Go', *Observer*, 12 January 1986.

6 'Education's Manchester School Liberal', The Terry Coleman interview, *Guardian*, 24 July 1985.

7 Quoted in Crossman, *Inside View*, p. 46.

8 Private information.

9 'Why I'm not the Prime Minister', James Prior interviewed by Jeremy Mayhew, *New Statesman*, 13 December 1985, pp. 12–14. Mayhew's interview was conducted as part of the preparation for Phillip Whitehead's *Writing on the Wall* series for Channel Four television.

10 'At Last Someone Says No, Prime Minister', leading article, *Observer*, 12 January 1986.

11 Private information.

12 Quoted in Peter Hennessy, 'From Woodshed to Watershed', *The Times*, 5 March 1984.

13 Conversation with David Howell, 21 February 1985.

14 Ibid.

15 Private information.

16 Private information.

17 Private information.

18 Private information.

19 Private information.

20 Letter from Sir Robert Armstrong to Peter Hennessy, 31 January 1985.

21 Private information.

22 Private information.

23 Private information.

24 Private information.

25 Private information.

26 Private information.

27 Private information.

28 Private information.

29 Private information.

30 Conversation with David Howell, 21 February 1985.

31 Private information.

32 Conversation with Sir Frank Cooper, 15 February 1985.

33 Private information.

34 Private information.

35 Private information.

36 'Howe: I Was Right and I Won't Resign', interview by Robin Oakley, *Daily Mail*, 6 February 1984.

37 Private information.

38 Private information.

39 'Deliberate Attempt Made to Avoid Discussing Issues', text of Michael Heseltine's resignation statement, *The Times*, 10 January 1986, p. 2.

40 *Panorama*, BBC1, 13 January 1986.

41 Peter Riddell, 'Thatcher Acts to Cool Row as Ministers Round on Heseltine', *Financial Times*, 11 January 1986, p. 1.
42 Resignation text.
43 Private information.
44 Adam Raphael and Ian Mather, 'The Point of No Return', *Observer*, 12 January 1986.
45 Resignation text.
46 Anthony Bevins, 'Brittan Apology to MPs over Westland Letter', *The Times*, 14 January 1986.
47 Ibid.
48 Resignation text.
49 'Westland Sets the Tories Spinning', *Economist*, 4 January 1986, p. 17.
50 Resignation text.
51 Ibid.
52 Ibid.
53 I am grateful to John Barnes of the London School of Economics for pointing this out to me over lunch at the Public Record Office on 31 December 1985.
54 Wilson, *The Governance of Britain*, p. 56.
55 Armstrong, CIPFA Centenary address.
56 *Panorama* BBC1, 13 January 1986.
57 Resignation text.
58 Heseltine, 'When I Knew I Had to Go'.
59 Clive Ponting, *The Right to Know* (Sphere, 1985), p. 173.
60 *Panorama*, BBC1, 13 January 1986.
61 Private information.
62 This is taken from the 1952 version of *Questions* as used in the Introduction.
63 See Peter Hennessy, 'Why Heseltine Finally Snapped', *The Times*, 10 January 1986.
64 Edmund Dell, 'Collective Responsibility: Fact, Fiction or Façade', RIPA lecture, 4 December 1979.
65 *Nine O'Clock News*, BBC1, 10 January 1986.
66 *News at Ten*, ITN, 10 January 1986.
67 Peter Riddell, 'An Irresistible Force at No. 10', *Financial Times*, 11 January 1986, p. 9.
68 London Weekend Television, *Weekend World*, 26 January 1986.
69 Tyne Tees Television, *Face the Press*, 26 January, 1986.
70 Private information.
71 Private information.
72 Hennessy, Morrison and Townsend, *Routine Punctuated by Orgies*, pp. 1–2.
73 Ibid., p. 85.

74 Ibid.
75 Conversation with David Howell, 21 February 1985. In fact, the head of the CPRS had had the right to sit on Cabinet committees since its foundation.
76 Private information.
77 Private information.
78 Private information.
79 *Falkland Islands Review. Report of a Committee of Privy Counsellors*, Cmnd 8787 (HMSO, 1983).
80 Quoted in Peter Hennessy, 'Whitehall Brief: The Unlearnt Falklands Lessons', *The Times*, 17 January 1984.
81 Private information.
82 *Falkland Islands Review*, p. 79.
83 Ibid.
84 Ibid., p. 83.
85 Private information.
86 Private information.
87 Maria Laura Avignolo, 'How Galtieri Got it Wrong', *The Sunday Times*, 17 November 1985.
88 Private information.
89 *Reflections*, BBC1, 20 October 1983.
90 Private information.
91 Conversation with David Howell, 21 February 1985. For an excellent account of the workings of OD(SA) and war Cabinets in general, see Seymour-Ure, 'British "War Cabinets" in Limited Wars'.
92 There had been criticism of Whitehall's failure to take adequate account of the vigorous anti-British campaign in the Argentinian press in the early weeks of 1982.
93 *Falkland Islands Review*, pp. 85–6.
94 Peter Hennessy, 'Duff Gets Top Security Job', *The Times*, 28 February 1983.
95 Peter Hennessy, 'Whitehall Brief: The Unlearnt Falklands Lessons'.
96 Ibid.
97 Private information.
98 Conversation with Nicholas Budgen, MP, 19 December 1984.
99 Peter Jenkins, 'The Last Chapter', *The Sunday Times*, 13 October 1985.
100 'Friday People', *Guardian*, 22 November 1985.
101 Private information.

Chapter 4 Cabinets and the Bomb

1 Mackintosh, *The British Cabinet*, p. 469.

2 PRO, CAB 130/101, GEN 464: Atomic Energy Development, 1st meeting, 13 April 1954.
3 Lord Wilson, interviewed in 'Smoking is not Compulsory', *The Quality of Cabinet Government*, BBC Radio 3, 27 June 1985.
4 Cooper, interviewed in 'The Price of Division', *The Quality of Cabinet Government*, BBC Radio 3, 4 July 1985.
5 Mackintosh, *The British Cabinet*, p. 496.
6 Margaret Gowing, *Independence and Deterrence: Britain and Atomic Energy 1945–1952*, Vol. I: *Policy Making*; vol. II: *Policy Execution* (Macmillan, 1974).
7 Ibid., vol. I, p. 1.
8 Ibid., pp. 1–2.
9 PRO, CAB 130/2, GEN 75, 1st meeting.
10 PRO, AIR 2/59 60: 'Draft Air Staff Requirement No. OR/230'.
11 PRO, CAB/30/16, GEN 163, 1st meeting, 8 January 1947: Confidential Annex, minute 1, 'Research in Atomic Weapons'.
12 Quoted in Hennessy and Arends, *Mr Attlee's Engine Room*, p. 19.
13 Letter from Professor George Jones to Peter Hennessy, 23 June 1985.
14 PRO, CAB 130/2, GEN 75, 15th meeting.
15 Peter Hennessy, 'How Bevin Saved Britain's Bomb', *The Times*, 30 September 1982.
16 PRO, CAB 130/16.
17 Ibid.: 'Note by the Controller of Production of Atomic Energy', 31 December 1946.
18 Ibid.
19 For details of Chevaline and its concealment, see Hennessy, *What the Papers Never Said*, pp. 113–19. For Sir Frank Cooper's evidence see, *Ninth Report from the Committee of Public Accounts, Session 1981–82*: 'Ministry of Defence. Chevaline Improvement to Polaris Missile System', House of Commons Paper 269 (April 1982) p. 13. Sir Frank joined the Air Ministry in 1948.
20 PRO, CAB 130/16.
21 Ibid.
22 Ibid.
23 H. Montgomery Hyde, *The Atom Bomb Spies* (Hamish Hamilton, 1980), p. 55.
24 Gowing, *Independence and Deterrence*, vol. I, p. 20.
25 Ibid., p. 21.
26 PRO, CAB 128/12, CM(48)31st Conclusions.
27 Gowing, *Independence and Deterrence*, vol. I, pp. 210–12.
28 Ibid., p. 210.
29 Ibid., p. 51.
30 Mackintosh, *The British Cabinet*, p. 496.

31 Gowing, *Independence and Deterrence*, vol. I, p. 211.
32 PRO, CAB 130/3, GEN 75/52.
33 Quoted in Henry Pelling, *The Labour Governments, 1945–51* (Macmillan, 1984), p. 126.
34 Gowing, *Independence and Deterrence*, vol. I, p. 230.
35 Ibid., p. 229.
36 That answer and the newspaper coverage it received can be found in Hennessy, *What the Papers Never Said*, pp. 17–29.
37 Bullock, pp. 3–49.
38 Private information.
39 Bullock, p. 847.
40 Gowing, *Independence and Deterrence*, vol. I, p. 405.
41 PRO, CAB 21/2281B: Prime Minister's Personal Minute serial no. M47c/51.
42 Ibid.: Prime Minister's Personal Minute, serial no. M140c/51, 8 December 1951.
43 Gowing, *Independence and Deterrence*, vol. I, p. 406.
44 Ibid., p. 407.
45 Ibid., p. 406.
46 PRO, CAB 130/100: 'Atomic Energy Estimates', note by the Minister of Supply, 3 March 1954.
47 Ibid.
48 Private information.
49 Ibid., GEN 464: Atomic Energy Development, 1st meeting.
50 Ibid.
51 PRO, CAB 128/27, pt 2, CC(54)47.
52 Ibid.
53 Ibid.
54 PRO, CAB 128/27, Ibid., CC(54)48, item 2.
55 Ibid.
56 Ibid.
57 Ibid.
58 Ibid.
59 Ibid.
60 *The Annual Register of World Events*, vol. 197 [for 1955] (Longmans, 1956), pp. 5–10.
61 Conversation with Sir Frank Cooper, 15 February 1985.
62 *Annual Register*, vol. 197, pp. 5, 10.
63 For a superb short account of the high politics of the British atomic programme and the special nuclear relationship, see Lawrence Freedman, *Britain and Nuclear Weapons* (Papermac, 1980). For his account of the restoration of Anglo-American collaboration, see pp. 6–7. See also Andrew Pierre, *Nuclear Politics: The British Experience*

with an Independent Strategic Force, 1939–70 (Oxford University Press, 1970).

64 Freedman, *Britain and Nuclear Weapons*, p. 7.

65 *Central Organisation for Defence* (HMSO, June 1963) Cmnd 2097, pp. 2–3.

66 Private information.

67 Private information.

68 Macmillan, *At the End of the Day* p. 360.

69 Ibid.

70 Harold Evans, *Downing Street Diary: The Macmillan Years 1957–63* (Hodder, 1981), p. 238.

71 Ibid., pp. 238–9.

72 Macmillan, *At the End of the Day*, p. 360.

73 Evans, *Downing Street Diary*, p. 240.

74 Macmillan, *At the End of the Day*, p. 360.

75 Ibid., p. 363.

76 Private information.

77 Freedman, *Britain and Nuclear Weapons*, p. 33.

78 *Let's Go With Labour for the New Britain* (Labour Party, September 1964), available in F. W. S. Craig, *British General Election Manifestos, 1918–1966* (Political Reference Publications, 1970). The section dealing with Labour's defence policy is on pp. 245–6.

79 Ibid.

80 Wilson, *The Labour Government 1964–70*, pp. 68–9.

81 Castle, *Diaries 1964–70,* p. 356.

82 Freedman, *Britain and Nuclear Weapons*, p. 32.

83 Ibid., p. 31.

84 Ibid., p. 32.

85 Ibid.

86 Crossman, *Diaries*, vol. II, p. 619.

87 Ibid.

88 Wilson informed President de Gaulle of the decision not to go for Poseidon at a meeting in Paris on 19 June 1967.

89 Castle, *Diaries 1964–70*, p. 306.

90 Private information.

91 Freedman, *Britain and Nuclear Weapons*, pp. 39–40.

92 Lord Wilson was referring to the ministerial group which in 1974 took the decision to proceed with Chevaline, which I had mentioned in my question to him. Presumably his remarks also apply to the group mentioned by Sir Solly Zuckerman over the lunch table to Mrs Castle in 1967.

93 Remember what Crossman reported Wilson as saying about Tam Dalyell and the need to campaign against British nuclear weapons in 1967.

94 Lord Wilson, interviewed in 'Smoking is not Compulsory', *The Quality of Cabinet Government*, BBC Radio 3, 27 June 1985.

95 Ibid.

96 Freedman, *Britain and Nuclear Weapons*, p. 44.

97 Private information.

98 Freedman, *Britain and Nuclear Weapons*, p. 48.

99 See Peter Hennessy, 'Whitehall Brief: £1000M Deterrent Fails to Get off the Ground', *The Times*, 30 June 1981.

100 Castle, *Diaries 1974–76*, p. 227n.

101 This was a larger body than the group of five. Either Wilson was citing it as the decision-making body as a cover for the smaller group, or the decision had gone to the DOPC between April and November 1974.

102 Castle, *Diaries 1974–76*, p. 227–8.

103 Ibid., p. 228.

104 Ibid.

105 Philip Webster, 'Updating of Polaris Regretted by Healey', *The Times*, 20 December 1982.

106 Quoted by Joel Barnett, MP, Chairman of the Public Accounts Committee, while examining Sir Frank Cooper on Chevaline, 9 December, 1981 (House of Commons Paper 269, para 121).

107 See Hennessy, *What the Papers Never Said*, pp. 113–39.

108 House of Commons Paper 269, p. v.

109 Private information.

110 Peter Hennessy, 'Whitehall Brief: Mr Callaghan's Secret Bequest to Mrs Thatcher. Planning for a Future Nuclear Deterrent', *The Times*, 4 December 1979.

111 Ibid.

112 Private information.

113 Hennessy, 'Whitehall Brief: Mr Callaghan's Secret Bequest'.

114 Ibid.

115 Ian Mather, 'Callaghan Wanted Trident', *Observer*, 20 July 1980. In the Commons debate on the 1981 Defence Estimates, Callaghan sketched 'the circumstances in which I might support it [Trident]': 'We might find that our allies had a surprising degree of understanding if we were to tell them that we wanted to bring home [from West Germany] at least 25,000 troops and that in doing that, we would maintain our naval and air strength. I must tell my hon. Friends that, that might involve retaining Trident. I might take a different view from some. However, if such a proposition involved retaining Trident, it would be a bargain that would be well worth making' (HC Deb, 20 May 1981, cols 316, 318).

116 Private information.

117 Dr Owen acknowledged being on Callaghan's committee of four, and his advocacy, during its discussions, of the cruise-missile option, on the Granada television programme *Under Fire* on 16 September 1985.

118 *The Labour Way is the Better Way* (Labour Party, 1979), pp. 37–8.
119 The existence of MISC 7 was revealed in Hennessy, 'Whitehall Brief: Mr Callaghan's Secret Bequest', 4 December 1979.
120 The membership of MISC 7 was revealed in Peter Hennessy, 'Cabinet's Atomic Bomb Minute Restored to File', *The Times*, 21 July 1980.
121 Private information.
122 Hennessy, 'Whitehall Brief: Mr Callaghan's Secret Bequest'.
123 Private information.
124 Private information.
125 Private information.
126 *The British Strategic Nuclear Force, July 1980. Texts of Letters Exchanged between the Prime Minister and the President of the United States and between the Secretary of Defense*, Cmnd 7979 (HMSO, 1980), p. 2.
127 Ibid., p. 3.
128 Quoted in Hennessy, 'Cabinet's Atomic Bomb Minute Restored to File'.
129 Dr Owen, interviewed in, *Under Fire*, Granada, 16 September 1985.
130 *Defence and Security for Britain* (Labour Party, 1984), pp. 27–8.
131 Prime Minister's speech to the Conservative Party Conference, Blackpool, 11 October 1985.
132 Simon Jenkins and Anne Sloman, *With Respect, Ambassador: An Inquiry into the Foreign Office* (BBC, 1985), p. 103.
133 Neil Kinnock, interviewed in *Under Fire*, Granada, 21 October 1985.
134 Private information.
135 Ibid.
136 Dr Owen, interviewed in *Under Fire*, 16 September 1985.
137 Duncan Campbell, 'Too Few Bombs to go Round', *New Statesmen*, 29 November 1985, p. 10.
138 Peter Hennessy, 'How Labour Might Disarm Britain', *The Times*, 15 May 1981.

Chapter 5   The Quality of Cabinet Government

1 Quoted in Lord Rothschild, *Meditations of a Broomstick* (Collins, 1977), p. 167.
2 Lord Wilson, interviewed in 'Smoking is not Compulsory', *The Quality of Cabinet Government*, BBC Radio 3, 27 June 1985.
3 The occasion was a meeting, which I attended, between officers of the Political Studies Association and Fleet Street political correspondents at the Royal Commonwealth Society on 5 December 1984.
4 Unless otherwise stated, all the extracts in this chapter are from the full, unedited transcripts of interviews carried out for *The Quality of Cabinet Government* series, broadcast on BBC Radio 3. Lord Wilson was

interviewed on 27 February 1985, Lord Home on 13 February 1985, Peter Shore on 12 March 1985, David Howell on 21 February 1985 and Sir Frank Cooper on 15 February 1985.

5 Lord Home mentioned his plans for Powell when the tape-recorder had been switched off on 13 February 1985. He subsequently gave permission for me to quote his remark, and it appeared in Peter Hennessy, 'The Quality of Cabinet Government in Britain', *Policy Studies*, 6, 2 (October 1985), p. 28.

6 Ernest Marples, a self-made businessman, had served as Postmaster General and as an ebullient, controversial Minister of Transport.

7 Peter Shore had the title slightly wrong. He was referring to R. H. S. Crossman, *The Charm of Politics and Other Essays in Political Criticism* (Hamish Hamilton, 1958).

8 That title had disappeared in 1970. Peter Shore was Secretary of State for Trade 1974–6.

9 Conversation with Lord Home, 5 November 1985.

10 Ibid.

11 So did Lord Home: 'I was a fifty years not a thirty years man' (conversation with Lord Home, 5 November 1985). R. A. Butler argued, when the change was mooted in 1966, for a 100-year rule. 'Rab' was one of the most accomplished Cabinet 'briefers'. Lord Home, who expressed not the slightest animosity towards Butler (the reverse, in fact) agreed with me that 'It was probably one of his elaborate jokes.'

12 Dame Evelyn Sharp.

Chapter 6   The Reform Agenda

1 A remark made at a meeting of officers of the Political Studies Association and Fleet Street political correspondents at the Royal Commonwealth Society on 5 December 1984.

2 Private information.

3 Conversation with Sir Frank Cooper, 15 February 1985.

4 Professor Gowing delivered this observation at a seminar held at the Institute of Historical Research in London on 13 November 1985.

5 Private information.

6 Simon Freeman and Barry Penrose, 'How Britain Would Have Coped if the Cabinet Had Been Killed', *The Sunday Times*, 21 October 1984.

7 Ibid.

8 King, 'Overload', p. 295.

9 Addison, *Now the War is Over*, p. 28.

10 King, 'Overload', p. 295.

11 Castle, *Diaries 1974–76*, p. 223.

12 Hennessy, Morrison and Townsend, *Routine Punctuated by Orgies*, p. 94.
13 Professor John Ashworth, 'Giving Advice to Governments', Lecture to the Royal Signals Institution, 23 November 1983.
14 Ibid.
15 Becoming a minister can actually increase a politician's constituency caseload. See Roy Gregory, 'Executive Power and Constituency Representation in United Kingdom, *Political Studies*, xxvii, 1 (March 1980), pp. 63–83.
16 The Terry Coleman interview, 'A Man at Home with Fact and Fiction', *Guardian*, 30 November 1985.
17 Lord Rothschild, 'The Best Laid Plans . . .', the first Israel Sieff Memorial Lecture, 4 May 1976; repr. in Rothschild, *Meditations of a Broomstick*, pp. 163–79. His remark on manifestos is on p. 171.
18 Ibid., pp. 173–4.
19 Dr Tessa Blackstone, 'Ministers, Advisers and Civil Servants', Gaitskell Memorial Lecture, University of Nottingham, 1979.
20 She drew these quotes from Maurice Kogan (ed.), *The Politics of Education* (Penguin, 1971), p. 109.
21 Ibid., p. 95–6.
22 Ibid., p. 161.
23 Sir John Hoskyns, 'Westminster and Whitehall: An Outsider's View', Institute for Fiscal Studies Annual Lecture, 12 October 1982.
24 Sir John Hoskyns, 'Conservatism is not Enough', Institute of Directors Annual Lecture, 28 September 1983.
25 Quoted from Lord Radcliffe's 1951 Reith Lectures, "Power and the State".
26 Professor John Ashworth, 'On the Giving and Receiving of Advice (in Whitehall and Salford)', Lecture to the Manchester Statistical Society, 16 November 1982. Professor Ashworth had by this time become Vice-Chancellor of Salford University.
27 See above, n. 13.
28 Hoskyns, 'Conservatism is not Enough'.
29 Sir Kenneth Berrill, 'Strength at the Centre – the Case for a Prime Minister's Department', the Stamp Memorial Lecture, University of London, 4 December 1980.
30 Lord Hunt of Tanworth, 'Cabinet Strategy and Management', CIPFA/RIPA Conference, Eastbourne, 9 June 1983.
31 Repr. in Douglas Wass, *Government and the Governed* (Routledge, 1984), pp. 21–40.
32 Sir Frank Cooper, 'Affordable Defence: In Search of a Strategy', Lecture to the Royal United Services Institute, 9 October 1985.
33 Peter Hennessy, 'Itching for Another Shot', *The Times*, 22 May 1984.

34 At my invitation, Professor Ashworth drew these points together from the implications of his two lectures. See Peter Hennessy, 'Whitehall Brief: Think Tank Rethink', *The Times*, 13 December 1983.

35 Dell, 'Collective Responsibility: Fact, Fiction or Façade', p. 28.

36 Tony Benn, 'The Case for a Constitutional Premiership' in King, *The British Prime Minister*, pp. 221–37.

37 David Lipsey (ed.), *Making Government Work*, Fabian Tract 480 (1982).

38 Norman Strauss, 'Why Whitehall Fails the Inner Cities', *The Times*, 6 November 1985.

39 Private information.

40 At the end of November, the breakdown of personnel and portfolios in the Downing Street Policy Unit was as follows.

Hartley Booth	environmental pollution, planning, home policy, drugs
David Hobson	export credits, Scottish and Welsh affairs, accountancy issues
Oliver Letwin	education, employment and local government
Christopher Monckton	housing and parliamentary affairs
Nicholas Owen	defence, competition policy, agriculture
Peter Warry	deregulation, pay, trade and industry
David Willetts	Treasury matters, health and social security
John Wybrew	energy, transport and the financial management initiative

The Prime Minister also has two very senior personal advisers separate from the Policy Unit though complementary to it: Sir Percy Cradock on foreign affairs, and Professor Sir Alan Walters (on an ad hoc basis) for economic affairs.

41 Ministry of Reconstruction, Report of the Machinery of Government Committee (HMSO, 1918), Cd 9230.

42 The phrase 'political R and D', alluded to here, was coined by Norman Strauss.

43 M. S. Schreiber and T. A. A. Hart, *Cabinets Ministeriels in France* (Civil Service Department, 1972), unpublished report, p. 11.

44 Sir Leo Pliatzky, *Getting and Spending, Public Expenditure, Employment and Inflation* (Basil Blackwell, 1982), p. 38.

Index